Thank you for your commitment to life and for your generous support for AUL's work!

Chris

PUSHING

Roe v. Wade

OVER THE BRINK

The Battle for America's Heart, the Human Right to Life, and a Future Full of Hope

Clarke D. Forsythe

Alexandra DeSanctis

Dedication

Thousands of Americans across the country have made possible the work of Americans United for Life, against all odds, since 1971. Many have persevered through decades of political and legal setbacks and the vicissitudes of election cycles. We know that much of their support over the years has been sacrificial. We are inspired by their love for life and their commitment to the equal dignity of every human being.

The team that works at Americans United for Life today knows well that its progress is based on the struggle of dozens of previous board and team members who have worked with Americans United for Life since 1971 and who sacrificed long hours and many years in the face of considerable opposition. We are grateful to them for their commitment which spurred their sacrifice and produced momentum that lifts our work today.

To these we dedicate this history.

Pushing *Roe v. Wade* Over the Brink

The Battle for America's Heart, the Human Right to Life, and a Future Full of Hope

Copyright © 2023 by Americans United for Life

ISBN 979-8-9869498-1-9

Published in the United States of America

by Americans United for Life

AUL.org

First Edition

Contents

Introduction

In May 2021, nearly 50 years after the U.S. Supreme Court imposed abortion on America with its decision in *Roe v. Wade*, the Court agreed to hear *Dobbs v. Jackson Women's Health Organization*, concerning Mississippi's protections for human persons after 15 weeks of pregnancy. On the morning of Friday, June 24, 2022, little more than one year after taking up the case, the Court handed down a decision that some had thought impossible: *Roe v. Wade* was overruled. The American people, democratically through Congress and the states, would now decide the issue for themselves.

Dobbs had been the first major challenge to the Court's abortion doctrine since *Planned Parenthood v. Casey* in 1992, and the case reached the Court only because of the tireless work of the American cause for the human right to life in the form of the pro-life movement. Since the Court's decision in *Roe*, pro-life Americans have never ceased advocating in the culture, in the law, and through the political process, demanding greater recognition for the dignity and natural rights of the prenatal human person. Abortion has always been the preeminent and most urgent cause for justice for pro-life Americans, although the human right to life has also always been understood to encompass a broad spectrum of issues pertaining to the human person throughout one's natural lifetime.

As the COVID-19 pandemic demonstrated, most Americans believe in the value of human life and the importance of protecting the wellbeing of every member of the human family. Since abortion was first imposed in our country by seven men in *Roe*, the American pro-life movement has been tireless in proclaiming that the preborn child is a truly an equal member of the human family who deserves the same moral recognition and equal protection of the law as each of us.

The truth of that principle is a matter of daily debate in our country. As the pandemic unfolded around us and hundreds of thousands of Americans lost their lives, we were reminded again by cultural and racial conflict that a notion of human dignity and equality is fundamental, a necessary component for a society ordered to the common good in which all of us can flourish. Over the past half-century, Americans United for Life has fought to keep that principle at the center of American law and society, with an unswerving emphasis on protecting the life of every human being in the law.

From the beginning of the modern abortion debate in the 1960s, through the euthanasia debate of the 1970s and 1980s, to modern debates over abortion financing and the proliferation of abortion pills, Americans United for Life has advocated a consistent bioethical vision for human thriving across the whole spectrum of every natural lifetime starting from the moment of conception.

Americans United for Life, inspired by the success of the NAACP's Legal Defense Fund, has worked to secure the human rights tradition upon which our nation was founded, especially in service of our most vulnerable brothers and sisters at the beginning and end of life. The work of Americans United for Life in culture, law, and policy and in courts, legislatures, and media has demonstrated the critical role of mediating institutions in American law and the democratic process. In playing that role, such organizations are constantly challenged with questions of political prudence and organizational effectiveness. What is leadership? How is success defined? How is momentum created in politics and in law and policy? Where can limited resources be most effectively applied? The questions, and the right answers, determine success or failure in shaping law and policy and renewing culture.

Founded in 1971, Americans United for Life has long sought the reversal of *Roe*, the abolition of abortion, and the revitalizing of the American human rights tradition upon which the Declaration's commitment to "Life, Liberty, and the pursuit of Happiness" rests. Although *Roe* has now been rightly thrown upon the ash heap of history, abortion remains a scourge from coast to coast and the nature of human rights and their protective scope must be continually articulated, defended, and upheld, and so the work of Americans United for Life will continue. We have come to recognize that the advancement of the human right to life and the protection and empowerment of Americans in culture, law, and policy is the work of every generation.

Pushing Roe v. Wade Over the Brink chronicles how three generations of committed leaders and team members at Americans United for Life have persevered in the fight not only to reverse *Roe* but also to foster a cultural and legal landscape in which the abolition of abortion is achievable and where the human right to life will truly mean that all are welcomed throughout life and protected in law.

By focusing America's moral gaze on the humanity of the preborn child and on the rights and responsibilities of mothers, fathers, and our entire political community, Americans United for Life champions a vision for upholding the equal dignity of every human being, building and sustaining a truly pro-life society that wins the battle for America's heart, the human right to life, and a future full of hope.

CHAPTER 1

The Bioethical Revolution
That Launched Americans United
for Life

The 1960s are well known as a decade of cultural upheaval, political activism, and social change in America. The Vietnam War was divisive, political unrest was widespread, and the 1968 Democratic National Convention in Chicago was engulfed by street protests. The tragic assassinations of President John F. Kennedy, Senator Robert Kennedy, and Dr. Martin Luther King, Jr., stoked fear, uncertainty, and turmoil. Social and family ties frayed.

But American society also witnessed at least one important positive change: The civil-rights movement, growing throughout the 1940s and 1950s, made significant gains in the 1960s through media, speeches, protests, court decisions, federal legislation, and the courage and prudence of its leaders.

As this enormous societal shift was unfolding, another significant change was taking place: the far lesser known "biological revolution." It was only as a result of this slowly unfolding set of changes in cultural attitudes and medical technology that the movement to legalize abortion was eventually able to find success in court.

As Berkeley Law professor David Louisell—who later became a board member of Americans United for Life—put it, the biological revolution of the mid-20th century included developments in "organ transplantation, permissive abortion, artificial insemination, sterilization, the pill, human including fetal experimentation ... and the possibilities of formal euthanasia, test-tube babies and genetic manipulation including cloning..."[1]

Of these many changes, Louisell believed that cloning was at the outer boundaries: "Cloning for humans at the moment remains but a fancy." In addressing the ethical problems that might arise concurrent with these developments, Louisell questioned the authority of the experts: "[t]o commit to the demographer, sociologist and other population expert primary concern for the population problem is not to excuse the rest of us from obligation as to what goes on in the meantime."[2]

Technological and bioethical developments continued apace throughout the 20th century. Life expectancy increased due to advances in medicine and public health. Technologically controlling fertility became a possibility when the birth-control pill—developed in part as a possible means of population control—hit the U.S. market in 1961.[3]

Advancements in technology have always shaped American law. At the beginning of the 20th century, when an abortionist was indicted for inadvertently killing a woman, a Maryland judge recognized the effects that medical technology might have in reducing maternal deaths from abortion:

> It is common knowledge that death is not now the usual, nor indeed the always probable consequence of an abortion. The death of the mother, doubtless, more frequently resulted in the days of rude surgery, when the character and properties of powerful drugs were but little known, and the control over their application more limited. But in these days of advanced surgery and marvelous medical science and skill, operations are performed, and powerful drugs administered, by skillful and careful men without danger to the life of the patient.[4]

During the 1960s, Louisell explored the existing legal constraints on organ transplantation.[5] In his view, among all the other prospects of the biological revolution, organ transplantation "likely enjoys, more than any other, the widest popular acceptability, indeed enthusiasm, the most significant scientific achievement with reasonable expectation of continuing progress, and the least substantial moral problems."[6] He was right. Louisell observed that heart transplantation, considered by some in 1966 to be a long way away, instead became a reality by the end of 1967, when a doctor in South Africa conducted the first heart transplant in which the patient regained full consciousness. The developments in biology and medicine resulted in the adoption of the Uniform Anatomical Gift Act, approved in 1968 and adopted by most states by the end of the 1960s.[7]

"Eugenic" sterilization, meanwhile, has had a long, sad history in America. Though the practice decreased in popularity as a result of World War II and the Nazi atrocities, it had not yet completely faded out of fashion in the U.S. by the 1960s. Princeton University Professor Paul Ramsey, who, like Louisell, went on to become an AUL board member, chronicled this reality in *Fabricated Man*.[8]

Some in the legal academy still believed that "evidence will indicate that need for a eugenics program exists if our quality of life is not to be seriously impaired through genetic deterioration," Ramsey wrote.[9] Artificial insemination by donor (AID), which was mostly unregulated in the 1960s, was viewed as one means to make eugenic goals more acceptable to the public. Another legal academic noted that "in 1966 twenty-six states had eugenic sterilization laws, of which twenty-three are compulsory. They apply to the mentally ill, the mentally retarded, epileptics and criminals." He suggested that the Supreme Court's infamous 1927 decision in *Buck v. Bell*,[10] which upheld compulsory-sterilization laws, was still "good law" and might support their constitutionality.[11]

Law professor Charles Kindregan warned, "In the coming decades humanity will be increasingly confronted with the prospect of technical control over the process of human reproduction" and cautioned about "the legal problems which will be raised by the biological revolution in the area of human fertility." In April 1971, *Time* magazine's cover story was entitled "The New Genetics: Man Into Superman."[12] At the end of the 1960s, law and bioethics were in turmoil, feeling the pressures of social, demographic, and technological change.

The two bioethical debates with the most enduring consequences were those over abortion and euthanasia. Technological and social change created a dynamic that enabled the legalization of abortion. Joseph Dellapenna, the world's foremost historian of abortion law, observed:

> The increasing safety of abortions for the pregnant woman, along with increasing pressures to limit the number of children in a family and the rather inadequate contraceptives available for doing so, combined to create a growing demand for abortion in the United States and the United Kingdom. Much the same was happening in other industrialized countries.[13]

That technological change was combined with social changes. Dellapenna added:

> The sudden transformation in the 1950s and 1960s of public thinking regarding abortion was rooted [in] a broad cultural change reflecting the political ascendance of a managerial elite that, in the United States, was committed to a pragmatic liberalism based on a political morality of rationality and efficiency.[14]

Advancements in medical technology had created bioethical conflicts in the protection of prenatal life. Technology in the 1950s and '60s had enabled a higher survival rate for babies born prematurely. In the 1950s, as Dellapenna found, an "extremely low birth weight" infant, one "weighing less than 1,000 grams (2.2 lbs) ... had barely a 2 percent chance of survival ... By 1960, survival rates ... had risen to 10 percent, and to 20 percent by 1970."[15]

At the same time, researchers were working on a chemical, prostaglandin F2 Alpha, that Upjohn Corporation of Kalamazoo, Michigan, was manufacturing and distributing for early abortions by 1972. W.N. Hubbard Jr., M.D., vice president and general manager of Upjohn's pharmaceutical division, acknowledged that "the medical profession is involved in the inhibition of life and here we look to the most effective and convenient means. Considering the pathology of population concentration and the futility of trying to keep up with an explosive birth rate by increasing productivity alone, the need for limitation of new human life becomes persuasive."[16]

By the early 1960s, Americans began to debate legalizing abortion, a debate that increased in intensity with each year that passed. Although the debate eventually made its way to the Supreme Court, it initially was highly decentralized and conducted at the local level in each state. Virtually every state legislature had its own debate over legalizing abortion, and most retained long-standing prohibitions on the procedure except when a mother's life was in danger.

By the end of the decade, the country was heading toward a crisis on the issue, both in the political arena and in the courts. As Chicago attorney Dennis Horan described it in his 1970 brief in the first modern Supreme Court abortion case, *United States v. Vuitch*, "Until the … current clamor for completely permissive abortion, the law's progress has been constant, and roughly parallel to the increase in scientific certainty of the nature of the unborn."[17]

Abortion challenged America's legal heritage that had protected unborn children. Louisell called it "the most threatening phase of the biological revolution because it has made something of a schizophrenic of our law."[18]

As a result of medical developments in the early 20th century, tort law (the law of civil wrongs) expanded to include legal protection against prenatal injuries, which technology helped to detect, and to protect prenatal human beings as persons from wrongful death. But this legal protection for prenatal human beings collided with the 1960s cultural upheaval clamoring for legal abortion.

Starting in the 1950s and 1960s, cultural elites across the country began a movement to legalize abortion, initially only in narrow circumstances. Doctors, law professors, and members of elite legal organizations, funded by wealthy individuals and foundations, began pushing to legalize abortion through state legislation.

The American Law Institute (ALI) drafted a model bill to legalize abortion in 1962. An early motivation of such laws was to increase professional discretion for doctors and to reduce the risk that doctors might be prosecuted for making the medical judgment to perform an abortion in life-threatening—or more permissive—medical circumstances.

Throughout the 1960s, the abortion debate was centered in state legislatures, and nearly every state continued to protect unborn children until 1967, when Colorado became the first state to adopt an abortion law with exceptions that went beyond saving the life of the mother. Thirteen states passed broader legal exceptions for abortion over the four years from 1967 to 1970.[19]

Initially, increasing interest in population control overshadowed these debates. It was a growing political issue in the 1960s, and the extent to which it captured public attention was reflected in a 1971 speech by Louisell. He was not one to exaggerate concerns, but in his remarks he referenced "two background-lurking bombs that do so much to charge our anxieties as well as set our rational fears: the hydrogen bomb and the population-explosion bomb."[20]

Louisell noted that, upon accepting the Nobel Prize for Peace in 1970 for "expanding food production in developing countries," Norman E. Borlaug had told the Nobel Committee, "We have only delayed the world food crisis for another thirty years. If the world population continues to increase at the same rate, we will destroy the species."[21]

At the same time, the National Academy of Sciences (NAS) was all-in for strict population control:

> "Family planning" is not equivalent to population control. Family planning is the rational and deliberate spacing of children in the number desired by the parents. But that number is determined by cultural considerations, family income, and ego satisfaction in the developed nations, and by the economic utility of children in the underdeveloped nations. Accordingly, large families are the norm among the affluent and among the ignorant poor. Population control demands that families be limited to the replacement rate.[22]

By 1968, the year that Planned Parenthood changed its formal position to favor legalized abortion, "population explosion" was a national political concern, so much so that in July 1969, President Richard Nixon delivered a "Special Message to the Congress on Problems of Population Growth."

The next March, Nixon signed a bill establishing a National Commission on Population Growth and the American Future. The group was named for its chairman, John D. Rockefeller III, an abortion activist and proponent of population control, who was active in funding efforts to further these causes. In March 1972, as Justice Harry Blackmun was writing his first draft opinions in *Roe v. Wade* and *Doe v. Bolton*, the Rockefeller Commission released its recommendations, advocating legalized abortion as a means of population control.

In a series of cases, the Supreme Court weighed in heavily on one side of the bioethical revolution. In 1965, in *Griswold v. Connecticut*,[23] the Court struck down Connecticut's criminal prohibition on the *marital use* of contraception—the one and only such law in the nation—and established a generalized "right to privacy" for the first time. Though *Griswold* was decided on a rationale of *marital* privacy, the decision was transformed within seven years into a platform for individualist expression. In 1972, the Court expanded *Griswold* and struck down limits on the sale of contraceptives to single individuals in *Eisenstadt v. Baird*,[24] decided by a 4-3 vote. These broad and ambiguous decisions served as crucial foundations for the Court when it addressed abortion.

One elite organization that would play an increasingly significant role in first legalizing abortion, and then influencing the Supreme Court to keep abortion unregulated, was the American College of Obstetricians and Gynecologists (ACOG), founded in 1951. In the summer of 1971, ACOG joined with other medical organizations to file an *amicus curiae* brief at the Supreme Court in the pending *Roe* and *Doe* cases, supporting abortion-on-demand.[25]

Ignoring substantial evidence to the contrary and contradicting its prior statements noting the risks of abortion, ACOG told the Court that abortion was more than 23 times as safe as childbirth, a figure they tied to Hungarian maternal-mortality numbers from the 1950s.

As Nancy Aries put it in a 2003 study, "Science was the ideological veneer for the profession's political position" in ACOG's campaign for legal abortion. ACOG's "policy-making process was deeply politicized and forced to respond to social demands beyond the medical establishment."[26] The group made the decision to file the brief "without sanction of the members of the College or even of their Board of Directors."[27]

A second bioethical issue at the center of public attention during the 1960s was death and dying, and more specifically, euthanasia.

The U.S. has a legal and cultural heritage specially protecting the lives of human beings over those of any other species, maintaining the 800-year-old tradition of homicide law, which is species-specific. Homicide law made the killing of a human being a felony, one of the most serious crimes. Anglo-American law also prohibited suicide for centuries. As Dennis Horan wrote in a 1975 article:

> Every civilized legal system considers euthanasia a crime. The law of England and America may consider it to be a more serious crime than any other legal system. The reason for this is rooted in Anglo-American common law which has traditionally placed the highest value on human life, regarding life as sacred and inalienable. The criminal law reflects this basic philosophy.[28]

For decades, euthanasia proponents in England and the U.S. pushed for legalization. In 1957, law professor and British eugenics advocate Glanville Williams gave a series of influential lectures at Columbia University, published as *The Sanctity of Life and the Criminal Law*, in which he advocated legalizing both abortion and euthanasia. In 1958, Yale Kamisar published a rebuttal to Williams, expressing skepticism about proposals for "mercy-killing" legislation.[29]

Despite these debates, initial legalization efforts were largely unsuccessful. In 1972, Louisell wrote that "no country in the world … permits euthanasia either of the voluntary or involuntary type," with the possible exception of "French and Swiss permissiveness" that allowed a physician to "provide but not administer poison at the request of a dying patient."[30]

Early proposals for legalization were ill-defined. Did euthanasia include both voluntary and involuntary cases? Were compulsory and involuntary the same? Were the motives of the patient important?

Ethical questions remained unsettled. What could be learned from Christian, Jewish, or Islamic traditions? Was it ethical for a physician to "administer drugs to alleviate pain even to the extent that may shorten life"? Was the traditional principle of double-effect part of the law?

Meanwhile, the question of living wills and advance directives had not yet been conceptualized or addressed in legislation. By the end of the 1960s, technology was advancing beyond ethical consensus, and legislators were falling behind in grappling with these bioethical problems. Most states had not expressly addressed most bioethical issues. Congress's power to legislate on many of these issues was doubtful. Public policy was thin and uncertain.

From 1967 to 1970, activists managed to loosen abortion restrictions in 13 states, adopting the ALI's model bill, including California, Georgia, and New York. Then the "reform" campaign sputtered in 1971 and 1972, just before the *Roe* decision, when no more legalization bills were enacted in the states. When abortion activists began to realize that the "reform" laws were not sufficiently broad, and that they could not achieve total repeal of abortion laws in the state legislatures, they took their advocacy into the courts.[31]

This growing political and legal campaign to legalize abortion nationwide and vanquish America's legal heritage protecting human life must have seemed inexorable by the time the founders of Americans United for Life started to organize in early 1971. Its founders envisioned AUL as an educational organization, but eventually the group began to adapt its strategy to the reality of the abortion debate in law and policy.

Chapter 1 Endnotes

1   David W. Louisell, *Biology, Law and Reason: Man as Self-Creator*, 16 Am. J. Juris. 1, 1 (1971).

2   *Id*. at 2.

3   Joseph W. Dellapenna, Dispelling the Myths of Abortion History 511 (2006) (hereinafter Dellapenna, Dispelling the Myths).

4   Worthington v. State, 92 Md. 222, 237–38 (1901).

5   David W. Louisell, *Transplantations: Existing Legal Constraints, in* CIBA Foundation Symposium on Ethics in Medical Progress 78, 80 (G. Wolstenholme & M. O'Connor eds. 1966); David W. Louisell, *The Procurement of Organs for Transplantation*, 64 N.W.U.L. Rev. 607, 625 (1969).

6   Louisell, *Biology, Law and Reason, supra* ch. 1 note 1, at 7.

7   *Id*.

8   Paul Ramsey, Fabricated Man: The Ethics of Genetic Control (1970).

9   *Id*. at 3, 8–9.

10 274 U.S. 200 (1927).

11 Homer H. Clark, Jr., *Law as an Instrument of Population Control*, 40 U. Colo. L. Rev. 179, 193 n.82 (1968) (citing Elyce Zenoff Ferster, *Eliminating the Unfit-Is Sterilization the Answer?*, 27 Ohio St. L.J. 591, 596 (1966)).

12 *The New Genetics: Man Into Superman*, Time, April 19, 1971, at 33.

13 Dellapenna, Dispelling the Myths, supra ch. 1 note 3, at 491.

14 *Id*. at 601.

15 *Id*. at 590.

16 *Upjohn's "Inhibition of Life" and a Response*, Newsletter of Americans United for Life, (Ams. United for Life, Chicago, Ill.), Sept.1974, at 5 (responding to Upjohn's editorial in the Journal of Reproductive Medicine (1972)).

17 Brief and Appendices of Dr. Bart Heffernan at 4, Amicus Curiae in Support of Appellant, United States v. Vuitch, 402 U.S. 62 (1971) (No. 84), *available at* https://aul.org/wp-content/uploads/2022/04/US-v.-Vuitch-Milan-Case-84-Brief-69-Pages.pdf.

18 Louisell, *Biology, Law and Reason, supra* ch. 1 note 1, at 19.

19 Paul Benjamin Linton, *The Legal Status of Abortion in the States if* Roe v. Wade *is Overruled*, 23 Issues In L. & Med. 3, 42 n.328 (2007).

20 Louisell, *Biology, Law and Reason, supra* ch. 1 note 1, at 2.

21 *Id*.

22 Comm. On Rsch. In the Life Scis., Nat'l Acad. of Scis., The Life Sciences: Recent Progress

AND APPLICATION TO HUMAN AFFAIRS: THE WORLD OF BIOLOGICAL RESEARCH REQUIREMENTS FOR THE FUTURE 446 (P. Handler ed. 1970).

23   381 U.S. 479 (1965).

24   405 U.S. 438 (1972).

25   "[A]bortion on demand … originated in the late 1960s among proponents of a freedom to abort as neatly encapsulating their political agenda." Dellapenna, DISPELLING THE MYTHS, *supra* ch. 1 note 3, at 929 & n. 214.

26   Nancy Aries, *The American College of Obstetricians and Gynecologists and the Evolution of Abortion Policy, 1951–1973: The Politics of Science,* 93 AM. J. PUBLIC HEALTH 1810 (Nov. 2003).

27   Thomas W. Hilgers, *The Medical Hazards of Legally Induced Abortion, in* ABORTION AND SOCIAL JUSTICE 57 (Thomas W. Hilgers & Dennis J. Horan eds., 1972).

28   Dennis J. Horan, *Euthanasia, Medical Treatment and the Mongoloid Child: Death as a Treatment of Choice?,* 27 BAYLOR L. REV. 76, 78 (1975).

29   Yale Kamisar, *Some Non-Religious Views Against Proposed Mercy-Killing Legislation,* 42 Minn. L. Rev. 969 (1958). Kamisar's influential article was later republished in DEATH, DYING, AND EUTHANASIA (Dennis J. Horan & David Mall, eds., 1977).

30   David W. Louisell, *Euthanasia and Biathanasia; on Dying and Killing, in* Death, Dying, and Euthanasia 383, 386 & n.13 (Dennis J. Horan & David Mall, eds., 1980).

31   Dellapenna, DISPELLING THE MYTHS, *supra* ch. 1 note 3, at 624–38.

CHAPTER 2

Into the Breach

At the heart of Frank Capra's 1946 film *It's a Wonderful Life* is the Bailey Brothers Building & Loan. Peter Bailey began the group in the fictional Bedford Falls as a non-profit organization to provide loans to his poor and middle-class neighbors who want to improve their living conditions. He does so out of personal conviction: "In a small way we are doing something important. Satisfying a fundamental urge. It's deep in the race for a man to want his own roof and walls and fireplace, and we're helping him get those things in our shabby little office."

Month by month, the group made progress incrementally, giving attention to "squeezing nickels and dimes" and working "to save three cents on a length of pipe." Over the course of decades, the group persevered against significant financial and economic obstacles to build "dozens of the prettiest little homes you ever saw, 90 percent owned by" their neighbors. By prudence, patience, and perseverance against considerable odds, they raised up the entire community.

The Bailey Brothers Building & Loan exemplifies a hallmark of America since the 18th century: the formation and proliferation of voluntary associations, as Alexis de Tocqueville highlighted in his classic study, *Democracy in America*, in the 1830s. Voluntary associations—many of which today are called non-profit organizations—have fostered immense legal, social, and religious change for the better.

In the 20th century, one of the most famous and successful of these organizations was the National Association for the Advancement of Colored People (NAACP). Founded in 1909, the NAACP litigated cases defending minorities accused of crimes and opposing racial segregation. Before Thurgood Marshall there was his mentor, Charles Hamilton Houston.[1]

After decades of litigation aimed at undermining the Supreme Court's 1896 decision in *Plessy v. Ferguson*,[2] which approved racial segregation in public accommodations, the NAACP won the landmark case of *Brown v. Board of Education*[3] at the Supreme Court in 1954. The Court unanimously declared that state-imposed racial segregation violated the Equal Protection Clause of the Fourteenth Amendment. For its courage, innovation, and successful strategy, the NAACP has been an inspiration for countless lawyers and non-profit legal organizations.

That included Americans United for Life. Apart from the U.S. Catholic bishops, AUL was the first national pro-life organization in America, incorporated in August 1971 in Washington, D.C., with its first office in the Washington Building at 15th & G Streets. AUL was incorporated by a group of advocates, including L. Brent Bozell Jr. of *National Review*, who wanted to educate Americans against abortion from a non-denominational, interdisciplinary perspective. Early board members were religiously diverse, including Catholics, Protestants, Unitarians, and Jews.

AUL's initial goal was a public-education campaign against abortion. Within 18 months of its founding, AUL had published *Abortion and Social Justice*, co-edited by Dr. Thomas Hilgers and Chicago attorney Dennis J. Horan.

Hilgers was a fellow in obstetrics and gynecology at the Mayo Graduate School of Medicine in Rochester, Minnesota, and had researched and written a report on *Induced Abortion* for the Minnesota legislature. During his residency, Hilgers circulated through Cook County Hospital for six months. While in Chicago, he met Horan, a member of the

Chicago Bar Association and American Bar Association and a lecturer in law at the University of Chicago Law School, who suggested collaborating on a book of essays to make the case against legalizing abortion.

Abortion and Social Justice was published by Sheed & Ward, "supported by a grant from Americans United for Life." The book's publication was delayed until after the decision in *Roe v. Wade.* It was finally published in 1973, a fortuitous delay that enabled the authors to include an epilogue leveling one of the first and strongest legal and medical critiques of the *Roe* decision.

The 19 essays combined law, medicine, history, and social-science data to advance a broad, pragmatic case against abortion. The book opened with a quote from Mahatma Gandhi: "It seems to me as clear as daylight that abortion would be a crime."[4]

The first chairman of the board of AUL was George Huntston Williams, the Hollis Professor of Divinity at Harvard University. An early AUL board member, Boston physician Dr. Joseph Stanton, recruited Williams to serve as the board's first chairman. Williams wrote the foreword, reflecting the prudential and democratic approach that would guide AUL's decades of work in the courts and legislatures. Williams, a Unitarian, described the aim of the book as:

> to present to the still open-minded, and concerned, the full range of argumentation against abortion: biological, medical, psychological, sociological, legal, demographic, and ethical ... Not a single essay or paper among the 19 is theological or programmatically religious, although undoubtedly a religious conviction informs many of the writers there of. The arguments against abortion as public policy can be cogently stated without resort to religious, ecclesiastical, or theological sanctions. And in a secular society, where state and church are constitutionally separated, it is entirely proper that we argue in the public domain against abortion in terms acceptable to humanists and theorists alike. ... We recognize that both law and education must complement each other, hence the stress in the collected essays of this volume.[5]

The contributors were "contending for the inviolability of all human life—from conception to natural death."[6] Williams understood that one's position on abortion would inevitably influence other social issues:

> A reverence for life within the womb is ultimately one with a reverent sense of responsibility and accountability for our global environment in the ecological concern of our time. But surely we will never be able to marshal the moral energy and self-discipline on an international scale to save some of the wilderness areas and to protect the myriad species of other forms of life now threatened with extinction if we do not have the ethical discernment and moral courage to oppose every facile acquiescence in individual and institutional violence against the mysterious sanctuaries of human life itself.[7]

Additional contributors included John T. Noonan Jr. and David Louisell, both professors at Berkeley Law School; Erma Clardy Craven, an African-American leader from Minnesota; Arthur Dyck, the Mary Saltonstall Professor of Population Ethics in the Center for Population Studies at Harvard University; Dr. Albert Liley, who had pioneered intra-uterine transfusion to treat the prenatal child; Marshall McLuhan, director of the Centre for Culture and Technology at the University of Toronto; and Victor Rosenblum, professor of political science and law at Northwestern University.

Horan and fellow lawyers Jerry Frazel, Tom Crisham, Dolores Horan, and John Gorby of John Marshall Law School joined Noonan and Louisell to contribute a chapter entitled "The Legal Case for the Unborn Child," an analysis of historical and contemporary legal protection for unborn children. Chicago physician Dr. Bart Heffernan assembled the facts and science of fetal development, including from the latest medical publications. He observed that "the phenomenon of 'quickening' reflects maternal sensitivity and not fetal competence."[8]

Hilgers contributed a 28-page chapter on "The Medical Hazards of Legally Induced Abortion," with a bibliography of more than 100 contemporary medical sources. He rebutted the claim that abortion was safer than childbirth, showing that the data from Eastern European countries and New York City were contradictory and unreliable. Hilgers also cited earlier, contradictory policy statements of elite medical organizations on abortion.

In an official statement of May 1968, the American College of Obstetricians and Gynecologists (ACOG) had declared, "It is emphasized that the inherent risk of such an abortion is not fully appreciated both by many in the profession and certainly not by the public."

A minority report published in May 1969 stated: "The inherent risks of a therapeutic abortion are serious and may be life-threatening; this fact should be fully appreciated by both the medical profession and the public. In nations where abortion may be obtained on demand, a considerable morbidity and mortality have been reported."

The March 1966 statement of the Council of the Royal College of Obstetricians and Gynaecologists in Great Britain, the 1970 statement of the Royal College, and the March 1970 statement of the Medical Society of the State of New York all mentioned the inherent risks.

Hilgers outlined contemporary data on immediate abortion complications—including infection, hemorrhage, perforation of the uterus, complications from hypertonic saline, anesthetic complications—and long-term complications that had been observed in foreign countries with legal abortion. No reliable American data were available during the time that abortion had been criminalized.

Hilgers described the medical literature on increased risk of ectopic pregnancy, miscarriage, sterility, and psychiatric problems following abortion. Even then, the problem with pre-term birth in future pregnancies after abortion was observable (and the evidence suggesting an increased risk has grown since then). Much, if not all, of Hilgers's points would later be cited in Horan's Supreme Court briefs in *United States v. Vuitch*, *Roe*, and *Doe v. Bolton*. These briefs launched a long-standing tradition in AUL's public education, emphasizing research that illustrates the negative effects of abortion for women.

Erma Clardy Craven contributed a chapter entitled "Abortion, Poverty and Black Genocide." Victor Rosenblum, a liberal Democrat, in a chapter entitled "Coercion in Liberation's Guise," criticized Supreme Court decisions in property and contract law that "all paid lip service to man's dignity and freedom but then reached decisions … that sanctioned … forms of economic coercion incompatible in practice with the freedom of contract principle."[9] Rosenblum applied this "realist" critique to judicial decisions on abortion that preceded *Roe*—*People v. Belous* from the California Supreme Court, *Vuitch* from the federal court in the District of Columbia, and *McCann v. Babbitz* from the federal court in Milwaukee.

Rosenblum emphasized Daniel Callahan's 1970 warning that "the credibility of advocates of legalized abortion under the banner of female freedom and 'the wanted child' is weakened when the zeal for change in the abortion laws is not matched by a comparable zeal to change those social conditions which force many women to choose abortion"[10] He observed that "economic pressures and social stigmas related to child-bearing today are as much instruments of force and coercion in ostensible choices of abortion as were the economic pressures and fears in ostensible choices not to join unions or to work at less than minimum wages in times past."[11]

Nearly 40 years later, Linda Greenhouse and Reva Siegel, in *Before* Roe: *Voices that Shaped the Abortion Debate Before the Supreme Court's Ruling,*[12] published excerpts from *Abortion and Social Justice* as an example of the significant voices that shaped the abortion debate before *Roe*.

In March 1972, in his capacity as AUL chairman, Williams sent a critical letter to President Richard Nixon, responding to the release of the Rockefeller Commission report. Williams denounced the commission's recommendation for the legalization of abortion, distinguished abortion from contraception, and denied that America had an overpopulation problem. He acknowledged that "public policy may appropriately attend to the global demographic problem and to the problem of natural resources and environmental health," but he wrote to "strongly oppose that part of the Commission's Report which endorses abortion as a licit means of public policy."

> A valid ecological and environmentalist concern for the so-called good of society cannot be grounded in calculated indifference to the civil liberty of the child in its mother's supposedly protective womb. I urge that the abortionist and anti-life part of the Report be firmly rejected in line with your own-expressed Constitutional respect for the inviolability of human life.[13]

Influencers

Abortion and Social Justice reflected an international network of collaboration by experts in law, medicine, and other learned professions who brought together reasoned civil arguments, based on careful study, intended to persuade. As Aristotle said more than 2,300 years ago, "Every failure of Truth to persuade reflects the weakness of its advocates."

It was an example of the reality that culture is shaped, for better or worse, by elites more than ordinary citizens and by networks more than solitary individuals. Culture is complex and isn't subject to ready change; it is hard to build and hard to alter. Talk of "transforming" culture is usually presumptuous. Cultural change demands informed, targeted strategies, sufficient resources, and long-term perseverance.

This emphasis has been with Americans United for Life since the beginning, and it became even more so when the AUL Legal Defense Fund was founded in 1974-75 and the disciplines of the legal profession influenced the culture of AUL.

In his book, *To Change the World: The Irony, Tragedy, and Possibility of Christianity in the Late Modern World*, sociologist James Davison Hunter sketches an original, sophisticated, and intricate description of what culture is and how it changes. He offers several propositions defining culture and cultural change.[14]

Hunter describes culture as "a normative order by which we comprehend others, the larger world, and ourselves and through which we individually and collectively order our experience … [T]hese norms define … what is good and evil, right and wrong, appropriate and inappropriate, honorable and shameful."[15]

He maintains that culture is "intrinsically dialectical," by which he means that "culture is a complex interaction of ideas and institutions" led by elites that organize human activity, as well as a complex interaction between individuals and the social order.[16] Symbols create culture, and those symbols are a form of capital, asset, or accumulated goods, including credentials, knowledge, accomplishments, and access.

Cultural capital is unevenly distributed in society. Just as there is economic inequality, there is cultural inequality. Hunter imagines culture as a structure in which capital is unevenly distributed at the center, with capital diminished as concentric circles get farther from the center. Individuals, networks, and institutions at the center have greater cultural capital, which may be imagined in terms of quality rather than quantity.

Hunter describes, too, that culture is formed by networks more than it is formed by individuals, even if they are brilliant and accomplished. This explains why those with the finest qualities and talents may be unknown, because they lack influence due to other constraints or limitations. Consequently, cultural change is more often produced by elites—influencers within society—than by changing the "hearts and minds" of average citizens.

Hunter, Janek Wasserman, and a host of other sociologists and historians have observed this unusual dynamic. As Edward Purcell recognized in *The Crisis of Democratic Theory*, between 1910 and 1970, "the recognized leaders of thought have increasingly been professionally trained university graduates, most of whom retained some close connection with the academies."[17]

History is replete with examples. Joseph Dellapenna, in his encyclopedic work, *Dispelling the Myths of Abortion History*, attributes "the first real challenge in the United States to the centuries old tradition condemning abortion" to British eugenicist and law professor Glanville Williams and his 1956 Carpentier Lectures at Columbia University Law School, published the following year as *The Sanctity of Life and the Criminal Law*.[18] Others point to Alfred Kinsey's report "as the source that reopened discussion of the acceptability of abortion" or "a book by ethicist Joseph Fletcher" or a conference by Planned Parenthood in 1955, the proceedings of which were published in 1958.[19] Whichever the source, all were the work of cultural elites.

A contemporary example is mask-wearing during the COVID-19 pandemic. Elites instructed people around the globe to wear masks, and people did so largely because those elites had told them to. Barton Swaim expressed this perspective in 2020:

> The coronavirus crisis has revealed at least this much: Elites hold more power over the lives of ordinary Americans than most of us appreciated. Somehow, brandishing only a few ill-understood statistics and the word "science," the well-to-do

influencers of our media, corporate and political spheres forced the nation's shopkeepers and wage-earners to bring their work activities and social habits to a dead stop for months on end. The few who questioned the wisdom of this orthodoxy were lampooned as idiots by their credentialed betters in respectable media outlets. It was an exercise of power I would have believed impossible six months ago.[20]

Elite influence is evident in plenty of social-reform movements. Janek Wasserman recently profiled the influence of the Austrian School of economics, which founded an approach to free-market economics in Vienna in the last quarter of the 19th century that influences American policy to this day. "The younger Austrians of the Hayek generation cemented the school's reputation in debates with socialists, Keynesians, and New Deal liberals," Wasserman writes. "They advanced a new defense of liberalism, often called neoliberalism, which still informs contemporary political discussions."[21] Austrian economists, like Friedrich Hayek (who won the Nobel Prize in 1974), Joseph Schumpeter, and Ludwig von Mises, who emphasized the importance of free-market economics, gained enormous influence by networking with international financial, business, and political elites. They positioned themselves "at the center of many of the most significant intellectual, economic, and political debates in Europe and the United States since its nineteenth-century inception." They established organizations, published books, and eventually "motivated a generation of American libertarian and free-market activists." By such "publications as Hayek's *Road to Serfdom*, Schumpeter's *Capitalism, Socialism, and Democracy*, and Mises's *Omnipotent Government*, Austrians brought their political values and worldviews to new audiences." They debated leading philosophers and economists, provided alternative ideas about economic problems, and proposed innovative policy approaches.

The Austrians "used their organizational acumen and networking savvy to create institutions to propagate their liberal, elitist thought style."[22] They were engaged in "intellectual work" and "movement building." They "courted journalists, (European) liberal politicians, and antistate, pro-business financial backers." They initiated conferences and graduate programs for Austrian economics. They made their ideas "more accessible by linking them to international—read: British and U.S.—trends."[23]

We can see similar dynamics at work today in the *Wall Street Journal* editorial and opinion pages, journals such as *National Review* and the *Atlantic*, and online outlets such as *Public Discourse, Daily Caller,* and the Heritage Foundation's *Daily Signal*.

The Importance of Networks

Hunter also observed that cultural change is not the result of the individual genius alone, but depends on individuals working within networks.

William Wilberforce, for example, was a British Member of Parliament (MP) who did heroic work to battle the slave trade in the British Empire between 1787 and 1833. While Wilberforce served as a voice for abolitionists in Parliament, he also worked with a network of abolitionists throughout England.

So, too, with the Austrian School of economics. Janek Wasserman wrote *The Marginal Revolutionaries* in order to launch "a renewed, critical engagement with this tradition [which] can be used to clarify how economics, politics, and power interact and how ideas, institutions, and influence intermingle to produce the orders in which we live."[24]

Wasserman shows that some projects did not produce substantial or immediate change until a network promoted them. For example, though Carl Menger's 1871 book *Principles of Economics* "offered a significant reformulation of core economic concepts like value, price and production, contributing to an incipient transformation in economics called the marginal revolution," it "was poorly distributed, found a limited readership, received middling reviews, and played a minor role in the vibrant economic discussions of the 1870s" and "quickly went out of print."[25] Still, Menger's book proved influential in the universities. A later network in Austria, connected with universities, took Menger's ideas, enhanced and disseminated them.

Abortion and Social Justice exemplified the legal, medical, and academic network that AUL developed and relied on for decades. Its contributors reflected AUL's network in 1971-72: diverse, interdisciplinary, and international. Several contributors joined AUL's board of directors in the

1970s, and some had an enduring effect on the organization, its mission, and its strategy.[26]

Dr. Joseph Stanton was sensitive to the power and reach of media. A tenacious advocate of Hippocratic medicine, he helped AUL publish statements and advertisements in the *New York Times* on abortion and other bioethical issues, including one in 1972 that reminded Americans of the traditional ethic of medicine, "do no harm" (primum non nocere), for all patients, born and unborn.

He organized another in the *New York Times* on January 22, 1983, memorializing the tenth anniversary of *Roe*. In October 1978, Stanton wrote and submitted testimony to the federal Ethics Advisory Board on in vitro fertilization, two years before the first IVF baby was born in the United States.

Stanton was limited by the effects of polio throughout his life and walked with the use of two canes, but at the age of 69 participated in a sit-in at an abortion clinic on Beacon Street in Brookline, Massachusetts, early on the morning of Saturday, March 5, 1989. With 200 others, he was arrested, handcuffed and jailed. When Stanton died in 1997, the church in Brookline was filled with mourners.

AUL's Values

A Judeo-Christian Ethic

Since its founding, AUL was inspired by the Judeo-Christian ethic. However imperfectly implemented by their followers, Judaism and Christianity have produced an ethic that significantly elevated the protection of human life and the dignity of men and women over several millennia. Colgate University political scientist Robert Kraynak wrote, "Among the great philosophies and religions of the world, Christianity may be said to make the loftiest claims on behalf of human dignity … Judaism and Islam, of course, also exalt humanity above other creatures and see the divine image in man."[27] That ethic provided the foundation for an "inviolability of life principle," as Justice Neil Gorsuch described it in his 2006 book *The Future of Assisted Suicide and Euthanasia*.

Likewise, Luc Ferry, an atheist and professor of philosophy at the University of Paris, acknowledged the impact of Christianity in his 2011 book, *A Brief History of Thought*:

> by resting its case upon a definition of the human person and an unprecedented idea of love, Christianity was to have an incalculable effect upon the history of ideas … [I]t is quite clear that, in this Christian re-evaluation of the human person, of the individual as such, the philosophy of human rights to which we subscribe today would never have established itself.[28]

This was an ethic William Wilberforce followed in the 1780s to fight the slave trade and slavery.[29] It prized human beings as uniquely valuable among all living creatures and declared the inherent dignity of every human being, without regard to race, sex, ethnicity, or human capacity. While Anglo-American law reflected that ethic in some ways, it did not do so fully. There was a constant need to improve and update the law to better embody that ethic.

Yet, the high regard for human life in Anglo-American law is recorded in Supreme Court justice James Wilson's account of the common law:

> With consistency, beautiful and undeviating, human life from its commencement to its close, is protected by the common law. In the contemplation of law, life begins when the infant is first able to stir in the womb. By the law, life is protected not only from immediate destruction, but from every degree of actual violence, and, in some cases, from every degree of danger.[30]

Yet, Wilson understood that the law—in the past, in different countries—did not protect human life to a high degree. He believed it was important to:

> show the anxiety, with which some legal systems spare and preserve human life; the levity and cruelty which others discover in destroying or sporting with it; and the inconsistency, with which, in others, it is, at some times, wantonly sacrificed, and, at other times, religiously guarded … [I]n Sparta, if any infant, newly born, appeared, to those who were appointed

> to examine him, ill formed or unhealthy, he was, without any
> further ceremony, thrown into a gulph near mount Taygetus
> ... At Athens, the parent was empowered, when the child was
> born, to pronounce on its life or its death ... [A]t Rome, the
> son held his life by the tenure of the father's pleasure ... .[31]

Abraham Lincoln reflected that same understanding of imperfection and moral progress in his application of the Declaration of Independence. Lincoln relied on the Declaration in the 1850s and 1860s to oppose the expansion of slavery, preserve the Union, and end slavery through the Thirteenth Amendment. He acknowledged that the Declaration had not yet been perfectly fulfilled:

> They [the authors of the Declaration of Independence] meant
> to set up a standard maxim for free society, which should be
> familiar to all, and revered by all; constantly looked to, con-
> stantly labored for, and even though never perfectly attained,
> constantly approximated, and thereby constantly spreading and
> deepening its influence, and augmenting the happiness and
> value of life to all people of all colors everywhere.[32]

Lincoln defended the natural rights principles of the Declaration as objectively true for all time, that human beings are endowed by their creator with certain inalienable rights, and that constitutional government by consent is morally right.

And yet, as C.S. Lewis noted in a 1958 essay, "Natural law, the value of the individual, the rights of man" were all "under assault in modern times."[33] These ideas, for Lewis, were prior to "the moral health and viability of second things, such as cultures, societies and governments."[34]

Dr. Martin Luther King, Jr also relied on "the majestic words of the Declaration of Independence" in 1963 in Birmingham in his campaign of "nonviolent direct action" against racial segregation. He appealed to "those great wells of democracy which were dug deep by the Founding Fathers in their formulation of the Constitution and the Declaration of

Independence," in order to more completely fulfill the goal of the Reconstruction Amendments in protecting civil rights in America.[35]

Persuasion

Abortion and Social Justice was AUL's initial effort at persuasion, another value that has driven the institution since its founding. Persuasion rests on the understanding that human beings have inherent purpose and dignity. Legal training teaches persuasion and seeks to instill skills that will help lawyers to achieve excellence in that virtue, so as to persuade clients, lawyers, judges, and legislators.

Persuasion is needed in an age of rage and rant, which reflects hatred in the human heart, a sign of cultural disease. The rage and rant we've witnessed in recent years has been the result of intentional training over the past few decades, starting with Saul Alinsky's 1971 book, *Rules for Radicals*, its Marxist ideology, and the proliferation of its ideology by radical left-wing billionaires such as George Soros. Alinsky abandoned persuasion for force, which rams ideas down people's throats. Seeking to persuade, by contrast, reflects respect for human beings and their dignity, and it is a necessary ingredient for self-government and civil society.

Bipartisanship

From its inception, AUL was bipartisan, in part due to its founders, but also because it reflected bipartisan support for human life in the major political parties at that time. As former AUL president Edward Grant has said: "there was nothing politically partisan in any of this. In fact, I'd say that [Horan's] leadership of AUL clearly directed us against such ties, except where tactically necessary."

Bipartisanship was smart politics when AUL was founded to work in state legislatures, because pro-life state legislators were found in both the Democratic and Republican parties in the 1970s and 1980s.

Ecumenical

Over the years, AUL's board and team have included Catholics, Evangelicals, Jews, Mormons, agnostics, and atheists. These members understood that they were *Americans* United for Life, and the name guided AUL's public voice and education efforts. In October 1986, AUL honored the late Nat Hentoff, jazz expert and long-time columnist of the *Village Voice*, for his commitment to the value of human life. AUL published his timeless essay, presented at an AUL Forum that fall, as a monograph entitled "The Indivisible Fight for Life."[36]

Resilience

At numerous points in AUL's history, its leadership has demonstrated remarkable resilience in the face of setbacks and criticism. After three years of intense work from 1970 to 1972 attempting to avert a Supreme Court decision legalizing abortion, Horan and other AUL leaders organized a network of experts and lawyers to challenge *Roe* and *Doe*, at a time when many thought the issue of abortion was settled. That resilience was on display time and again: after Supreme Court decisions such as *Diamond v. Charles*, after *Thornburg v. American College of Obstetricians and Gynecologists*, after *Webster v. Reproductive Health Services*, after *Planned Parenthood of Southeastern Pennsylvania v. Casey*, after *Stenberg v. Carhart*, after *Whole Woman's Health v. Hellerstedt*.

How does each of these principles fare 50 years after AUL's founding?

On July 16, 2020, the U.S. State Department's Commission on Unalienable Rights, chaired by Harvard Law Professor Mary Ann Glendon, released a report advocating three primary ideas:

1. The importance of the Universal Declaration of Human Rights adopted by the United Nations in 1948 and how it was influenced by the principles of the American Founding;

2. What's important for the protection of human rights is not "global governance" or "transnational organizations" but sovereign nation states protecting human liberty;

3. We will advance human rights by emphasizing the rights articulated and affirmed by a global consensus in the Universal Declaration in 1948.[37]

Though the report did not mention abortion, its emphasis on "unalienable, God-given rights grounded in sovereign nation-states" identifies a secure foundation for championing human rights.

In some quarters, the case for the dignity of human life is being made in a more compelling manner in the public square, and competing arguments have not fared well.[38] In a 2006 essay, Jurgen Habermas, the 91-year-old German philosopher and sociologist, noted that "universalistic egalitarianism, from which sprang the ideals of … human rights and democracy, is the direct legacy of the Judaic ethic of justice and the Christian ethic of love … To this day, there is no alternative to it…"[39]

The life and teachings of Bertrand Russell likewise show that "the centuries-long struggle to devise a morality from within merely human resources has now proven itself a failure," as philosopher Dallas Willard has described the modern philosophical legacy.[40] As one young woman at Harvard asked her professor, "What's the point of knowing good, if you don't keep trying to become a good person?" But as Willard points out, even "knowing good is not seriously proposed in college or university courses today. Any 'knowing' in such matters is thought to be totally impossible… both knowing good and being good are for the most part treated with open scorn in the academic settings which determine so much of our lives. That is the outcome of the long effort to establish a secular ethic in the modern period."[41]

The founders of AUL knew that a modern, secular ethic could not provide an ethical foundation for protecting human life, from conception to natural death, in the law.

In his 2012 book *Mind & Cosmos: Why the Materialist Neo-Darwinian Conception of Nature is almost Certainly False*, New York University philosopher Thomas Nagel offers two propositions for respecting human life and dignity: It is "undeniable … that our clearest moral and logical reasonings are objectively valid" and "somehow the world generates conscious beings capable of recognizing reasons for action and belief … We don't know how this happens but it is hard not to believe that there is some explanation of a systematic kind—an expanded account of the order of the world."[42] Nagel wonders if the "dominance of materialist naturalism" may be "nearing its end" and explores "what might replace it."[43]

These values have been necessary to the legal and policy goals of the cause for life in America, but they have not guaranteed success, because ideas alone are not enough. Leadership, strategy, and resources are crucial for implementing ideas and values, and the early leaders of AUL knew they needed an organizational structure to advance their mission.

Dennis Horan's Visionary Leadership

Attorney Dennis Horan was part of the AUL network before he was part of AUL. He collaborated with Hilgers on *Abortion and Social Justice* and replicated that collaboration with many publications.

Born in 1932, Horan served as a Marine during the Korean War. He was a 1957 graduate of Loyola University and a 1963 graduate of Loyola University Law School and subsequently joined the law firm Hinshaw, Culbertson, Moelmann & Fuller in Chicago. Horan eventually became managing partner and during his tenure the firm tripled in size.

In addition to his legal practice, Horan became an instructor in law at the University of Chicago Law School, where he taught trial advocacy and medical law. He was vice-chairman of the Medicine and Law Committee of the American Bar Association, a fellow of the American College of Trial Lawyers, and chairman of the tort-law section of the Illinois State Bar Association. His initial specialty was medical malpractice, which helped him establish relations with experts such as David Louisell and gave him command of medical studies and data.

Horan's medical-malpractice expertise and affiliation with doctors formed a natural network for legislation and litigation on bioethics. As Dr. Bart Heffernan later put it, Horan "saw abortion not only as a violent tragedy for women and unborn children, but as an ominous threat to the value of human life itself. He saw early on that it would lead, as we now see, to infanticide and euthanasia. He fought with increasing energy to reverse this trend which he saw as a threat to civilization itself." Heffernan eulogized Horan as "a man of letters whose poetry was published frequently; he was a student and teacher of the law; a practical man who saw to its just application."

The First Modern Supreme Court Abortion Case

Horan brought to AUL the skills and strategic perspective of a litigator. Jack Gorby recalled that, early in their relationship, Horan asked a rhetorical question: "What's the first thing you do when you prepare your case for trial?" Horan's answer: "I write my final argument." Horan imagined how he would argue the case to the jury and then constructed the trial work to support that final argument.

Even before AUL began, Horan was involved in abortion litigation in state and federal courts. He saw the threat of abortion cases in the federal court pipeline and involved himself in at least three abortion cases in federal court and two abortion cases in state courts from 1970 to 1972.

Horan filed a brief in the landmark New York abortion case, *Byrn v. New York Health & Hospital Corp.*[44] In 1970 Horan's brief in *Byrn*, filed with attorneys Jerome A. Frazel, Jr., Thomas M. Crisham, Dolores B. Horan, and Jack Gorby, presented the historical case against a right to abortion.

After the Chicago chapter of the American Civil Liberties Union filed *Doe v. Scott*[45] in February 1970, challenging the 1828 Illinois abortion law, Horan was drawn into the case, one of more than 20 abortion cases filed as test cases challenging state abortion prohibitions.[46] Horan tried to avert the legalization of abortion by the courts and believed that the Illinois case was the best vehicle for the Supreme Court to address the issue.

He was alerted to the case by Bart Heffernan, his brother-in-law and a cardiologist in Chicago. Working over the weekend, they prepared and filed a motion on Wednesday, March 11, 1970, asking the court to appoint Dr. Heffernan as the guardian for the class of unborn children throughout Illinois.[47] Heffernan was granted intervention in March 1970 by federal Judge William Campbell.

Horan predicated his motion for the appointment of a guardian *ad litem* on Federal Rule of Civil Procedure 17(c), which, in 1970 read: "The Court shall appoint a Guardian *Ad Litem* for an infant or incompetent person not otherwise represented in an action or it shall make such other order as it deems proper for the protection of the infant or incompetent person."

Of the more than 20 abortion cases filed in federal court between 1968 and 1973, *Scott* was virtually the only one in which the court appointed a guardian *ad litem* to represent unborn children. In June 1970, the district court, on its own initiative, issued a critical order, effectively short-circuiting the case, "that there are no factual issues in dispute and the legal issue of the constitutional questions presented may best be fully heard and considered on motions to dismiss or for summary judgment" and announced that it would decide whether the statute was "unconstitutionally vague and indefinite" and "constitutes an invasion of privacy."

The court never allowed discovery in the case. Horan objected to the summary proceeding but filed the motions and briefs as ordered and asked the district court to "declare that the United States Constitution and the Constitution of the State of Illinois protect and guarantee to the class of unborn children ... due process of law and equal protection of the law for the preservation and protection of their lives."

Meanwhile, the Supreme Court was moving to hear its first modern abortion case, *Vuitch*.[48] Dr. Milan Vuitch was an abortionist in Washington D.C. and Maryland, and the case was his constitutional challenge to the District of Columbia's abortion prohibition, first enacted by Congress in 1901 and readopted in 1953, which prohibited abortion "unless ... necessary for the preservation of the mother's life or health."[49] *Vuitch* tested the constitutionality of the term "health" in the D.C. law, which, when adopted by Congress, was virtually unique among abortion laws in America. Before trial, federal judge Gerhard Gesell dismissed the case, holding that the D.C. abortion law was unconstitutionally vague.[50] (Vuitch was prosecuted in Maryland before *Roe* had been decided and successfully sued for abortion malpractice in D.C. after *Roe*.[51]) One stain that has characterized the Supreme Court's abortion doctrine since 1970 has been the unscrupulous abortionists who have so often been the named plaintiffs to headline the major abortion cases.

After judge Gesell struck down the abortion statute in the District of Columbia in November 1969,[52] the case moved directly to the Supreme Court. On July 13, 1970, Horan, Louisell, and colleagues filed their *amicus curiae* brief in the Supreme Court on behalf of Heffernan, noting that he was guardian *ad litem* in *Scott* for "the class of all unborn children in the State of Illinois who will be adversely affected by the abolition of the abortion statute in Illinois."

Their 61-page brief was a scholarly analysis replete with legal, historical, and scientific authorities. It emphasized legal protection for the unborn child in property law, growing protection in tort law, and fetal medicine, including "the burgeoning scientific knowledge of the realities of fetal life [that] has worked a dramatic revolution in tort law." It also contained photographs of a prenatal child at various gestational ages up to 28 weeks.

Horan's brief sought to complement the brief filed by the U.S. Solicitor General, Erwin Griswold, in defense of the D.C. abortion prohibition. Horan argued that Congress intended to protect the prenatal child through the D.C. abortion prohibition. The appendix contained a medical bibliography of 60 medical authorities on fetal medicine. The Supreme Court heard oral arguments in *Vuitch* on January 12, 1971, an oral recording of which is still available online.[53]

Back in Illinois, on January 29, 1971, the three-judge district court ruled 2-1 in *Scott* that the Illinois abortion law was unconstitutional because it was unduly "vague" during the first twelve weeks of pregnancy but not thereafter.[54] This was an odd conclusion because the Illinois abortion law had been enacted in 1828, and hundreds of abortionists had been convicted under that law in the past century. Why twelve weeks? Because, Horan reasoned, abortion activists argued that abortion in the first twelve weeks was safer than childbirth, relying on Planned Parenthood researcher Christopher Tietze citing Eastern European numbers from the 1950s.

Judge William Campbell, the dissenter from the 2-1 ruling, raised an objection that would later be directed at *Roe* and the Supreme Court's abortion doctrine:

> No individual right or freedom is ever advanced in this country through an unwarranted intrusion of the judiciary into the proper province of the legislature. Indeed, in these days of pressure groups regularly seeking from courts that which only legislatures can properly give, constitutional government is weakened each time courts place their personal philosophical views above the law.[55]

Horan quickly filed an appeal on behalf of Heffernan to the Supreme

Court. At the time, seven other abortion cases were pending in the Supreme Court.

Three weeks later, Horan's vision, expertise, networking, and litigation strategy were captured in a historic, day-long medical-legal conference on abortion sponsored by Illinois Right to Life and held on Sunday, February 21, 1971, at Loyola University Medical Center in Maywood, Illinois. Jack Gorby attended the Loyola conference and introduced himself to Horan for the first time, which began a decade long collaboration with Horan and AUL on human rights law and litigation in the Supreme Court.[56]

The three attorneys involved in the Illinois abortion case, Horan, Frazel, and Crisham, spoke at the conference, along with Illinois State Representative Henry Hyde, then Majority Leader of the Illinois House of Representatives, and other lawyers and doctors. At the time, approximately 13 states had liberalized abortion law by legislation in the 1960s.[57] "If abortion is legalized in the U.S.," Horan told the conferees, "we will see the issues of euthanasia and infanticide in 5 years," quoting from a bill introduced in Florida in Oct. 1969, designated "an act relating to the right to die with dignity." "This fight might take 25 years," Horan warned. He had no illusions that the battle would be brief.

Two months later, the Supreme Court issued a badly splintered 5-4 decision in *Vuitch* on April 21, 1971.[58] The majority opinion by Justice Black held that the D.C. abortion law *was not unconstitutionally vague.* The decision was muddled by at least seven separate opinions and complicated by a procedural dispute over the federal Criminal Appeals Act.

The next day, April 22, the justices voted to hear *Roe* and *Doe* in the fall of 1971.

Unknown to Horan and his colleagues, the Court initially agreed to hear *Roe* and *Doe* not to address abortion—as most assume—but to determine the application of *Younger v. Harris*, which the Court had decided on February 23, 1971. *Younger* limited the circumstances under which state court criminal defendants could take their cases into federal court, the type of procedural scenario presented in some of the federal court abortion cases, like *Roe* and *Doe*. The Court decided to hear *Roe* and *Doe* to see how *Younger* applied to the factual situation in *Roe* and *Doe*. They left Horan's appeal in *Scott* in limbo.[59]

Like few others, Horan recognized the negative implications of *Vuitch*. Although the Court ruled that the D.C. abortion law was not unconstitutionally vague, it did so by giving an expansive interpretation to the "health" exception in the D.C. law. justices Douglas and Stewart signaled that they supported some notion of abortion rights. *Vuitch* demonstrated to Horan that the Court might indeed move to legalize abortion. It did not bode well for *Roe* and *Doe*, and Horan warned the leaders of AUL that the Court might issue a ruling legalizing abortion.

Horan's *amicus* brief filed in *Roe* and *Doe* in the summer of 1971 launched AUL's legal and scholarly emphasis on the negative impact of abortion on women.[60] The lengthy medical bibliography of 173 articles compiled by Dr. Hilgers contained in the Appendix to Horan's brief in *Roe* and *Doe*, and its critique of the New York City abortion data and Eastern European abortion data, were never rebutted by the justices.

The brief was filed on behalf of more than 224 physicians, professors and fellows of ACOG, including Drs. Mildred Jefferson, Joseph Stanton, Herbert Ratner, Eugene F. Diamond, Edward Kilroy, who at one time or another were AUL board members. Also listed were Drs. Leo Alexander, Alex Barno, Watson Bowes, Laura Edwards, Marjorie Hartig, Barbara Hastings, Marilyn Johnson, Albert Liley, Richard T.F. Schmidt, Hymie Gordon, Bart Heffernan, Andre Hellegers, Fred Mecklenburg, Konald Prem, Barbara Rockett, Mildred Shelley, Gloria Volini, John C. Willke, Doris Wright, and numerous professors of medicine from university medical schools at Harvard, Minnesota, Denver, Tufts, Colorado, Tulane, Cincinnati, Ohio State, Baylor, Northwestern, Georgetown, University of Texas-Houston, New Jersey, Louisiana State, Vanderbilt, Stritch-Loyola, UCLA, Mayo, New Mexico, Mississippi, UCSF, Utah, University of Chicago, SUNY Buffalo, Yale, Pittsburgh, Missouri, Purdue-Indianapolis, Connecticut, USC, Texas Southwestern, Creighton, Boston University, Illinois, Case Western, University of Washington-Seattle, University of South Carolina, Oklahoma, Louisiana State, Toledo, Michigan, Loma Linda, Penn, Emory, and the University of Illinois.

ACOG had filed a counter brief in the Supreme Court in support of a right to abortion, listing 178 physicians. Most were from Minnesota, including three from the Mayo Clinic, where Justice Blackmun had been resident counsel in the 1950s. The ACOG brief claimed that the 120-year-old law was "unconstitutionally vague," emphasized the impact on medical practice, and deceptively characterized the issue at stake as "the performance of medically indicated therapeutic abortions."[61]

In September 1971, the Supreme Court was plunged into crisis when justices Black and Harlan abruptly retired due to ill health. That removed two justices who would likely have voted *against* a national right to abortion and created two vacancies which flipped the balance of the Court to 4-3 pro-abortion. That temporary 4-3 majority was able to move to hear *Roe* and *Doe* in December and to seek to use the cases to sweep away the abortion laws before the two vacancies could be filled in January 1972.[62]

Americans United for Life filed a separate *amicus* brief in *Roe* authored by Notre Dame law Professor Charles Rice, who had published books and articles on bioethical issues during the 1960s.[63] Rice argued in the brief that unborn children were persons protected by the Fourteenth Amendment.

Horan, Frazel, and Crisham filed a similar brief in two Illinois abortion cases, *People v. Frey* and *People v. Mirmelli*, which originated in Chicago (Cook County), in support of the state's enforcement of the 1828 Illinois abortion law against two abortionists for doing first trimester abortions. Mirmelli was a doctor; *Frey* was not. The Illinois Supreme Court held the cases until *Roe* was decided and then, two months later, reversed the convictions, concluding that *Roe* invalidated the Illinois abortion law.[64] Showing the confusion about *Roe* at the time, the court dismissed the case against the lay abortionist, *Frey*. Decisions like *Frey* necessitated the Court's clarification of *Roe* in *Connecticut v. Menillo* in November 1975, in which the Court had to make clear that *Roe* applied to doctors and that "non-physicians" could still be prosecuted.

When *Roe* was issued in January 1973, Horan was undoubtedly frustrated that he had anticipated most of the arguments for abortion in *Vuitch* and *Roe*, and rebutted the legal arguments that Justice Blackmun eventually relied upon in his majority opinion in *Roe*. His frustration showed in his epilogue in *Abortion and Social Justice*, with Gorby and Hilgers, which laid out an early legal and medical critique of the *Roe* opinion.

The Need for a Public Interest Law Firm

The genesis of the AUL Legal Defense Fund began with Horan. After *Roe* was decided, he urged Stanton and Rosenblum that a legal defense fund, on the order of the NAACP, was needed to counter the Supreme Court's decision in *Roe*. Horan outlined this need in a speech to diocesan attorneys in 1974.[65]

Horan became a board member of AUL in 1973. Following Horan's leadership, AUL moved to Chicago by August 1974 and opened its first office in Chicago in the Carbon and Carbide Building at 230 N. Michigan Avenue, Suite 515, just south of the Chicago River.[66] AUL became the first pro-life public interest law firm in America.

As Ed Grant recalled, Horan "saw such precedents in the NAACP Legal Defence Fund, and the 'Americans United for Separation of Church and State' LDF, and he knew the pro-life movement needed something similar." Horan's "idea of a Legal Defense Fund was clearly linked to the NAACP's example."[67] A thorough effort to understand and adapt a strategy to overturn *Roe* to the strategy and tactics of the NAACP "was initiated after the O'Connor 'collision course' opinion in *Akron*," which Professor Kenneth Ripple and Professor Richard Myers addressed at the 1984 *Reversing Roe* Conference.[68] However, between *Roe* and 1984, "the strategy of 'cabining-in *Roe*'" was consciously applied.

An independent, public interest law firm or "legal defense fund" was necessary for several reasons. It could zealously pursue its public interest mission, independent of numerous countervailing forces. It could advise legislators and create test cases. It could work independently of other law firms and organizations. It could work nationally, across all 50 states, and internationally. It could litigate in federal and state courts. It could raise tax-exempt and tax-deductible funding and not be dependent on client fees, as private law firms are. And, as would become clear within a few years, pro-life law professors would become increasingly ostracized as the legal academy got swept up with abortion as a "right" and the American Bar Association (ABA) endorsed a "right" to abortion at its annual meeting in August 1992.[69] Pro-life professors could not carry on such a legal project within most law schools. Pro-life advocacy would have to be done by a tax-exempt organization that could aggressively and independently pursue the mission.

AUL's Leadership

As the chairman of AUL between 1978 and 1988, Horan was, colleagues recognized, "at the peak of his powers." Fellow board member Dr. Eugene F. Diamond recalled dozens of board meetings at which Horan would keep the discussion in line, saying, "Stick to the point!" or "Follow the agenda!" Diamond described him, with affection and admiration, as a "hard-nosed man" with a "built-in lawyer's scold."

Horan recruited leading law professors, such as Louisell and Noonan, to the AUL board. Louisell was "of counsel" on Horan's Supreme Court brief in *Vuitch* in 1970, joined the AUL board in August 1974, and served until his death in August 1977.[70]

Noonan was a professor at the University of California at Berkeley and wrote a series of influential legal books. When nominated to the U.S. Court of Appeals for the Ninth Circuit in 1984, Noonan resigned from the AUL board to serve as a federal appeals court judge for three decades. Upon Noonan's death in 2017, Harvard law professor Andrew Kaufman recalled his experience with Noonan while they were students at Harvard Law School:

> John was indomitable. I first saw that quality when he was a student at Harvard Law School taking Dean Griswold's course in Taxation. John was then a rare kind of student, for he already had a Ph.D. from Catholic University. He was also a member of the Law Review and decided that, with all the things he was interested in doing while at law school, he could either do all the work in Taxation or he could attend all the Taxation classes but not both. He decided to do the former. At the end of the year Dean Griswold advertised for a research assistant to help him with a brief over the summer. Undeterred by the fact that he had never gone to class, John applied. When asked whose tax course he had taken, John replied "yours." When Griswold said that he didn't recognize John, John explained his choice. Griswold, also an indomitable sort, then said that he would read John's exam—this was in the days before anonymous

grading—and get back to him. John got an A and the job.[71]

Professor Victor Rosenblum was an early board member who served as vice-chairman and later chairman, from 1972 to 2006. In a 2004 interview, Rosenblum recalled that he had been asked to attend a meeting with Dr. Herbert Ratner of Oak Park, Illinois, and Dr. Stanton to "talk about an organization that would be different from The Value of Life Committee [founded by Dr. Stanton in Boston in 1970] and wouldn't be limited to physicians. It would draw upon professionals of all kinds of backgrounds, religious, non-religious, with primacy of commitment to human life."

That organization became AUL. It was Rosenblum who recruited Northwestern Law students, Paige Cunningham and Ed Grant, to work for AUL. After Rosenblum died in March 2006, Supreme Court Justice Antonin Scalia gave a memorial tribute to him at Northwestern University Law School.[72]

AUL's first legal team from 1974 to 1976 was part-time, consisting of Horan (by then a partner at Hinshaw Culbertson), Rosenblum (professor at Northwestern), Louisell (professor at University of California at Berkeley), and John Gorby (professor at John Marshall Law School in Chicago). None could serve full-time. AUL needed a full-time legal team.

In a November 3, 1975 letter to AUL chairman George Williams at Harvard Divinity School, Horan reported on the status of several priority AUL projects.[73] The translation of the West German abortion decision by Jonas and Gorby was completed.[74] Horan was still trying to communicate with Dr. Ernst Benda, president of the Federal Constitutional Court for the Federal Republic of Germany, to schedule him for a speech in America. Benda eventually gave that speech at Harvard University on April 27, 1977, during a lecture tour sponsored by the John Marshall Law School. Horan and Gorby coordinated that tour. Benda's article on the West German abortion decision was eventually published in *Human Rights*, a journal of the American Bar Association's Section of Individual Rights and Responsibilities, in 1977.[75]

Horan also reported to Williams that the manuscript for *Death, Dying and Euthanasia* was moving forward slowly and that he was hoping it would be published by June 1976. Horan and colleagues were working on an *amicus* brief to be filed in "the Missouri cases" (*Danforth*).[76] Horan believed that "next to *Roe v. Wade* the Missouri case will have the greatest impact on the Movement." They had received a grant from Our Sunday Visitor to cover the printing cost of the *amicus* brief in *Danforth*. Melvin Morgan was found not guilty in a prosecution for fetal homicide in Cook County, Illinois, a prosecution which had been aided by a legal memo prepared by Jack Gorby and "AUL Legal Defense Fund Lawyers, which convinced the State Attorney of Cook County that the homicide law of Illinois did protect a viable unborn child." (A decade later, Illinois enacted a fetal homicide law, drafted in significant part by AUL, which explicitly protected the unborn child from conception outside the context of abortion.)

The fundamentals of what AUL would become, and the role it would play in the broader pro-life movement, were set in motion by Horan and the earliest board members in the 1970s. As opportunities opened up and obstacles shifted, the group would rise to the challenge with strategic adjustments.

Chapter 2 Endnotes

1   *See generally* Richard Kluger, Simple Justice (1975).

2   163 U.S. 537 (1896).

3   347 U.S. 483 (1954).

4   Abortion and Social Justice, *supra* ch. 1 note 27, at ii (citing All Men Are Brothers: Life and Thoughts of Mahatma Gandhi (Krishna Kripalani, ed. 1972)).

5   George H. Williams, *Foreward: The Democratization of a Near Constant in History to* Abortion and Social Justice, *supra* ch. 1 note 27, at ix, xiv.

6   *Id*. at xvii.

7   *Id*. at xviii.

8   Bart T. Heffernan, *The Early Biography of Everyman, in* Abortion and Social Justice, *supra* ch. 1 note 27, at 15.

9   Victor G. Rosemblum, *Coercion in Liberation's Guise, in* Abortion and Social Justice, *supra* ch. 1 note 27, at 151.

10   *Id*. at 153.

11   *Id*. at 153.

12   Linda Greenhouse & Reva B. Siegel, Before *Roe v. Wade*: Voices that Shaped the Abortion Debate Before the Supreme Court's Ruling 88–94 (2d ed. 2012).

13   On file with author.

14   James Davison Hunter, To Change the World: The Irony, Tragedy, and Possibility of Christianity in the Late Modern World 32–47 (2010).

15   *Id*. at 32.

16   *Id*. at 34.

17   Edward A. Purcell, Jr. The Crisis of Democratic Theory: Scientific Naturalism & the Problem of Value x (1973). *See also* Darel E. Paul, From Tolerance to Equality: How Elites Brought America to Same-Sex Marriage (2018).

18   Dellapenna, Dispelling the Myths, *supra* ch. 1 note 3, at 586–89.

19   *Id*. at 586–87.

20   Barton Swaim, *The People vs. Their Betters: The Red-Blue Dance of the Working Man and the Overclass, Diagrammed at Last,* Wall St. J. (Jan. 24, 2020), https://www.wsj.com/articles/political-books-the-people-vs-their-betters-11595626826?mod=searchresults&page=1&pos=2.

21   Janek Wasserman, The Marginal Revolutionaries: How Austrian Economists Fought the

WAR OF IDEAS 3 (2019).

22   *Id*. at 14.

23   *Id*. at 39.

24   *Id*.

25   *Id*. at 17.

26   In 1972, the board included George H. Williams; Victor Rosenblum; Louise Summer-hill; Donald McClane; Dr. John Hildebrand; John Archibold; Notre Dame law professor Charles Rice; Dr. Eugene Diamond; Georgetown University professor Germain Grisez; Drew University professor Will Herberg; Dr. Edward Kilroy, Kenneth Mitzner, Ph.D.; Dr. Herbert Ratner, director of public health in Oak Park, Illinois; and Dr. Joseph Stanton. Actress Loretta Young was the board's honorary chairman. In a 2005 interview, Mitzner confirmed that he had attended the founding meeting of AUL with Brett Bozell in Washington DC in 1971, along with Herbert Ratner, who had helped to organize the meeting and invited Mitzner.

27   IN DEFENSE OF HUMAN DIGNITY: ESSAYS FOR OUR TIMES 81 (Robert P. Kraynak & Glenn Tinder, eds., 2003).

28   LUC FERRY, A BRIEF HISTORY OF THOUGHT: A PHILOSOPHICAL GUIDE TO LIVING 60 (2011).

29   *See* CLARKE D. FORSYTHE, *Wilberforce's Perseverance, in* POLITICS FOR THE GREATEST GOOD: THE CASE FOR PRUDENCE IN THE PUBLIC SQUARE 78 (2009) (hereinafter Forsythe, PFTGG).

30   *Id*. at 218 (citing JAMES WILSON, *Lectures on Law, in* THE WORKS OF JAMES WILSON 596–97 (Robert G. McCloskey ed., 1967)).

31   *Id*. at 217.

32   Abraham Lincoln, *Speech on the Dred Scott Decision at Springfield, Illinois, June 26, 1857, reprinted in,* ABRAHAM LINCOLN SPEECHES AND WRITINGS, 1832–1858 398 (Don E. Fehrenbacher ed.,1989).

33   JUSTIN DYER & MICAH WATSON, C.S. LEWIS ON POLITICS AND THE NATURAL LAW 134 (2016). *See* C.S. Lewis, *Willing Slaves of the Welfare State*, THE OBSERVER, July 20, 1958, at 6, *reprinted in* C.S. LEWIS, GOD IN THE DOCK: ESSAYS ON THEOLOGY AND ETHICS 314 (Walter Hooper ed., 1970).

34   DYER & WATSON, C.S. LEWIS ON POLITICS AND THE NATURAL LAW *supra* ch. 2 note 33, at 146. *See also* O. CARTER SNEAD, WHAT IT MEANS TO BE HUMAN: THE CASE FOR THE BODY IN PUBLIC BIOETHICS (2020).

35   Martin Luther King, Jr., *Letter from Birmingham City Jail, reprinted in* MARTIN LUTHER KING, JR., WHY WE CAN'T WAIT, 77–100 (1963).

36   Nat Hentoff, *The Indivisible Fight for Life,* AMS. UNITED FOR LIFE (Oct. 19, 1986), http://groups.csail.mit.edu/mac/users/rauch/nvp/consistent/indivisible.html.

37   COMM'N ON UNALIENABLE RTS., U.S. STATE DEP'T, REPORT OF THE COMMISSION ON UNALIENABLE RIGHTS (2020).

38   *See generally* Snead, *supra* ch. 2 note 34; JOHN F. KILNER, DIGNITY AND DESTINY: HUMANITY

IN THE IMAGE IF GOD (2015); MICHAEL J. SANDEL, THE CASE AGAINST PERFECTION: ETHICS IN
THE AGE OF GENETIC ENGINEERING (2007); WESLEY J. SMITH, CONSUMER'S GUIDE TO A BRAVE
NEW WORLD (2004); THE PRESIDENT'S COUNCIL ON BIOETHICS, BEING HUMAN: READINGS FROM
THE PRESIDENT'S COUNCIL ON BIOETHICS (2003); IN DEFENSE OF HUMAN DIGNITY, *supra* ch. 2
note 27; FRANCIS FUKUYAMA, OUR POSTHUMAN FUTURE: CONSEQUENCES OF THE BIOTECHNOLOGY
REVOLUTION (2002); LEON KASS, LIFE, LIBERTY AND THE DEFENSE OF DIGNITY: THE CHALLENGE
FOR BIOETHICS (2002).

39   JÜRGEN HABERMAS, TIME OF TRANSITIONS 150–151 (2006), *reprinted in* Thomas Gregersen,
      A Misquote About Habermas and Christianity, POL. THEORY – HABERMAS & RAWLS (June
      8, 2009), http://habermas-rawls.blogspot.com/2009/06/misquote-about-habermas-
      and.html.

40   DALLAS WILLARD, THE DIVINE CONSPIRACY 184 (1998).

41   *Id*. at 185.

42   THOMAS NAGEL, MIND & COSMOS: WHY THE MATERIALIST NEO-DARWINIAN CONCEPTION OF NATURE
      IS ALMOST CERTAINLY FALSE 31 (2012).

43   *Id*. at 15.

44   286 N.E.2d 887 (N.Y. 1972), *appeal dismissed for want of substantial federal ques-
      tion*, 410 U.S. 949 (1973).

45   321 F. Supp. 1385 (N.D. Ill. 1971), *vacated and cases remanded for further consider-
      ation in light of* Roe v. Wade, 410 U.S. 113 (1973).

46   *See* CLARKE D. FORSYTHE, *The Road to* Roe*: Taking Abortion into the Courts, in* ABUSE OF
      DISCRETION: THE INSIDE STORY OF *ROE V. WADE* 55 (2013).

47   There are different kinds of guardians in the law. Horan specifically filed for ap-
      pointment of a guardian *ad litem*, which is "a guardian appointed by a court … to
      prosecute or defend for an infant … ." *Guardian ad Litem,* BLACK'S LAW DICTIONARY
      834 (Rev. 4th ed. 1968).

48   402 U.S. 62 (1971).

49   D.C. Code Ann. § 22-201 (1901) (repealed 2004).

50   United States v. Vuitch, 305 F. Supp. 1032 (D.D.C. 1969).

51   Furr v. Vuitch, 482 A.2d 811 (D.C. 1984).

52   *Vuitch,* 305 F. Supp. 1032.

53   *Vuitch*, 402 U.S. 62; *United States v. Vuitch*, OYEZ, https://www.oyez.org/cas-
      es/1970/84 (last visited June 30, 2023).

54   321 F. Supp. at 1395.

55   *Id*. at 1396.

56   Life, Liberty, & Law, *Jack Gorby on the Early Days of Americans United for Life,*
      Roe v. Wade *and Strategies to Advance Human Rights, and the Future,* AMS. UNITED
      FOR LIFE (Oct. 19, 2020), http://podcasts.apple.com/us/podcast/life-liberty-and-law/

id1472791329.

57   Paul Benjamin Linton, *Enforcement of State Abortion Statutes After* Roe*: A State-by-State Analysis*, 67 U. Det. L. Rev. 157, 158–60 (1990) ("Pre-*Roe* statutes may be divided into five broad categories: (1) thirty states allowed abortion only to save the life of the mother; (2) two states and the District of Columbia allowed abortion to preserve the life or health of the mother; (3) one state allowed abortion to save the mother's life or to terminate a pregnancy resulting from rape; (4) thirteen states adopted § 230.3 of the American Law Institute's Model Penal Code' or some variant thereof; (5) four states allowed abortion on demand but set limits in terms of the age of the fetus.")

58   402 U.S. 62.

59   Heffernan v. Doe, 401 U.S. 969 (1971); Hanrahan v. Doe, 39 U.S.L.W. 3438 (1971).

60   Motion and Brief Amicus Curiae of Certain Physicians, Professors and Fellows of The American College of Obstetrics and Gynecology in Support of Appellees, *Roe*, 410 U.S. 113 (No. 70-18) & Doe v. Bolton, 410 U.S. 179 (1973) (No. 70-40), *available at* http://aul.org/wp-content/uploads/2022/01/Horan-brief-in-Roe-Doe-filed-on-behalf-of-physicians-professors-fellows-of-ACOG-Oct.-15-1971-complete.pdf.

61   On file with author.

62   Forsythe, Abuse of Discretion, *supra* ch.2 note 46, at 17–54.

63   Brief of Americans United for Life, Amicus Curiae, In Support of Appellee, *Roe*, 410 U.S. 113 (No. 70-18), *available at* http://aul.org/wp-content/uploads/2019/03/1971-Roe-v.-Wade.pdf.

64   People v. Frey, 294 N.E.2d 257 (Ill. 1973).

65   Dennis J. Horan, *Abortion and the Conscience Clause: Current Status*, 20 Catholic Law. 289 (1974).

66   AUL's September 1974 newsletter identified AUL's headquarters at 230 N. Michigan Avenue. Newsletter of Americans United for Life, *supra* ch. 1 note 16.

67   Interview with Edward R. Grant, Former President, Ams. United for Life (2020).

68   *See* Abortion and the Constitution: Reversing *Roe v. Wade* Through the Courts (Dennis J. Horan, et al. eds., 1987).

69   *See* Associated Press, *Endorsement Puts ABA in Thick of Abortion Fray,* Deseret News (Aug. 12, 1992), https://www.deseret.com/1992/8/12/18999143/endorsement-puts-aba-in-thick-of-abortion-fray.

70   Christopher B. Mueller, *David W. Louisell—In Memoriam*, 66 Cal. L. Rev. 921 (1978).

71   Andrew Kaufman, *John T. Noonan '54: 1926–2017,* Harvard L. Today (Apr. 25, 2017), https://today.law.harvard.edu/john-t-noonan-54-1926-2017/.

72   Justice Scalia said, in part: "It is Vic Rosenblum's character that justifies my calling him a great man. He had his priorities right—and at the top was his faith and his family … Where Vic's character most vividly shown forth, it seems to me, was in

his tireless devotion to the pro-life cause. No law professor devoted more time and energy to protection of the unborn ... When someone like Vic Rosenblum leaves our midst, I am struck for us with a great sense of loss, and then with a great sense of wonder. How does such a man come to be? How have we deserved to have him among us? And will he be followed by others of equal worth? For the sake of our profession, and of our nation, I pray that he will." On file with the author.

73   On file with the author.

74   Robert E. Jonas & John D. Gorby, *West German Abortion Decision: A Contrast to* Roe v. Wade, 9 JOHN MARSHALL J. PRAC. & PROC. 605 (1976).

75   Ernst Benda, *The Impact of Constitutional Law on the Protection of Unborn Human Life: Some Comparative Remarks*, 6 HUM. RTS. 223 (1977).

76   Motion and Brief, Amicus Curiae of Dr. Eugene Diamond and Americans United to Life, Inc., In Support of Appellees in 74-1151 and Appellants in 74-1419, Planned Parenthood of Cent. Mo. v. Danforth, 428 U.S. 52 (1976) (Nos. 74-1151), *available at* https://aul.org/wp-content/uploads/2018/10/1976-PP-v.-Danforth.pdf.

CHAPTER 3

Roe v. Wade Shatters
American Law and Politics

oe v. Wade radically changed, in virtually every way, the abortion issue in America. Directed by the Supreme Court, and applied for 49 years by the lower federal courts in all 50 states, *Roe* dictated the legal, political, financial, and social structures that have shaped the abortion issue for more than four decades. To respond effectively to *Roe*, AUL needed a thorough understanding of the decision.

The first great difficulty of the Court's ruling was understanding what it meant. The vast scope of the "right" in question was obscured by the Court's own words, the length and complexity of the *Roe* and *Doe* opinions, and by the media's inaccurate descriptions of the decisions. For instance, the *New York Times* ran a headline on January 23, 1973, the day after the case was decided, announcing that the "right" was limited to the "first three months" of pregnancy.

The criticism of *Roe* over the years, from judges and scholars, has been enormous.[1] Pro-abortion Harvard Law Professor Mark Tushnet wrote in 1983: "It seems to be generally agreed that, as a matter of simple craft, Justice Blackmun's opinion for the Court was dreadful."[2] Or as

Rutgers law professor Earl Maltz wrote: "The opinion [in *Roe*] exemplifies Blackmun's work product. It is best described as ponderous—a fifty-page exegesis … But its treatment of the legal issues is conclusory and generally unsatisfying."[3]

In *Roe*, the Court ruled that states could not prohibit abortion before fetal viability, and defined "viability" as the capacity of a fetus to survive outside the womb, which was at roughly 28 weeks of pregnancy as the Court understood it in 1973. But the Court went farther, ruling that the states could not prohibit abortion even after viability, if the abortion was considered "necessary … for the preservation of the life or health of the mother."

Who determined whether the abortion was "necessary"? The abortionist.

What did the critical exception for "health" mean? The Court defined "health" in the companion decision of *Doe v. Bolton*—which is often overlooked and little understood—to include "all factors—physical, emotional, psychological, familial, and the woman's age—relevant to the well-being of the patient. All these factors may relate to health."[4]

Roe and *Doe* together—as the Court held they must be read—mean that the 50 states must allow abortion for any reason related to "well-being," at any point before birth.[5]

Inside the womb, killing the fetus at any time is treated as a lawful abortion; outside the womb, the killing may be treated as infanticide—though if the live birth is preceded by a failed abortion attempt, it is questionable whether the state could prosecute the abortionist.

Before *Roe*, most states had prohibited abortion, except to save the life of the mother, since colonial times, and they were continuing to enforce abortion laws up to January 1973.[6] With *Roe*, the Court wrested the abortion issue from the hands of the people and centralized its control, regulation, and management in the nine justices. In short, the Court stripped all 50 states of authority over the issue of abortion, except in strict circumstances specified by the Court, as of January 22, 1973.

Roe prevented states from enforcing abortion *prohibitions*—at any stage of pregnancy. *Roe* created a private right to kill innocent prenatal human beings, a shocking precedent in American constitutional law.

The obstacles to the passage and enforcement of abortion prohibitions could not be lifted as long as *Roe* remained in effect, because federal courts applied that prohibition in every state, and state and federal officials obeyed it.

Roe posed an unprecedented challenge. Though it was fairly clear that the states could not prohibit abortion prior to fetal viability, it wasn't immediately clear what state or federal limits would be permitted under the ruling. Its meaning would become clearer only as the Court continued to decide related cases over four decades. While the Court allowed marginal regulations in some states—like parental notice and consent laws or informed consent laws—the Court also allowed abortion activists to challenge in court virtually any pro-life law passed by the states. With virtually every subsequent decision, the Court continued to shrink the authority of states to limit abortion.

The limbo in which Horan's Illinois abortion case was stuck ended with the *Roe* decision. A month after the Court ruled in *Roe* and *Doe*, the justices rejected a number of abortion cases, including Horan's appeal on behalf of Dr. Heffernan from Illinois.[7] That was the end of the road for *Doe v. Scott* and Horan's effort to avert the Court's legalization of abortion.

After a decade of public debate over abortion, at the time that *Roe* came down, 31 states had rejected legalization and retained legal prohibitions on abortion except to save the life of the mother. *Roe* swept these away, along with every other state abortion law.

Meanwhile, the Court had opened the door to "back alley" abortionists, who could hang out a shingle on Main Street and continue business. Abortionists quickly opened their doors as "abortion providers." Kermit Gosnell of Philadelphia, Richard Ragsdale of Rockford, Illinois, Ulrich Klopfer of South Bend, Indiana, and Warren Hern of Colorado opened the doors of their now-legal businesses shortly after *Roe*.

Roe was broad and vague, leaving much unclear as to what would be permitted, which the Court admitted in their next abortion decision, *Danforth* in 1976. On the whole, *Roe* seemed to mean that the people, through their elected representatives, could not limit abortion, other than with marginal regulations.

Chief Justice Burger's concurring opinion in *Roe* supported this broad interpretation, and the pro-abortion Family Planning Perspectives, published by the abortion-advocacy group, the Alan Guttmacher Institute, noticed the loophole: "Even New York's law appears to be overbroad in proscribing all abortions after 24 weeks except to preserve the woman's life, since the Court has held that an exception must also be made for the preservation of the woman's heath (interpreted very broadly)."[8]

In *Roe*, the Court took complete control of abortion. The attorney general of Wisconsin, for example, issued an "advisory opinion" on January 31, 1973, to state district attorneys, indicating that *Roe* and *Doe* "have effectively rendered unconstitutional and unenforceable the Wisconsin abortion statute."

The Court's decision in *Roe* undoubtedly encouraged some nations to legalize abortion, but few went as far as the Supreme Court. Even 40 years later, the United States was one of only seven nations to allow abortion for any reason after 20 weeks, and one of only five to allow abortion for any reason after fetal viability, along with China, North Korea, Vietnam, and Canada.[9]

In *Roe*, the Court adopted an unprecedented and comprehensive role successively described by Justices Byron White, Sandra Day O'Connor, William Rehnquist, and Clarence Thomas as "the nation's *ex officio* medical board with powers to approve or disapprove medical and operative practices and standards throughout the United States."[10]

The issue of abortion was centralized in and completely controlled by the Court, which declared the right, policed its boundaries, and dictated state policy. The Court became, in effect, the national abortion control board.

By eliminating the abortion laws of all 50 states, *Roe* immediately created a legal and public-health vacuum. Unless states acted to fill that vacuum, it continued. Unless states enacted legislation placing conditions or limits on the right, none existed. Without legislative requirements for informed consent, parental notice, or sanitary conditions, there were none. Justice Blackmun realized to a limited degree that *Roe* would create this vacuum, telling his colleagues ahead of time that the Court should release its decision timed for the start of the 1973 state legislative sessions, so that the states could act in response.[11]

Roe also empowered abortionists to challenge every new abortion limit a state might adopt. Abortionists immediately attempted, through court cases, to require that public facilities and public funding be used for abortion, to push viability as late in pregnancy as possible, and to oppose legislative regulations on the procedure.[12] Given the complexity and ambiguity of the Court's two opinions, totaling nearly 78 pages, much was clarified only by years of cases, allowing the Court to explain what it had decided in *Roe* and *Doe*.

In subsequent cases, the Court made the work of abortionists even easier. In 1976, the justices allowed abortionists to represent women in court via "third-party standing"—the abortionists could stand-in for women—a practice not allowed in the law for any other medical procedure. The Court made an exception for abortion, empowering abortionists to claim in court that women don't need health and safety regulations, that women don't need informed-consent laws, that minors don't need to notify or seek consent from a parent, and that public-health data about abortion are unimportant and don't need to be reported, collected, or analyzed.

The Court next allowed abortionists to challenge abortion laws in their totality, otherwise known as a facial challenge, rather than as applied to specific circumstances. This allowed judges to avoid the work of determining the facts—such as the woman's medical condition or her reasons for seeking an abortion—in any given abortion case.

Despite the backlash to *Roe*, prestige reinforced the power the Court had concentrated in itself. Government officials obeyed the Court, and *Roe* had the support of political organizations, foundations, wealthy individuals, and the media, all of which helped to slow public opposition in the first decade after *Roe*.

AUL's Prudential Strategy

When Horan refocused AUL's mission through the Legal Defense Fund, it allowed the group to pursue a prudential strategy shaped by the disciplines of the American legal system.[13]

A famous Supreme Court case exemplifies this philosophy and tradition. In 1839, 45 enslaved Africans on a Spanish slaveship, *The Amistad*, sailing from Havana, Cuba, freed themselves and took command, killing some of the crew during the uprising. The ship, sailing off the coast of the eastern United States, was eventually captured near the eastern tip of Long Island, Montauck Point, by a U.S. naval ship in January 1840. *The Amistad* was towed to New London, Connecticut, where the slaves were jailed pending a court hearing, which instigated a legal case that was appealed to the Supreme Court in 1841.[14]

At the outset of the case, a wealthy New York businessman, banker, evangelical philanthropist, and abolitionist, Lewis Tappan, interviewed Roger S. Baldwin, an attorney in Connecticut, to help free the enslaved Africans. Baldwin proposed that the key to winning the case, and freedom for the slaves, was based in property law—the question of ownership. Baldwin wanted to show that the property was seized illegally by the slavers, as this would allow a court to direct a legal remedy.

Tappan dismissed the strategy as immoral, saying, "This war must be waged on the battlefield of righteousness." Tappan was disturbed by Baldwin's proposition that the key to the case was proving that the slaves were "illegally acquired," resulting in the "wrongful transfer of stolen goods." "It would be against everything I stand for," Tappan said, "to let this deteriorate into an exercise in the vagaries of legal minutiae. These are people, Mr. Baldwin, not livestock." Tappan and Baldwin disagreed about the goals and the means. Tappan wanted to stand on religious truth alone in an American court of law. But Baldwin eventually prevailed in the courts on his legal theory, and the Supreme Court declared the slaves free in 1841.[15]

The cause for life in America, before and after *Roe*, faced unique legal, political, and constitutional challenges that required a unique sense of prudential engagement in changing law and policy. Translating moral principles into law is a difficult enterprise, requiring practical wisdom, or prudence, which Thomas Aquinas defined as "right reason about what is to be done."[16]

As an intellectual virtue, prudence requires discernment, understanding the problem, deliberation about the solution, a clear decision about what to do, and effective execution of the decision. Each stage is complex, and greater experience and understanding may lead to renewed deliberation, new decisions, and better strategies.

As a political virtue, prudence is oriented toward the moral good in politics and public policy. Prudence asks four questions of political leaders: Do they pursue good goals (moral purpose) in politics? Do they exercise wise judgment as to what's possible? Do they successfully apply means to ends? Do they preserve the possibility of future improvement when all of the good cannot be immediately achieved?

Prudence is practical wisdom, not theoretical wisdom. It is about action. It looks to opportunities to advance moral purpose in politics and seeks to overcome obstacles. As practical wisdom oriented toward the moral good, prudence must guide goals, priorities, strategies, and tactics to achieve success. It compels us to anticipate obstacles, plan ahead, understand the limit of our resources, and apply them to achieve our goals. Prudence provides an effective balance to the oft-repeated religious aphorism, "God *doesn't* expect us to win; he just expects us to be faithful." Prudence is oriented toward achieving moral goals in politics and daily life.

Prudence is, unfortunately, often confused with other philosophies. It is neither pragmatism nor incrementalism, in the sense that prudence is not rigidly committed to gradualism or rigidly defined steps. Rather, it seeks the largest steps possible toward moral improvement, accounting for opportunities and obstacles.

Prudence may involve the choice between two or more goods or a choice between two or more evils. Yet prudence may—in the light of existing opportunities and obstacles—counsel a tactic of incremental steps. As Henry Hyde said during congressional debate in 1976 over his amendment which prohibited federal taxpayer funding for abortions, "I do support this amendment, not because it is perfect, but because it is the best attainable. Many human lives will be saved, and this is no small achievement."[17]

It is a legitimate debate as to whether more could be achieved in any particular circumstance, but prudence grounds a campaign for justice in the natural law, the cardinal virtues, and a focus on moral purpose for the common good, radically different from the modern political focus on rage and power.

In the 1990s, leading social commentators taught that "rage and despair are an essential element in the struggle for justice."[18] The philosophy of Saul Alinsky, reflected in his 1971 influential book, *Rules for Radicals*, instills a nihilistic focus on conflict and power. In the late 1990s, the philosopher Dallas Willard had already observed "a nation increasingly sick with rage and resentment of citizen toward citizen,"[19] on display in national elections, reaching its crescendo in the elections of 2016 and 2020.

Prudence, by contrast, is an acquired ability and requires learning how law can be changed in the face of obstacles. Prudence also counsels citizens to consider the effect of politics on future generations. The great British statesman Edmund Burke properly understood the social contract as binding "those who are living, those who are dead, and those who are to be born."[20]

Effective Responses to *Roe* and *Doe*

Before *Roe*, pro-life Americans sought to preserve the traditional legal prohibition against abortion except to save the life of the mother. In 31 states, despite nearly a decade of public debate, that prohibition was preserved at the time the Supreme Court issued *Roe*. In some states, exceptions were introduced into the law, some narrow, some broad. "Repeal" and "reform" laws passed in 1967, 1968, 1969, and 1970, *but no such laws passed in the states in 1971 or 1972*, a sign of the pro-life movement's building momentum.

Roe completely changed the legal and political landscape by sweeping aside all state abortion limits. The Court created a vacuum and assumed states would enact regulations based on a reading of the opinion. But state legislation in 1973 and succeeding years immediately sparked opposition from abortionists, who filed test-case litigation in the courts. A very slow process.

Rhode Island attempted to induce the Court to quickly and completely reconsider. When that failed in 1974, the Court ruled on substantive abortion issues in *Planned Parenthood v. Danforth* in 1976. During those years, the Court's vacuum expanded and, for decades, the vacuum for health-and-safety regulations continued. This was demonstrated once again in 2020, when the Court struck down Louisiana's admitting-privileges requirement for abortion clinics, a requirement which applies to virtually all other ambulatory surgical centers in the U.S.. Another abortion exception.

In a world of limits and constraints on time and resources, prudence counseled a multi-faceted political and legal response. There was uncertainty as to the precise implications of *Roe*, and when complete prohibition of a social evil is not possible due to countervailing obstacles, it is prudent to limit the evil as much as possible.

Overturning a controversial Court decision that has the support of large segments of society is one of the hardest things to do in the American constitutional system, but beginning in 1973, the pro-life movement undertook several strategies. Members of Congress filed constitutional amendments on abortion. Rhode Island enacted a complete prohibition on abortion. Other states, including Illinois, Minnesota, Missouri, and Utah, enacted limits on abortion when complete prohibition was not possible.

Pro-life advocates could attempt to repeal *Roe* or take it apart piece by piece. In the face of massive opposition and uncertainty, they attempted both and identified the most promising strategies by trial and error.

Trained as a lawyer, and as a serious Catholic intellectual, AUL's Dennis Horan instinctively pursued a prudential approach, knowing that incremental change is hard-wired into the American judicial system, as legal scholar Bryan Garner has noted,

> Our system deals with questions of law by increment, by degree, and on specific facts litigated from the bottom up. This system allows for a greater degree of fine-tuning and refinement—and constant improvement.[21]

As Notre Dame Law professor and later-judge Kenneth Ripple wrote in his book, *Constitutional Litigation*, "constitutional doctrine unfolds incrementally."[22]

Horan and Rosenblum shaped their strategy with a prudential realism about how law changes. Horan's legal and litigation experience, with briefs in *Bryn*, *Vuitch*, and *Roe*, lent realism to his perspective. While law professors such as Joseph Witherspoon, Charles Rice, and Robert Byrn pushed for constitutional personhood through a judicial ruling, AUL focused on legislation and litigation that could produce test cases to attract Court review. AUL believed that, if *Roe* could be overruled through a Supreme Court reversal, it would be through a federalism decision rather than a "personhood" ruling under the Fourteenth Amendment.

Congress and Constitutional Amendments on Abortion

ROUND 1

Within weeks of the *Roe* decision, members of Congress introduced numerous constitutional amendments to overturn it.[23]

The dominant goal among pro-life leaders was a "Human Life Amendment," though there was extensive debate among them over the text, including over what, if any, exceptions would be included.[24] A states' rights amendment was disfavored, as many pro-life leaders preferred a human life, personhood approach. Berkeley Law professor John Noonan, who drafted a "congressional powers" amendment, was ostracized for a time by some leaders in the movement, many of whom believed that the key to undoing *Roe* was the declaration of "personhood." Both Catholic theology and the language of the Fourteenth Amendment influenced that attitude from different perspectives.[25]

In 1974, Horan was involved in efforts to craft one possible constitutional amendment, and he organized a meeting of pro-life lawyers, under the auspices of the National Right to Life Committee, to produce a Human Life Amendment. This was eventually introduced in Congress as S.J.R. 141 and H.J.R. 132.

AUL supported both a personhood amendment and, later, a federalism amendment, favoring whichever had the greatest chance of passing Congress and curtailing or overturning *Roe*. In the wake of *Roe*, Horan's prudential approach was exemplified in his support for the morality of imperfect legislation, doing whatever can be done to secure the greatest possible protection for life. As he told Catholic diocesan attorneys in 1974:

> I am not a believer in legislation that is an outright disavowal of the court, as we witnessed in the Rhode Island case [*Doe v. Israel*, which the Supreme Court refused to hear on May 13, 1974]. I am a believer in attempting to achieve the maximum possible with legislation, e.g., even if the statute complies with *Roe v. Wade* and *Doe v. Bolton*. [T]here is no reason it cannot

contain a preamble which states that the unborn child is a human person from conception, that the statute is passed of necessity, allowing abortions only because of those cases, but that in all other areas of the law the unborn child shall be treated as a person.[26]

In the first phase of the battle, before Jimmy Carter's presidency, AUL board member David Louisell testified on July 8, 1975, before the Subcommittee on Constitutional Amendments of the U.S. Senate Committee on the Judiciary (the Bayh Committee).[27] Carter's election, and Senate elections of November 1976 in the aftermath of Watergate, put constitutional amendments on hold between 1977 and 1980.

ROUND 2

With the election of Reagan in 1980, Republicans captured the Senate for the first time in 30 years, making a constitutional amendment on abortion seem feasible. Pro-life leaders were largely united in the primary goal of passing such an amendment.

AUL was again involved in congressional hearings on the subject from 1981 to 1983 and showed flexibility in supporting different measures, including the Human Life bill and a constitutional amendment. AUL worked closely with Senator Orrin Hatch (R., Utah) and Senator John East (R., N.C.) during this time.

During the Reagan presidency, Horan and Rosenblum both testified before Congress on constitutional amendments. AUL supported both a personhood amendment and the Hatch-Eagleton Federalism Amendment between 1981 and 1983. As vice chairman of AUL's board of directors, Rosenblum presented testimony on the personhood of the unborn child under the Fourteenth Amendment before the Subcommittee on Separation of Powers of the U.S. Senate Committee on the Judiciary on June 1, 1981.[28]

Later that year, as AUL chairman, Horan presented testimony on November 16, 1981, in support of the Hatch Amendment, S.J. Res. 110, before the Subcommittee on the Constitution of the U.S. Senate Committee on the Judiciary.[29] S.J. Res. 110 provided: "A right to abortion is not secured by this Constitution. The Congress and the several States shall

have the concurrent power to restrict and prohibit abortions: *Provided,*
That a law of a State which is more restrictive than a law of Congress
shall govern." Rosenblum testified later that day in support of S.J. Res.
110.[30]

Congressional hearings resumed in 1983. AUL presented testimony to
the Subcommittee on the Constitution of the U.S. Senate Committee on
the Judiciary in support of S.J. Res 3, which provided: "A right to abortion is not secured by this Constitution. The Congress and the several
States shall have concurrent power to restrict and prohibit abortion.
Provided, That a provision of a law of a State which is more restrictive than a conflicting provision of a law of Congress shall govern." In
February and March of that year, several AUL lawyers including Horan,
Rosenblum and AUL board member and Brigham Young University
Law School professor Lynn Wardle, testified in support of S.J. Res. 3 to
reverse *Roe.*[31]

Three months after those hearings closed, the Supreme Court issued
its decision in *City of Akron v. Akron Center for Reproductive Health*[32]
on June 15, 1983, a blockbuster decision because Justice O'Connor, in
her first abortion case, dissented from the majority decision striking the
City of Akron's abortion limits. Justices White and Rehnquist, the two
original dissenters in *Roe*, joined her opinion, which mounted a strong
and thorough critique of the *Roe* decision.

Two weeks later, the Hatch-Eagleton Human Life Federalism Amendment died on the Senate floor in a 49-50 vote, when two-thirds support
was needed. *Akron* likely influenced some senators to vote against
the Hatch Amendment, convincing them that the Court was changing
and an amendment wasn't needed. The effort to pass a constitutional
amendment on abortion died that day. No major pro-life organization
would actively support a new amendment campaign in Congress until
Roe was reversed.

Chapter 3 Endnotes

1   *See, e.g.*, Clarke D. Forsythe, *A Survey of Judicial and Scholarly Criticism of* Roe v. Wade *Since 1973: Legal Criticism and Unsettled Precedent,* Ams. United for Life (Jan. 2022), https://aul.org/wp-content/uploads/2022/01/A-Survey-of-Judicial-and-Scholarly-Criticism-of-Roe-v.-Wade-Since-1973.pdf.

2   Mark V. Tushnet, *Following the Rules Laid Down: A Critique of Interpretivism and Neutral Principles,* 96 HARV L. REV. 781, 820 (1983).

3   EARL M. MALTZ, THE CHIEF JUSTICESHIP OF WARREN BURGER, 1969-1986 19 (2000).

4   410 U.S. at 192.

5   *Id.*

6   *See* Clarke D. Forsythe, *The Effective Enforcement of Abortion Law Before* Roe v. Wade, *in* THE SILENT SUBJECT: REFLECTIONS ON THE UNBORN IN AMERICAN CULTURE (Brad Stetson, ed., 1996).

7   Heffernan v. Doe, 410 U.S. 950 (1973).

8   Editorial, *Abortion: The High Court has Ruled,* 5 FAM. PLAN. PERSP. i (1973).

9   *See* Forsythe, ABUSE OF DISCRETION, *supra* ch. 2 note 46, at 126-127 (listing data).

10 *Danforth*, 428 U.S. at 99 (White, J., concurring in part and dissenting in part); Webster v. Reprod. Health Servs, 492 U.S. 490, 519 (1989) (Rehnquist, C.J.) (plurality opinion) (citing *Danforth*, 428 U.S. at 99); City of Akron v. Akron Ctr. for Reprod. Health, 462 U.S. 416, 456 (1983) (O'Connor, J., dissenting) (citing *Danforth*, 428 U.S. at 99); Whole Woman's Health v. Hellerstedt, 136 S. Ct. 2292, 2326 (2016) (Thomas, J., dissenting) (citing Gonzales v. Carhart, 550 U.S. 124, 164 (2007)). *See also Gonzales,* 550 U.S. at 164 (describing *Webster* as "criticizing *Roe's* trimester framework because, *inter alia*, it 'left this Court to serve as the country's *ex officio* medical board with powers to approve or disapprove medical and operative practices and standards throughout the United States" (citation omitted)).

11 *See The Public Health Vacuum the Justices Created, in* Forsythe, ABUSE OF DISCRETION, *supra* ch. 2 note 46, at 211–244.

12 Hodgson v. Anderson, 378 F. Supp. 1008 (D. Minn. 1974), *dismissed for want of jurisdiction sub nom.*, Spannaus v. Hodgson, 420 U.S. 903 (1975). *See also* LYNN D. WARDLE, THE ABORTION PRIVACY DOCTRINE (1980) (discussion early abortion cases decided by the federal courts in the 1970s) *and* JOHN NOONAN, A PRIVATE CHOICE: ABORTION IN AMERICA IN THE SEVENTIES (1979).

13 AUL's prudential strategy is described in detail in Forsythe, PFTGG, *supra* ch. 2 note 29.

14 United States v. Libellants and Claimants of The Schooner Amistad, 40 U.S. 518

(1841).

15 AMISTAD (DreamWorks Pictures 1997).

16 Forsythe, PFTGG, *supra* ch. 2 note 29 at 263 (citing THOMAS AQUINAS, SUMMA THEOLOGICA I-II, q. 57, a. 4).

17 McRae v. Califano, 491 F. Supp. 630, 766 (E.D.N.Y. 1980).

18 DALLAS WILLARD, THE DIVINE CONSPIRACY: REDISCOVERING OUR HIDDEN LIFE IN GOD 150 (1998).

19 *Id.* at 150–51.

20 GREG WEINER, OLD WHIGS: BURKE, LINCOLN & THE POLITICS OF PRUDENCE 50 (2019). *See also* John M. Breen, *Modesty and Moralism: Justice, Prudence, and Abortion: A Reply to Skeel & Stuntz*, 31 Harv. J. L. & Pub. Pol'y 219 (2008); Anthony T. Kronman, *Alexander Bickel's Philosophy of Prudence*, 94 YALE L.J. 1567 (1985).

21 Bryan Garner, *Introduction* to THE LAW OF JUDICIAL PRECEDENT 1, 10 (Bryan Garner, ed., 2016).

22 KENNETH RIPPLE, CONSTITUTIONAL LITIGATION 122 (1984). *See also* Richard Myers, *Pro-Life Litigation and the American Civil Liberties Tradition, in* ABORTION AND THE CONSTITUTION, *supra* ch. 2 note 68 (the American judiciary "rarely takes a giant step to establish a new doctrine or definitively reject an old one"); VANESSA A. BAIRD, ANSWERING THE CALL OF THE COURT: HOW JUSTICES AND LITIGANTS SET THE SUPREME COURT AGENDA 5 (2007) (referring to "the iterative nature of lawmaking in the judicial process: cases are built on the legal arguments of previous ones."); AMANDA HOLLIS-BRUSKY, IDEAS WITH CONSEQUENCES: THE FEDERALIST SOCIETY AND THE CONSERVATIVE COUNTERREVOLUTION 59–60 (2014) ("Ultimately, as the various narratives and analyses throughout this book show, it is in this incremental fashion that constitutional change actually comes about.").

23 Stephen B. Presser & Clarke D. Forsythe, *Restoring Self-Government on Abortion: A Federalism Amendment*, 10 TEX. REV. L. & POL'Y 301 (2006). *See* I HUM. LIFE REV. 1 (Spring 1975) (debating abortion following *Roe v. Wade*) *and* I HUM. LIFE REV. 24 (Winter 1975).

24 *See e.g.*, James L. Buckley, *A Human Life Amendment*, 1 HUM LIFE REV., 7, 7-20 (1975).

25 Interview with Thomas J. Marzen, Former General Counsel, Ams. United for Life (2004).

26 Horan, *Abortion and the Conscience Clause, supra* ch. 2 note 65, at 294–95.

27 David W. Louisell, *The Burdick Proposal: A Life-Support Amendment*, I HUM. LIFE REV. 9, 12 (1975).

28 Rosenblum criticized the *Roe* decision and its reliance on the advocacy of Cyril Means, the general counsel for NARAL. He emphasized the common law protection for the unborn child, the growth of state legislative protection in the nineteenth century, and modern tort law protection. He deftly employed the recently published history of abortion by James Mohr, highlighting evidence in Mohr showing that the states in the nineteenth century were concerned with protecting the life of the unborn child, but criticizing Mohr for (1) failing to "acknowledge the background of

new biological research and discovery which convinced these doctors [in the nineteenth century] that early abortion takes the lives of human beings" and (2) failing to recognize that the nineteenth century state legislative advances were consistent with common law protection, not anomalous. With the nineteenth century scientific understanding as background, Rosenblum argued that "[t]he contemporaneous attitude of the state legislatures and public is of relevance to the understanding of the framers and ratifiers of the Fourteenth Amendment with regard to whether the unborn were to be included as 'persons' protected by it ... The 'spirit' of this Amendment demands that members of the human species before birth be acknowledged before the law ... ." Testimony *reprinted in* Victor G. Rosenblum, *Abortion, Personhood and the Fourteenth Amendment, in* AUL Studies in Law and Medicine (Ams. United for Life., Ser. No. 11, 1981).

29 S.J. Res. 110 provided: "A right to abortion is not secured by this Constitution. The Congress and the several States shall have the concurrent power to restrict and prohibit abortions: Provided, That a law of a State which is more restrictive than a law of Congress shall govern." *See Constitutional Amendments Relating to Abortion: Hearings on S.J. Res. 17, S.J. Res. 18, S.J. Res. 19, S.J. Res. 110 Before the Subcomm. on the Constitution of the S. Comm. on the Judiciary*, 97th Cong. (1981); *Id.* at 753 (testimony of Dennis J. Horan).

30 *Id.* at 847 (testimony of Victor Rosenblum).

31 *See Legal Ramifications of the Human Life Amendment; Hearings on S.J. 3 Before the Subcomm. on the Constitution of the S. Comm.on the Judiciary,* 98th Cong. (1983) (containing testimony of Steven (Rick) Valentine, Executive Director of Americans United for Life, Lynn Wardle, and prepared statements by Dennis J. Horan and Victor G. Rosenblum).

32 462 U.S. 416.

CHAPTER 4

The Supreme Court Splinters

Justice Harry Blackmun wrote his opinion in *Roe v. Wade* with the expectation that states would fill the public-health vacuum created by the *Roe* decision during the 1973 legislative sessions. This was proven naive; the Court in *Roe* had given too much license to abortion activists.[1] Using *Roe* as a sword to challenge any state abortion regulation, abortionists rejected any limits on *Roe*'s expansive right, before or after fetal viability, and challenged abortion limits passed by the states in 1973 and 1974 and in the following decades.

Important test cases on abortion were dismissed by the Court in 1974 and 1975. The first major abortion case that the Court agreed to hear involving substantive limits, *Planned Parenthood v. Danforth*, didn't take place for three years. *Danforth* dealt with issues that hadn't been addressed in *Roe*, which the Court expressly acknowledged. The declaration of a "right" in *Roe* was one thing, but the justices splintered when faced with the question of practical limits on abortion.

In January 1976, Dennis Horan, Jack Gorby, and Dolores Horan filed a brief in *Danforth* on behalf of Americans United for Life and Dr. Eugene F. Diamond, a Chicago pediatrician and AUL board member. The brief described AUL as "a national educational foundation organized to educate and promote better understanding of the humanity of the unborn child and the value of human life" with a "membership [that] includes approximately 20,000 persons located in every state of the union."

The brief was one of the first assignments given to Tom Marzen, a law student at IIT-Chicago Kent Law School: to write in support of the spousal-consent provision in *Danforth* and to write on the facts of fetal development for the brief. Marzen first volunteered for AUL before joining the legal team after his graduation.

At the time, Dr. Diamond was an intervening defendant in the cases pending in the federal appeals court in Chicago, which involved the constitutionality of the 1975 Illinois Abortion Act.[2] In the same way as Dr. Heffernan served in *Doe v. Scott* in 1970, Dr. Diamond was appointed guardian *ad litem* for the class of unborn children in Illinois.

The 1975 Illinois Abortion Act, passed in response to *Roe*, was enacted on November 19 of that year. The Illinois Senate voted 36-15 and the Illinois House voted 109-40 to override Governor James Thompson's veto of the bill. Like the Missouri legislation at issue in *Danforth*, the Illinois law contained provisions dealing with parental consent, spousal consent, informed consent, and protections for viable prenatal children.

Horan and colleagues opened their brief in *Danforth* arguing that the Missouri statute was constitutional under *Roe* but also that the "decision handed down by this Court in *Roe v. Wade* is not constitutionally sound, should be carefully reconsidered and should be narrowed rather than broadened in its implications."

The brief's introduction enumerated reasons why the Court should confine *Roe* to its narrowest boundaries, including a summary of the abortion decision issued by the federal constitutional court of West Germany in 1975.[3] The West German decision represented a significant departure from the reasoning of *Roe* and a dramatically different way of viewing abortion, one that was more respectful of prenatal human beings.

Professor Jack Gorby worked for two years to translate that decision for the John Marshall Law Review, eventually publishing, with his collaborator Robert Jonas, commentaries in one of the John Marshall law school's journals.[4] The West German court was united in its conclusion that there existed a legal obligation by the state to protect the prenatal child. In fact, it held "that the State has an affirmative duty to protect the unborn life at all stages of pregnancy."[5] The "issue over which the constitutional Court split … concerned *how* the state fulfills its affirmative duty to protect unborn human life."[6]

The dissenting opinion neither questioned the constitutional personhood ("legal value") of the unborn nor did it quarrel with the legal necessity for protecting unborn life. Instead, it said that "the life of each individual human being is self-evidently a central value of the order of justice."[7] The AUL attorneys hoped that the West German decision would influence the direction of the U.S. Supreme Court's abortion doctrine.

The rest of AUL's brief in *Danforth* supported the constitutionality of each of the eight provisions of Missouri's law: "Plaintiff admitt[ed] in their brief (p. 26) at 19 weeks maternal mortality for abortion exceeds maternal mortality for live birth." The brief supported the constitutionality of the definition of viability in section 2(2), the physician's standard of care and duty to protect any infant born alive in section 6(1), the requirement of "the written informed consent of the patient" as a proper exercise in the states interest in maternal health" in section 3(2), the spousal-consent provision in section 3(3), the parental-consent requirement in section 3(4), the termination of the rights of aborting parents in the case of an infant born alive after abortion in section 7, the prohibition of saline abortions after the first trimester in section 9, and the recordkeeping and reporting in sections 10 and 11. The Missouri law was much like Illinois's 1975 abortion statute. As the Court decided abortion cases in the 1970s and 1980s, and with medical and social experience with the abortion issue, some states would leave these intricate issues behind and move on to others, like partial-birth abortion, in the 1990s.

The Court issued its decision in *Danforth* on July 1, 1976, just before the bicentennial of American independence. The majority upheld a general informed-consent requirement but struck down Missouri's spousal-consent requirement. Justices Byron White, William Rehnquist, and

Chief Justice Warren Burger dissented in part. *Roe*'s 7-2 majority had shrunk to 6-3.

The case also elicited skepticism from Justice Potter Stewart about the accuracy of information women receive in abortion clinics. Summarizing the record in the case, Stewart noted: "It seems unlikely that [a minor] will obtain adequate counsel and support from the attending physician at an abortion clinic, where abortions for pregnant minors frequently take place."[8] In case after case over the decades, from *Danforth* to *City of Akron* to *June Medical Services v. Russo*, the justices have disregarded facts such as these about the reality of abortion practice.[9]

The same day as *Danforth*, the Court issued its decision in *Singleton v. Wulff*,[10] also from Missouri, a split decision, in which a bare *plurality* held that abortionists could represent their patients in court using "third-party standing."[11] Justices Powell, Burger, Stewart, and Rehnquist dissented, arguing that abortionists could not represent the interests of women in *any* case other than one involving a proscription of abortion.[12] The issue of abortionists' standing was still contested 44 years later and remained unsettled, as Justice Clarence Thomas pointed out in his dissent in *June Medical Services*.[13]

Parental Authority Over the Medical Care of Minor Daughters

Parental rights are derived from the prior special duty of parents towards their children. As Dennis Horan described it in his 1975 Baylor Law Review article, "Under the law there is a peculiar legal relationship that exists between a parent and child which matures and changes as the child matures, until the roles ultimately reverse themselves."[14] In virtually all other areas of medicine in the 1960s, parents had the right to consent before their minor children could undergo medical treatment, a legal and ethical principle anchored in the common-law tradition.[15]

Preserving the parental right to notice and consent for an underage daughter's abortion was another critical question left open by *Roe*. In response, numerous states enacted parental-consent or parental-notice laws in the years immediately following *Roe*.

The Court first addressed the subject in *Danforth*. Missouri's statute required one-parent consent during the first twelve weeks of pregnancy if the girl was unmarried and under 18, unless a physician certified that the abortion was "necessary in order to preserve the life of the mother." The majority in *Danforth* viewed Missouri's statute as a "parental veto" and declared it unconstitutional. Another exception for abortion.

Three years later, the Court addressed Massachusetts' parental-consent law, when the Court established its general framework for "abortion rights" for minors. In that case, (*Bellotti II*), AUL filed a brief on behalf of Dr. Eugene Diamond, the pediatrician and AUL board member who, at the time, was an intervening defendant in the litigation in Illinois, *Wynn v. Carey*, to defend Illinois's parental-consent law.[16] AUL's brief argued that parental rights were fundamental, derived from the common law, and overrode any "abortion right" of minors. In a badly-fractured opinion in July 1979, the Court split 4-4-1 in *Bellotti II* with four different opinions.[17] Justice Powell introduced an "undue burden" standard that balanced the minor's right to abortion against parental rights and, if the parents objected to the abortion, allowed a judge to approve an abortion if it was in the "best interests" of the minor, so-called "judicial bypass."

The Court first decided the question of parental *notice* in 1981 in *H. L. v. Matheson*,[18] a case from Utah. AUL filed a brief defending Utah's law, and the Court upheld it by a 5-1-3 vote, with Justices Marshall, Brennan, and Blackmun dissenting.

This is obviously a deeply-felt, heartrending issue for parents, and, in the wake of *Danforth* and *Bellotti*, most states moved ahead with parental-notice and parental-consent legislation. The legal struggle to preserve parental rights continued through *Akron* and *Ashcroft* in 1983 and *Casey* in 1992. In those cases, the Court decided that one-parent or two-parent consent laws needed to include a judicial-bypass process. The *Hodgson* case from Minnesota in 1990 decided that two-parent notice required judicial bypass. The question of whether *one-parent notice* requires judicial bypass was still undecided in 2022.

By the 2000s, at least 43 states had enacted and were actively enforcing parental-notice or parental-consent laws. As of 2019, 38 were in effect and five had been enjoined by court injunction. Several were struck down by activist state courts, including in Alaska, California, Montana, and New Jersey. Some, such as Indiana's, were in litigation. Abortion activists oppose parental rights, whether of consent or notice, and challenged them wherever possible. The divisions in the Court kept the issue unsettled, and it remained unsettled when the Court addressed *Dobbs* in 2021.[19]

Protecting Viable Prenatal Children

Roe established a sweeping right to abortion, and by international standards it is still extraordinary today. It was unclear after *Roe* whether and to what extent states could protect the prenatal child. Could states protect prenatal children once they became viable outside the womb? Many states attempted to do that, including Pennsylvania through its 1974 law and Illinois through its 1975 law.

In Illinois, AUL actively defended the Illinois abortion laws and amendments throughout the 1970s, representing Dr. Eugene Diamond as an intervenor in defense of the 1975 Illinois abortion law and in defense of the 1977 Illinois parental consent law.

After the Illinois Abortion Act of 1975 was struck down,[20] the federal appeals court invalidated the Illinois parental-consent law and 48-hour waiting period. AUL appealed in 1978, seeking to defend the Abortion Act of 1975, and several of its provisions, including the requirement for fetal death certificates to precisely track abortions as a matter of public health, and the informed consent requirement. These questions weren't answered in *Danforth*. Unfortunately, the Supreme Court dismissed the appeal in October 1978.[21]

But the Court eventually took up the question of Pennsylvania's protection for the viable child in what became *Colautti v. Franklin*. After the federal court in Illinois in *Wynn v. Scott* upheld a similar Illinois law—which sought to protect a viable prenatal child by requiring that an abortion be done in whatever manner was most likely to result in a live birth—AUL filed a brief in the Supreme Court on June 6, 1978 in support of Pennsylvania's law, which sought to protect viable prenatal children.[22] AUL's brief argued that the Pennsylvania statute was constitutional because it did not burden the right to abortion but rather regulated the "manner or context in which the abortion is performed."

The Court finally decided *Colautti v. Franklin*[23] on January 9, 1979, a 6-3 decision with the majority opinion written by Justice Blackmun.

The Court in *Colautti* applied *Roe*'s viability rule rigidly and struck down Pennsylvania's definition of viability, declaring that the definition was vague and therefore unconstitutional.[24] Justice White's dissent was joined by Chief Justice Burger and Justice Rehnquist. *Roe*'s 7-2 majority had been reduced again. Six years after *Roe*, the Court refused to defer to a state's marginal limitation on late-term abortions.

Even so, the question of protecting viable prenatal children would not go away; states persisted in trying to prevent late-term abortions.

The Court arbitrarily adopted the viability rule in *Roe* based on the pragmatic goal of increasing "access" to abortion.[25] In expanding the abortion right to viability, the justices considered fetal growth but not the effects of late-term abortion on maternal health nor the possibility of late-term abortion resulting in live births, which became an immediate problem with the *Edelin* case in Massachusetts and others.[26] As Horan described *Edelin*, "At issue ... were the duties and responsibilities of a physician who performs a legal abortion which produces a viable fetus. Must he employ all reasonable means to preserve that life? If he does not, has he committed a crime?"[27] *Roe* did not necessarily mean that an abortionist had the right to kill a viable fetus born alive. Or did it?

After the Court's 2007 decision in *Gonzales v. Carhart*, which upheld the federal Partial-Birth Abortion Ban Act and expressed concern about late-term abortion, at least 23 states, starting with Nebraska, passed various limits at 18-20 weeks gestation. A five-month limit combined both a sensible restriction to protect fetal life along with a medically-reasonable goal of protecting maternal health. In 2004, a widely cited medical journal article by Linda Bartlett and others showed a greatly increased rate of maternal mortality from abortions after 20 weeks of pregnancy.[28]

The ambiguity of *Roe*'s viability rule has fostered continuous debate since 1973 over the issue of late-term abortions. *Roe*'s protection of late-term abortions led to countless babies being born alive after an attempted abortion, which led to scandals such as that of Dr. Kermit Gosnell in Philadelphia. Our heated debates over partial-birth abortion, the Born-Alive Infant Protection Act (BAIPA)[29] in Congress and the states, and 20-week limits on abortion are the direct result of the scope and ambiguity of *Roe* and *Doe* and the Court's inability or unwillingness to deal with the issues those cases created.[30]

Limits on Public Funding of Abortion

In the immediate aftermath of *Roe*, AUL's most significant and consequential litigation involved preventing the use of tax dollars to fund abortions. This was a question left open by *Roe*. Obviously, it would be imperative to build a fence around the decision, lest the right to abortion be expanded to require public endorsement or public funding. In that uncertainty, AUL prioritized legislative prohibitions on government funding of abortion, which inevitably led to litigation. States quickly began to pass legislation to prevent government funding of abortion, and Congress followed for the first time with the Hyde Amendment in 1976. The battle over public funding eventually established the first significant limits on abortion that the Court permitted to remain in place. From 1975 to 1979, AUL was involved in several public-funding cases, stepping stones which laid the foundation for the landmark victory in *Harris v. McRae*.

The first major case began in St. Louis, where *Roe* forced Mayor John Poelker, like thousands of governors and mayors across the country, to decide how to manage public hospitals and public funding and whether to allow elective abortions. Poelker decided to exclude elective abortions—those not medically indicated—from the St. Louis public hospital. As a result, he was engulfed in years of litigation. At the intermediate stage, a federal court of appeals imposed a judgment for attorneys' fees for the plaintiffs' attorneys against Poelker *personally* because the court believed he was too stubborn.

The decision in *Roe* garnered the votes of seven justices, but the application of *Roe* to discrete issues in the next series of decisions—*Danforth, Poelker, Beal, Maher,* and *Harris*—quickly divided the justices. Justices Blackmun, Brennan, and Marshall went off in one extreme direction seeking to expand abortion rights. Justices Stewart, Powell, and Burger sought to moderate *Roe* and allow some marginal limits. Justices White and Rehnquist maintained their deep disagreement with *Roe*. This division, prompted by new cases raising new issues, kept *Roe* unsettled.

After the Court decided *Danforth* and *Singleton* on July 1, 1976, it immediately took up three more abortion cases: *Poelker* from St. Louis, *Beal* v. *Doe* from Pennsylvania, and *Maher* from Connecticut, each dealing with aspects of public financial support for abortion.

The U.S. Court of Appeals for the Eighth Circuit ruled that the St. Louis' policy of excluding elective abortions from public hospitals was a violation of equal protection, "finding that the provision of publicly financed hospital services for childbirth but not for elective abortions constituted invidious discrimination." The court "mandated that the hospital provide abortion facilities and services even to the extent of hiring physicians who would agree to perform abortions."

AUL took an important strategic turn in *Poelker*. [31] Unlike its brief in *Danforth*, AUL's *amicus* brief in *Poelker* did not attempt to relitigate *Roe* but sought to uphold the St. Louis policy within the context of the framework of *Roe*. AUL's primary argument was "that Equal Protection does not require abortion on demand nor does it require public hospitals to perform abortions which are not medically indicated."

The policy in St. Louis was constitutional because it was "rationally related to the valid interests involved." The city's policy distinguishing medically-indicated from non-medically indicated (elective) abortions was "a reasonable allocation of medical resources."

AUL's brief emphasized that the evidence in the case showed that abortion was not medically necessary: "Most first trimester abortions are not performed in hospitals anywhere in America. Instead they are performed in free standing clinics."

As a result, the policy should be subject to a rational-basis test and not strict scrutiny because the policy did not interfere with the private "right" to abortion: "A right to be free from governmental interference in private matters does not imply a reciprocal right to public implementation of private decisions."

Poelker,[32] *Maher*,[33] and *Beal*[34] were argued together at the Supreme Court on January 11, 1977, ten days before president-elect Jimmy Carter took office. In a 6-3 vote, with Justices Blackmun, Brennan, and Marshall dissenting, the Court upheld the St. Louis restriction on public funding for abortion. The Court concluded that "the constitutional question presented [in *Poelker*] is identical in principle with that presented by a State's refusal to provide Medicaid benefits for abortions while providing them for childbirth," the issue before the Court in *Maher*, which the Court also upheld. There, Connecticut successfully defended the state's Title XIX Medical Assistance Program which did not provide for funding elective abortion, only those found to be "medically or psychiatrically necessary."[35]

In *Beal*, AUL filed a brief in support of the Pennsylvania limit on public funding.[36] The Court issued a joint opinion for six justices upholding the Pennsylvania policy. Justices Blackmun, Brennan and Marshall vigorously dissented in *Poelker*, *Maher*, and *Beal*. In the run-up to *Harris* in 1980, *Beal*, *Maher*, and *Poelker* provided a solid foundation of Court decisions for the fight over the Hyde Amendment. [37]

Defending the Hyde Amendment

After Congress debated numerous constitutional amendments on abortion between 1973 and 1975, a second controversy pitting one branch of the federal government against another erupted in 1976 when Congress passed the Hyde Amendment, sponsored by Congressman Henry Hyde (R-Il), later a board member of AUL. The amendment prohibited federal funds from being used to pay for abortion "except where the life of the mother would be endangered if the fetus were carried to term."[38]

In the spring of 1976, Patrick Trueman joined AUL as executive director, the first full-time member of the legal team. Living in Chicago at the time, Trueman, like some other lawyers who came to work for AUL, had a job offer from a private law firm. Out of commitment to AUL's mission, he decided to forego the more lucrative opportunity and came to work with AUL.[39]

Trueman spearheaded AUL's involvement in defending the Hyde Amendment and other legislation and litigation between 1976 and 1982. He was succeeded in 1982 by Steven (Rick) Valentine as executive director, until Rick left in 1983 to join the staff of Sen. John East (R-NC) in Washington.

Trueman collaborated with local New York attorneys Larry Washburn and Gerry Bodell, and intervened in the New York federal court challenge to the Hyde Amendment, in which Trueman and AUL represented Hyde, Sen. James Buckley (R-NY), and Sen. Jesse Helms (R-NC) as intervening defendants in federal court in New York before Judge John Francis Dooling, to establish that Congress did not have to fund abortions through the Medicaid program.[40] That litigation lasted for four years, during which time Congressman Hyde was tailed and shadowed at church in an effort to prove the amendment that bore his name was motivated by his religious beliefs. Attorney Bob Destro, later an AUL board member, also filed briefs representing *amici curiae*.

Judge Dooling in Manhattan declared the Hyde Amendment unconstitutional on October 22, 1976 and ordered the federal department of Health, Education, and Welfare (HEW)—the predecessor to today's Department of Health and Human Services—to continue to fund elective abortions.[41]

AUL appealed the case to the Supreme Court, but after deciding *Beal*, *Maher* and *Poelker*, the Court on June 29, 1977 sent *Harris* back to the lower court and ordered it to reconsider in light of those decisions.[42] Two and half more years of litigation ensued, and Judge Dooling again declared the Hyde Amendment unconstitutional on January 15, 1980.[43]

In the meantime, a case was filed challenging the Illinois version of the Hyde Amendment, which prohibited the use of public funds for abortion unless necessary to preserve a mother's life. At stake was the question of whether taxpayers could be compelled to fund abortion. The plaintiffs claimed that opposition to abortion was merely religious and that the law amounted to an establishment of religion in violation of the First Amendment and constituted "invidious discrimination" in violation of the Equal Protection Clause.

In the Illinois case, *Williams v. Zbaraz*, AUL represented Drs. Jasper Williams and Eugene Diamond as intervening defendants. The federal court in Chicago struck down the Illinois law in April 1979.[44]

The Supreme Court decided on February 19, 1980 to hear *Harris* and *Williams* together, and it set an expedited briefing schedule with 29 days for AUL to file its opening brief for Buckey, Helms, and Hyde.[45]

Dennis Horan tapped AUL board member and Northwestern Law School professor Victor Rosenblum to argue *Williams* on behalf of AUL's clients who had intervened, which pitted two friends against one another. Rosenblum and Robert (Bob) Bennett were both professors at Northwestern and close friends. Prior to the Supreme Court argument in April 1980, Northwestern Law School hosted a practice argument between the two professors for the benefit of students. At the Supreme Court, Bennett argued the challenge to the Illinois law on behalf of the plaintiffs and Rosenblum argued in defense of its constitutionality.

The Court's landmark decision in *Harris*, delivered on the last day of June in 1980, upheld the Hyde Amendment, while the Court in *Williams* upheld Illinois' prohibition on public funding for abortion, vindicating AUL's four-year fight.[46] The Court again divided 6-3 in *Harris* and *Williams*. The majority opinion by Justice Potter Stewart rejected the claim that government limits on public funding violated the Establishment Clause or the Equal Protection Clause. The Court rejected and isolated the extreme position of Justices Blackmun, Brennan, and Marshall, who would have compelled public funding by taxpayers on the same basis as public funding for childbirth.

Many would say that *Harris* was the most significant pro-life victory at the Supreme Court in the wake of *Roe*. It established important constitutional limits on *Roe*, substantially curtailed the amount of public dollars funding abortion, and limited the possibility that the Court would further endorse abortion by compelling public support. A 2016 statistical analysis by Dr. Michael New concluded that the Hyde Amendment has saved 2,000,000 lives since it was first enacted at the federal level in the 1976.[47]

After *Harris*, Horan and then-AUL staff counsel Tom Marzen published a second law review article on taxpayer funding of abortion entitled "The Supreme Court on Abortion Funding: The Second Time Around."[48] The article addressed the implications of *Harris* and *Williams* for "the entire field of abortion jurisprudence." The article defended "the Supreme Court's rationale for its decisions in these cases" and examined "some of the potential implications for future legislation and litigation."[49] *Harris* was a landmark decision because it recognized that the state could favor childbirth over abortion and "increase[d] the tension in the law between two views on the nature of the human fetus."[50] The Court in *Roe* had admitted that precedent did not support a right to abortion and that abortion was different from prior privacy decisions,[51] and the majority reiterated that in *Harris*,[52] concluding that the legislature could treat abortions uniquely because they are "inherently different from other medical procedures, because no other procedure involves the purposeful termination of a potential life."[53] This was starkly different from the barren vision of Judge Jon O. Newman that Justice William Brennan endorsed in his dissent in *Beal*:

> The view that abortion and childbirth, when stripped of the sensitive moral arguments surrounding the abortion controversy, are simply two alternative medical methods of dealing with pregnancy may be gleaned from the various opinions in *Roe* and *Doe*."[54]

Horan and Marzen highlighted the significance of the resulting rationale in *Harris*:

> As a practical matter, the *Harris* decision makes it unmistakably clear that the state may disfavor abortion and favor protection of fetal life as a matter of social and economic policy. As a result, the government may freely terminate all forms of direct financial support for abortion services and may offer positive economic inducements to forgo abortion without providing similar assistance or inducement to procure abortion.[55]

Harris gave a green light to state prohibitions on public funding of abortion, and AUL strongly promoted these limits at the federal and state levels. The decades since *Roe* would have been much more difficult and more contentious had the Court required nationwide taxpayer funding for abortion.

Harris was a watershed decision. Knowing its significance, abortion activists always have refused to accept *Harris*, fighting to at least limit *Harris* or to overturn it and compel state and federal funding of abortion. During a June 2016 debate at the National Constitution Center in Philadelphia between AUL senior counsel Clarke Forsythe, law professor Mary Ziegler, and Kathryn Kolbert, the ACLU attorney who argued and won *Casey*, Kolbert expressed confidence that Hillary Clinton would win the 2016 presidential election and go on to nominate Supreme Court justices who would overturn *Harris* and require publicly funded abortion.[56]

The Next Turning Point

Ronald Reagan defeated Jimmy Carter in the November 1980 presidential election. When Justice Potter Stewart, one of the seven justices who joined the Court's decision in *Roe*, retired four months after Reagan's inauguration, the president fulfilled his campaign promise to nominate the first woman to the Court, selecting Sandra Day O'Connor.

O'Connor wrote two compelling dissents to the logic of *Roe*, first in *City of Akron v. Akron Center for Reproductive Health* in 1983 and again in *Thornburgh v. American College of Obstetricians and Gynecologists*[57] in 1986. These dissents indicated a serious threat to the future of *Roe* and encouraged *Roe*'s critics. They signaled a change on the Court, though it was far from clear whether O'Connor's criticisms would lead to overturning *Roe* itself.[58] O'Connor's criticisms of *Roe* remained accurate, despite the fact that she later flip-flopped and voted to reaffirm *Roe* in *Casey* in 1992 and voted in 2000 to strike down state-level bans on partial-birth abortion in *Stenberg v. Carhart*.[59]

Three cases that the Court decided in 1983, *Ashcroft*, *Akron*, and *Simopoulos*, led to a significant shift in legal strategy. AUL's brief in *Akron*[60] urged the Court to limit *Roe* by shifting from the tough strict-scrutiny analysis of state abortion laws to a more lenient "substantial" or "undue burden" standard.[61] The brief argued that strict scrutiny should be reserved for protecting fundamental rights expressed in the text of the Constitution.

This proposition was argued by Solicitor General Rex Lee and roughly adopted by Justice O'Connor in her dissent, joined by Justices White and Rehnquist. The AUL brief also cited the infamous undercover investigation of Chicago abortion clinics conducted by the *Chicago Sun-Times* and published as "The Abortion Profiteers." Justice Powell cited this series in his majority opinion in *Ashcroft* but, unfortunately, did not heed its lessons.

Akron was the opportunity for the first of five direct conflicts over *Roe* between the Reagan and Bush administrations and the Supreme Court. When the U.S Solicitor General argues before the Court, the Solicitor plays a unique role, acting in a sense as the president's attorney before the Court, representing the administration, but is also expected to give frank counsel to the justices.

In *Akron*, Reagan's Solicitor General Rex Lee filed a brief supporting state limits on abortion, challenging the Court's abortion doctrine and urging substantial revision in favor of deference to the states. But his brief did not expressly urge the Court to overturn *Roe*.

At the oral argument on November 30, 1982, Justice Blackmun was so troubled by the brief that he asked Lee,

> Q: "Mr. Solicitor General, are you asking that *Roe v. Wade* be overruled?
>
> A: I am not, Mr. Justice Blackmun.
>
> …
>
> Q: "Mr. Lee, did you write this brief personally?"
>
> A: "Very substantial parts of it, Justice Blackmun."[62]

After *Akron*, the Reagan and Bush Administrations continued to challenge the Court's abortion doctrine, expressly urging that *Roe* be overruled in five cases, *Thornburgh*, *Webster*, *Hodgson*, *Rust*, and *Casey*.

AUL's brief in *Ashcroft* defended the constitutionality of three provisions of the Missouri law: the requirement of a second physician's opinion for post-viability abortions, the pathology-report requirement for all abortions, and the hospitalization requirement for abortions after the first trimester.[63]

AUL's brief in *Simopoulos v. Virginia* defended Virginia's hospitalization requirement because it was reasonably related to the protection of maternal health, which the Court in *Roe* had found to be a compelling interest after the first trimester. AUL cited 23 states that required hospitalization for abortions performed during the second trimester, and

Justice Powell cited this fact from the AUL brief in his majority opinion in *Akron*.[64]

The Court issued its decisions in *Akron*, *Ashcroft*, and *Simopolous* on the same June day in 1983, striking down most of the regulations but upholding some. Although six justices struck down *Akron*'s abortion regulations, the decisions were overshadowed by the dissent of O'Connor, joined by White and Rehnquist, the two dissenters in *Roe*. The count of justices who had criticized *Roe* now reached four—the three dissenters in *Akron*, plus Burger's earlier criticisms.

In the wake of *Akron*, *Ashcroft*, and *Simopolous*, AUL published a ten-year retrospective on abortion legislation and litigation, written by Cunningham, Marzen, and Quinlan, *Where Are We Now: The Supreme Court Decisions Ten Years After Roe v. Wade.*[65] Cunningham, a graduate of Taylor University and Northwestern University Law School, had become executive director and general counsel of AUL, Marzen was chief staff counsel, and Quinlan, a graduate of the University of Notre Dame Law School, was staff counsel. The introduction noted that detailed informed-consent legislation, "the real heart of abortion regulation and deterrence," was taken off the table for the foreseeable future by the decisions in *Akron* and *Ashcroft*.

Although AUL was disappointed by the results in these three cases, it was encouraged by the "forceful dissent by the sole woman on the Supreme Court: Justice Sandra Day O'Connor," joined by White and Rehnquist. AUL's analysis focused on the majority opinions, the O'Connor dissent, and the legislative outlook.

The Court reaffirmed *Roe* based rigidly on *stare decisis* but "apparently felt unconstrained to explain or justify the actual legal reasoning and constitutional foundations of that decision." The majority barely acknowledged "the fierce political and academic controversy generated by *Roe*." The majority was still inclined to give great deference to abortion providers. The Court at the time deferred to the standards of the National Abortion Federation, the American College of Obstetricians and Gynecologists, and the American Public Health Association (APHA) "as the chief evidence of what constitutes 'accepted medical practice.'" Even so, the Court turned around in *Ashcroft* and lightly acknowledged that "not all abortion clinics, particularly inadequately regulated clinics, conform to ethical or generally accepted medical standards."[66] The Court in *Ashcroft* even cited the infamous 1977-78 series by the *Chicago Sun-Times* on "The Abortion Profiteers."[67] But the Court would not tolerate detailed informed-consent requirements that offered a competing medical view to the abortionist's.

Advancements in medical technology would be important going forward. In *Ashcroft*, the Court upheld a parental-consent requirement that provided a judicial alternative. *Ashcroft* upheld the second physician requirement for a post-viability abortion because it was reasonably related to the State's compelling interest in protecting a viable child. The Court also upheld the pathology examination requirement.

The majority deferred to pro-abortion organizations to determine what was "accepted medical practice," which in effect gave abortion activists veto power over abortion legislation. If abortion activists changed their "standards" to rule out legislation that had formerly conformed to "standards"—as they did in 1982 between the start and the conclusion of the *Akron* litigation—the Court would defer to that change.

Justices Blackmun, Brennan, Marshall, and Stevens would have struck down even marginal abortion-related requirements. Blackmun insisted that "*the woman's health must always prevail over the fetus' life and health when they conflict*," and he reiterated his opposition to any form of parental or judicial consent.

AUL noted that O'Connor's dissent "laid bare the fallacies of both the majority opinion and its precedent, *Roe v. Wade*." The three dissenting justices would have upheld all of the regulations challenged in the three cases, on the basis that none constituted an "undue burden."

Turning to the future and the legislative outlook, AUL noted that the Court had addressed nine abortion-policy issues and concluded that detailed informed-consent requirements, waiting periods, and second-trimester hospitalization were "probably fruitless" in the short term. Instead, AUL recommended "strict reporting laws that keep track of maternal morbidity and mortality" as necessary to establish future medical standards. AUL also recommended carefully-drafted statutes mandating the humane disposition of fetal remains. These did not become a practical reality for many states until 2019, however, when the Supreme Court threw out the challenge to Indiana's humane disposition law in

Box v. Planned Parenthood of Indiana and Kentucky, Inc.,[68] enacted after the May 2015 revelations of Planned Parenthood's sale of the tissue of aborted babies.

AUL recommended state legislation that wouldn't run into the buzzsaw of the federal courts and would have some chance of taking effect and being enforced. That included parental consent or notice laws, though consent laws required a judicial-bypass mechanism. At that time, AUL argued that a spousal-*notice* requirement might pass court review, and it strongly advocated prohibitions on public funding of abortion and supported funding for abortion alternatives. States could require general but not detailed informed consent, which did not become a realistic possibility until *Casey* in 1992.

Although it was a difficult time for pro-life legislation in the states because the Court's Blackmun majority was so hostile to state legislation, one bright spot was legislation protecting the unborn child as a person in the non-abortion context, including fetal homicide, prenatal injury, and wrongful-death statutes.[69] AUL also drafted and recommended a statutory prohibition on novel "wrongful birth" suits, by which doctors could be sued for failing to advise or enable an abortion. Perseverance was necessary until the Blackmun majority left the Court.

AUL's 1984 Conference on Reversing *Roe* Through the Courts

June 1983 was a strategic turning point in the drive to overturn *Roe*, with two major developments that shifted the focus from overturning *Roe* through constitutional amendments to overturning *Roe* through the courts.

The first was the *Akron* decision and O'Connor's strong dissent, so sharply critical of *Roe* and the Court's abortion doctrine.[70] It gave pro-life leaders and legislators hope that the Court was changing and would continue to change with new justices nominated by President Reagan.

Second, the amendment effort in Congress came to an end in June 1983, two weeks after *Akron*. The Senate, in a 49-50 vote, failed to approve the Hatch-Eagleton Human Life Amendment on June 28, 1983, killing the ten-year effort to overturn *Roe* by constitutional amendment.[71] Because O'Connor's dissent signaled that the Court might be changing to some extent, it may have influenced some senators to vote against the Hatch-Eagleton Human Life Federalism Amendment, believing it to be unnecessary.

Following these two major events, the obstacles and opportunities changed, and momentum shifted toward the only other effective means in America's constitutional system of overturning a Court decision interpreting the Constitution: through the courts, by setting up a test case that would provide the vehicle for the Court to correct its disastrous constitutional interpretation and self-inflicted wound in *Roe*. The dissent from O'Connor, White, and Rehnquist encouraged more test case litigation against *Roe*.

Recognizing this as a turning point, AUL organized and hosted a national conference in Chicago at the Palmer House Hotel in March 1984, "Reversing *Roe v. Wade* Through the Courts," to devise a more focused and concerted litigation strategy.

From its founding, AUL's board, team, and strategy have been influenced by social and legal reformers and shaped by the examples of their prudential strategies, including the anti-slavery leader William Wilberforce and his allies in England, U.S. anti-slavery advocate Frederick Douglass, and civil-rights leaders such as Dr. Martin Luther King, Jr.

But no leader or organization more closely reflected the legal mission of AUL than the NAACP. Before Thurgood Marshall and his colleagues, who won *Brown v. Board of Education* in the Supreme Court in May 1954, there was his mentor Charles Hamilton Houston, dean of the Howard University Law School, first special counsel at the NAACP, and one of the most important architects of the NAACP's legal strategy against segregation.

Just months before the AUL Legal Defense Fund was founded by Dennis Horan in Chicago, Horan told the diocesan attorneys in May 1974 in Washington, D.C., "We should create a national Legal Defense Fund, similar to the NAACP Legal Defense Fund, the ultimate purpose of which will be the reversal of the judge-made law of *Roe v. Wade* and *Doe v. Bolton*."[72]

How did the NAACP devise their strategy? What were their strengths and weaknesses? How did they persevere? The NAACP and its strategy were so influential to AUL that, within three months after joining AUL in February 1985, AUL counsel Clarke Forsythe read *Simple Justice*,

Richard Kluger's 778-page monumental history of the litigation strategy that led to *Brown v. Board of Education*.

The speakers at AUL's Chicago conference in March 1984 included law professors and practicing litigators who could focus on dissecting *Roe*, addressing the elements of a successful strategy and the roadblocks involved. The conference focused on two primary questions: What influences the Supreme Court in overturning past decisions, and how do those lessons apply to *Roe*? Professors Kenneth Ripple and John Noonan spoke, and when they were nominated to the Seventh and Ninth Circuit appeals courts respectively, new authors finished and published their papers. Professors added critiques of Blackmun's historical analysis in *Roe*. Ripple and Professor Richard Myers applied the lessons of the NAACP to abortion litigation.

The biggest gap in the conference, which can be attributed to the state of medical data in 1984, was the absence of a thorough examination of existing data on short-term and long-term risks to women from abortion, a gap that would be filled to some extent in subsequent years.

Horan, AUL director of education Steve Baer, Tom Marzen, and Paige Cunningham shaped the conference. Ed Grant took a major role in editing the papers, and they were published by Georgetown University Press as *Abortion and the Constitution: Reversing Roe v. Wade Through the Courts*, with a forward by the president of Notre Dame, Father Theodore Hesburgh. The conference enabled AUL to shape a general plan two years before Antonin Scalia joined the Supreme Court.

The next year, AUL was one of the "conservative social" litigation groups featured in Lee Epstein's book *Conservatives In Court*. Epstein noted that AUL was established in the early 1970s in Washington, D.C., to educate citizens on the "harmful effects" of abortion.[73]

> Prior to *Roe* and *Doe*, anti-abortion groups had successfully lobbied against repeal. Now that those legislative victories had no meaning [after *Roe*], groups opposed to abortion had no choice but to fight the court's decision. *Roe* and *Doe* acted as catalysts for the formation of the right to life movement ...[74]

> The AUL Legal Defense Fund, whose ultimate objective is to

overturn *Roe* and *Doe*, has also made some progress. Initially, it was impatient; it wanted the court to overrule its 1973
decisions immediately. But over time it has learned that by
whittling away at those decisions through funding and consent
restrictions it could severely limit *Roe*'s impact. ...[75]

After the 1973 abortion decisions, anti-abortion groups became
acutely aware of the utility of litigation. Although there are
several groups that now represent the right to life position in
the courts, the AUL Legal Defense Fund, which was founded in
1975, is the movement's only full-time public interest law firm.[76]

The last Illinois abortion litigation in which AUL was directly involved
was *Keith v. Daley*, an ACLU court challenge to Illinois House Bill 1399,
which amended the Illinois Abortion Act of 1975 and had been passed
by the General Assembly over the governor's veto on June 30, 1984.[77]
The Illinois Pro-Life Coalition sought to intervene to defend the Illinois
law, which the federal court denied.

An appeal went to the U.S. Court of Appeals in Chicago, where AUL
counsel Maura Quinlan represented the Pro-Life Coalition and argued
the appeal. In June 1985, the U.S. Court of Appeals affirmed the denial
of intervention.[78] *Keith*—and the denial of a right to appeal in *Diamond
v. Charles*[79] at the Supreme Court the following year—signaled the end
of the line for the tactic of pro-life intervention in abortion cases, which
Horan had spearheaded in 1970.

Thornburgh: Last Hurrah of the Blackmun Majority

Another major turning point came in 1985 and 1986. For a decade, AUL
was immersed in the enactment and defense of the Illinois Abortion
Law of 1975 and its amendments in the 1970s and 1980s, which AUL
had played a significant role in drafting.[80] The federal appeals court in
Chicago issued a decision on November 30, 1984,[81] once again striking
down the law. After the Seventh Circuit ruled, AUL informed Illinois
attorney general Neil Hartigan that AUL intended to appeal on behalf of
intervenors Drs. Diamond and Williams. Hartigan's office was not forth-
coming about its intent to appeal. AUL filed its appeal in the Supreme

Court by the deadline of February 28, 1985. The next day, AUL was
stunned to find out that Hartigan had failed to file.

While AUL was encouraged that the Supreme Court agreed in May to
hear the case[82]—combining the case with Pennsylvania's appeal in
Thornburgh v. ACOG and scheduling the the oral arguments together—
AUL was left alone, heading to the Supreme Court representing private
parties, without the support of Illinois, an awkward and uncertain
position. AUL nevertheless proceeded with the appeal, combined with
Thornburgh.

AUL briefed the *Diamond* case and Dennis Horan argued it before the
Supreme Court on November 5, 1985. Because Illinois failed to appeal,
it was a difficult argument.[83] Though Horan sought to argue the merits
of the Illinois abortion law, it was clear that the pro-abortion justices
would question AUL's "appealable interest" as a private party. Blackmun, Marshall, Stevens, and Brennan asked Horan questions exclusive-
ly about the intervenors' interest in the appeal for nearly half of the
argument.

> Justice Marshall: Are you qualified to give us the position of
> the state of Illinois?
>
> Horan: In the court below and before the Seventh Circuit, the
> State was a party, did litigate the issues, and we jointly filed
> joint briefs, so that the position of the State on each one of
> these issues was stated in those briefs. The Attorney General
> has filed a statement with this Court under Rule 10.4 that he
> does have an interest in the outcome of this case. ...
>
> Justice Marshall: Well, what is the position of the State now,
> and how do you know?
>
> Horan: Because the State filed a letter which was referred
> to in the brief of the Appellees and a copy of which is in an
> appendix to our reply brief, stating that they have an interest
> in the outcome of the case. They did not state the reason why
> they did not file a notice of appeal. My understanding is that
> the reason was simple inadvertence.

White asked three questions. Burger, Powell, Rehnquist, and O'Connor asked none. An ominous sign.

The more consequential case turned out to be *Thornburgh*, argued the same morning as *Diamond* by the Pennsylvania attorney general's office. *Thornburgh* provided an opportunity for the Reagan Administration to directly challenge *Roe* and urge the Supreme Court, for the first time, to overrule it. The brief for the United States was written by Acting Solicitor General Charles Fried and assistant attorney generals Richard Willard and Carolyn Kuhl. Fried's 30-page brief was a thorough critique of the constitutional foundations of *Roe*, its shoddy reasoning, and its negative effects on the nation.

In April 1986, the Court dismissed *Diamond* because—as AUL feared—Illinois had failed to file an appeal in the case.[84] That didn't prevent AUL's clients, the intervenors, from facing an attorneys' fees judgment of $200,000 because the district court struck down the Illinois law. Senator Strom Thurmond (R., S.C.) introduced a bill on behalf of the Reagan Administration that would have ended the assessment of attorneys' fees against intervenors under federal law, and AUL executive director and general counsel Ed Grant was in touch with the White House during 1985 about the implications of the bill. The attorney-fees litigation continued until 1988, culminating in a $200,000 judgment against Dr. Diamond, payable to the ACLU.[85] Congress never passed an amendment to the federal Civil-Rights Attorneys' Fees Act and that judgment chilled intervention in state abortion litigation for many years.

Two months after dismissing *Diamond*, the Court issued its decision in *Thornburgh*, on June 11, 1986, indicating that the threat to *Roe* was growing stronger. Blackmun's opinion for a 5-4 majority including Brennan, Marshall, Stevens, and Powell was the last hurrah of the *Roe* Court. The pro-*Roe* majority had shrunk from 7-2 in *Roe*, to 6-3 in *Akron*, to 5-4 in *Thornburgh*.[86]

O'Connor again filed a strong dissent, joined by White and Rehnquist, her second major criticism of *Roe* and the Court's application of it.

In a major development, Chief Justice Burger, who originally joined the *Roe* majority, dissented separately. Burger wrote that he agreed "with much" of the dissents filed that day by White (joined by Rehnquist) and O'Connor (joined by Rehnquist). Burger indicated that his skepticism about the implications of *Roe* and its expansion had blossomed into fundamental doubt that it should survive:

> I regretfully conclude that some of the concerns of the dissenting Justices in *Roe*, as well as the concerns I expressed in my separate opinion, have now been realized ... today the Court astonishingly goes so far as to say that the State may not even require that a woman contemplating an abortion be provided with accurate medical information concerning the risks inherent in the medical procedure which she is about to undergo and the availability of state-funded alternatives if she elects not to run those risks. Can anyone doubt that the State could impose a similar requirement with respect to other medical procedures? Can anyone doubt that doctors routinely give similar information concerning risks in countless procedures having far less impact on life and health, both physical and emotional than an abortion, and risk a malpractice lawsuit if they fail to do so?
>
> Yet the Court concludes that the State cannot impose this simple information-dispensing requirement in the abortion context where the decision is fraught with serious physical, psychological, and moral concerns of the highest order. Can it possibly be that the Court is saying that the Constitution *forbids* the communication of such critical information to a woman? We have apparently already passed the point at which abortion is available merely on demand. If the statute at issue here is to be invalidated, the "demand" will not even have to be the result of an informed choice. ...
>
> In discovering constitutional infirmities in state regulations of abortion that are in accord with our history and tradition, we may have lured judges into "roaming at large in the constitutional field." The soundness of our holdings must be tested by the decisions that purport to follow them. If *Danforth* and today's holding really mean what they seem to say, I agree we should reexamine *Roe*.[87]

Then the next shoe dropped. A week later, on June 18, Burger announced that he would retire and chair the Commission on the Bicentennial of the United States Constitution. When Reagan announced he would nominate Rehnquist for chief justice and Judge Antonin Scalia to fill Rehnquist's seat, AUL attorneys practically danced down Dearborn Street in Chicago celebrating.[88]

Defending the Adolescent Family Life Act

Meanwhile, the Reagan Administration was complementing work in the states by changing the direction of family planning in federal programs. AUL defended the constitutionality of federally-funded programs that taught an inviolability of human life ethic in the mid-1980s. The ACLU filed suit against the Reagan Administration's Adolescent Family Life Act (AFLA), a family planning program that taught abstinence and excluded abortion-advocacy organizations from the program. The AFLA limited federal funding to "programs or projects which do not provide abortions or abortion counseling or referral" and to "projects or programs which do not advocate, promote, or encourage abortion."

The ACLU argued, in essence, that religious organizations must be excluded from federal funding, that abstinence in the AFLA's care services and prevention services promoted religious beliefs, and that federal funding of such teaching amounted to an "establishment" of religion that violated the First Amendment. AUL represented United Families of America as intervening defendants in the federal court in the District of Columbia.

From 1985 to 1988, AUL and local counsel Paul Arneson were heavily involved in the trial court litigation. In April 1987, the district court struck down the program as unconstitutional, holding that the AFLA had "the primary effect of advancing religion," which prompted a direct appeal to the Supreme Court.

AUL asked then-University of Chicago Law Professor Michael McConnell to argue the case for AUL's intervenors in the Supreme Court. McConnell was a conservative legal scholar who had clerked for J. Skelly Wright in the D.C. Circuit and then for Justice William Brennan at the Supreme Court. After his clerkship, McConnell had worked at the Office of Management and Budget (OMB) and joined the faculty at the University of Chicago Law School, where he quickly developed a national reputation as a premier scholar of religious liberty. He agreed to argue the appeal for the intervenors. AUL attorneys Grant, Forsythe, and affiliated attorneys Paul Arneson and Michael Woodruff, helped McConnell with the briefs and his preparation for oral argument.

McConnell defended the federal program, sharing oral argument time with Solicitor General Charles Fried, and won the appeal in June 1988 as the Reagan Administration was coming to an end. In a 5-4 decision, with the majority opinion by Chief Justice Rehnquist, the Court held in *Bowen v. Kendrick* that the AFLA was not invalid on its face and sent the case back to the federal district court.[89] Justices Blackmun, Brennan, Marshall, and Stevens dissented. The hostile *Roe* majority had dissolved.

The *Webster* Opportunity

Tragically, Horan didn't live to see the fruits of his long labor. Horan died suddenly on May 1, 1988 at the young age of 56. Horan's energy, vision, and leadership had guided AUL from 1974 to his untimely death, and he had an enormous influence on legal debate and changes in abortion and euthanasia law, and other bioethical issues, during his final two decades.

AUL didn't have to wait long to return to the Supreme Court. In July 1988, a federal appeals court invalidated Missouri's abortion regulations,[90] setting up the first direct showdown over *Roe*. Missouri attorney general William Webster was willing to defend the statute at the Supreme Court, and AUL was willing to help.

Though AUL had not drafted the Missouri statute, AUL had filed a brief in support of the law in the appeals court because it presented important legal limits on abortion: a declaration (preamble) that human life begins at conception, a viability-testing requirement, and limits on the use of public facilities to promote abortion—including a provision struck down by the Eighth Circuit, which forbade "the use of public facilities, employees, or funds to encourage or counsel certain abortions."[91] AUL's brief at the appeals level helped to establish a relationship with the Missouri attorney general's office.

The looming threat to *Roe* was clear, signifying that *Roe* was unsettled. Two weeks before the Eighth Circuit ruled, the journal of the American Bar Association published an article entitled "Will *Roe v. Wade* Be Overruled?"[92] After the Supreme Court agreed to hear *Webster*, Blackmun told first-year law students on September 13, 1988, that it was a "distinct possibility that *Roe* would be overturned this Term."[93]

Forsythe traveled to Jefferson City, Missouri, to meet with Webster and Jerry Short, Webster's principal assistant, who had argued the *Webster* case in the Eighth Circuit. Webster asked Forsythe to write a draft of the jurisdictional statement, and a discussion ensued as to whether Missouri should ask the Court to overrule *Roe*.[94] A U.S. assistant attorney general in the Reagan Administration, Brad Reynolds, prevailed on Webster and Short to present the overruling question among the questions presented in Missouri's appeal.

During the fall of 1988 and winter of 1989, AUL organized the *amicus* briefing effort in *Webster*, including a brief by the state of Louisiana, joined by Arizona, Idaho, Pennsylvania, and Wisconsin. Had there been more time, more states likely would have joined.

In February 1989, AUL attorneys Paul Linton and Forsythe filed a brief in the Supreme Court on behalf of 259 legislators from 13 states urging that *Roe* be "overruled and the authority to regulate abortion … restored to the States."

Webster argued the case at the Supreme Court on April 26, 1989, sharing time with U.S. Solicitor General Charles Fried, who argued that *Roe* should be overruled.

For the next two months, the debate among the justices was intense. The wait for a ruling in *Webster* extended beyond the normal end of the Court's term. The Court finally released its decision on July 3, 1989.[95] Rehnquist wrote an opinion for five justices, and the supporters of an unlimited abortion right in *Roe* were reduced to four: Justice Blackmun dissented, joined by Brennan and Marshall, and Stevens dissented separately.

The initial vote by the Justices after the April 26 argument included a majority to overturn *Roe*. But O'Connor ultimately dropped out and published a concurring opinion in which she joined to uphold the Missouri regulations but stated that *Roe* did not need to be reconsidered in this case, kicking the can down the road. Though it was disappointing that the Court did not overturn *Roe*, four strong votes for overturning *Roe* was encouraging, and it was gratifying to see Justice O'Connor cite

AUL's brief on behalf of the American Association of Pro-Life Obstetricians and Gynecologists (AAPLOG).[96] In *Webster*, a plurality of the Court expressly rejected central tenets of the *Roe* doctrine.

Only later did AUL find out how close it had come. While *Webster* was pending but before the decision was announced, Justice Anthony Kennedy wrote to Chief Justice Rehnquist on May 22, 1989: "I am in substantial agreement with your excellent opinion in this case. As you know, in my view the case does provide a fair opportunity to assess the continuing validity of *Roe v. Wade*, and I would have used the occasion to overrule that case and return this difficult issue to the political systems of the states."[97] Lacking was the fifth and decisive vote of Justice O'Connor.

Public Opinion and Abortion

One of the tragedies of *Roe* is that the Supreme Court, without constitutional authority, removed the abortion issue from the hands of Americans. Since colonial days, abortion had been considered a crime, decided through the democratic process, by the people through their elected representatives. That was true through the adoption of the Constitution of 1787 and through the Reconstruction Amendments after the Civil War. Abortion laws were actively enforced by the states until the eve of *Roe*, and that enforcement was effective.[98]

Because laws protecting human life were centered in the states—what used to be called state police power—public support was important for effective law enforcement and the legal protection of human life. That's true for virtually all bioethical issues. With the sole exception perhaps of contraception and the Supreme Court's *Griswold* and *Eisenstadt* decisions, *Roe* was unique in removing the decision about a controversial bioethics issue from the American people. In 1997, the Supreme Court rejected a national right to assisted suicide and left that issue to the democratic process. Virtually all other bioethical issues are decided, first and foremost, at the state level. If the cause for life in America is to build on its momentum, it must focus on democratic action and nurture public opinion on abortion.

After the *Webster* decision, which for the first time since *Roe* gave significant deference to the states on abortion, AUL organized and sponsored a Gallup poll on abortion in 1990, entitled "Abortion and Moral

Beliefs." This was and remains the most comprehensive survey ever taken of American attitudes toward abortion. The survey instrument was written and designed by University of Virginia sociologist James Davison Hunter.

Hunter subsequently analyzed the polling data from the 1990 Gallup poll in detail in his book, *Before the Shooting Begins.*[99] The survey found that a majority of Americans believed that abortion takes a human life but also found that Americans did not understand what the Court did in *Roe* or *Webster.* Without such an understanding, polls asking Americans whether Americans "support *Roe*" or "whether *Roe* should be overturned" cannot produce reliable results.

Ragsdale Litigation: Chicago's Abortion Clinics and Conditions

Webster was a jolt, heightening AUL's expectations as to what might be possible. The Court gave some leeway to states and decided the same day to take up three additional abortion cases, raising hopes that the Court might overturn *Roe* entirely in the next series of cases.

The three cases included a major one from Illinois that laid out the long, sordid history of substandard conditions and providers in Chicago's abortion clinics. *Roe* created a public-health vacuum, as Justice Blackmun had anticipated. In the first few years after *Roe*, the Court refused to approve health-and-safety regulations passed by state and local governments in a series of cases, including the *Friendship Medical Center* case from Chicago.[100]

AUL first demonstrated its commitment to protecting women from the physical and psychological harms of abortion in Horan's briefs in *Vuitch* and *Roe* and in *Abortion and Social Justice.* It influenced AUL to draft health and safety regulations for abortion clinics, starting with Illinois in the 1970s—a commitment that continued through AUL's work in *June Medical* in 2020.

Informed consent is a principle of medical ethics, embedded in American law for at least the past half century: the principle that women should be fully informed of the nature, risks, and alternatives to abortion, including an understanding of the short- and long-term risks.

The medical risks were described in detail in the 2016 documentary *Hush.*[101]

The terrible conditions in Chicago abortion clinics in the years after *Roe* were first exposed in a five-month investigation by the Better Government Association (BGA) and the *Chicago Sun-Times*, published in a multi-part series by the *Sun-Times* between November 12, 1978, and December 1978, entitled *The Abortion Profiteers*. The five-month probe focused on four abortion clinics that accounted for more than one-third of the abortions performed in Illinois in 1977.

The series was followed by legislative hearings in Springfield and a December 13, 1978, report of the Illinois House Human Resources Committee's subcommittee on health. The investigation uncovered twelve abortion-related deaths between 1973 and 1978 that had gone unreported. One of the abortionists covered by the *Sun-Times* investigation was Ulrich Klopfer, who died in 2019, leaving 2,400 fetal specimens from aborted human beings in his garage and car near Crete, Illinois, south of Chicago.[102]

A decade after the *Sun-Times* investigation, Pam Zekman, one of the reporters who contributed to the 1978 series, reported that "since 1985, the state has been powerless to even license the outpatient surgicenters that specialize in abortions." That was due to the lower court decision in *Ragsdale v. Turnock* in 1985 that was heading to the Supreme Court.[103]

AUL worked with those who helped the *Sun-Times* expose the Michigan Avenue "clinics." As Ed Grant recalled, "AUL labored on the legislation for years before it was enacted, and then worked very closely with the professional staff at the Illinois Attorney General's office to defend the law. At that time, the Illinois legislature was pro-life, and clinic regulation legislation, drafted by AUL, was enacted in 1985."

The ACLU in Chicago enlisted abortionist Richard Ragsdale to act as a plaintiff,[104] and the law was declared unconstitutional by both the federal trial court and appeals court.[105] Illinois appealed, seeking review by the Supreme Court, and on the same day that the Court decided *Webster*, it agreed to hear *Turnock v. Ragsdale* in the Fall of 1989.[106]

AUL immediately set to organizing the briefing in the appeal. In August 1989, Ed Grant and Paige Cunningham filed a brief at the Supreme

Court on behalf of Feminists for Life and AAPLOG in support of the Illinois regulations, documenting the tragic history of abortion practice in Illinois. AUL counsel Paul Linton filed a second brief in *Ragsdale* on behalf of Illinois representatives and senators, addressing whether Illinois could enact abortion-specific regulations of clinics.[107]

This led to great hope that the next case the Court would hear would be one in which the pro-life position held the highest ground—a clinic-regulations statute, enacted after a public exposé of terrible clinic conditions, and with a Court moving away from the absolutist position of striking down virtually every form of abortion regulation. Illinois filed its brief, relying on the *Webster* decision in July 1989 and arguing that the Illinois clinic regulations "do not unduly burden the abortion decision."

Unfortunately, AUL faced its second collision with Neil Hartigan. The Illinois attorney general was positioning himself to make a second run for governor and had abandoned his pro-life position. (Hartigan became the Democratic nominee for governor in 1990 but lost to Republican Jim Edgar.)

Oral argument in *Ragsdale* was scheduled for December 5, 1989 but it never happened. As Grant recalled,

> The acid test was whether [Hartigan] would pursue this appeal in the Supreme Court—the other side was apoplectic that we might win this case before the Court. Hartigan knuckled under, the case was settled over the course of the next several few years on a consent decree providing minimal safeguards for clinics, and the case before the Supreme Court withdrawn.[108] So, instead of getting a good law upheld, and making incremental progress with the Court, we lost everything.

On November 22, 1989, the parties filed a joint motion to defer further proceedings in the Supreme Court, pending submission of a proposed consent decree to the district court. The federal appeals court approved the consent decree in August 1991, gutting the Illinois law and ending the fight over clinic regulations in the state.[109] The Supreme Court granted the parties' joint motion to defer the appeal on December 1,

1989,[110] and dismissed the case in March 1992, after the Illinois attorney general caved to the ACLU.[111]

Grant recalled, "The history here is important for several reasons. Clinic regulations work. As the Philadelphia District Attorney's [2012] report bluntly concludes, Pennsylvania stopped being in the business of enforcing its own clinic regulations when a pro-abortion Republican (Ridge) replaced a pro-life Democrat (Casey)."

Grant pointed out that, as Jillian Melchior demonstrated in a piece for *National Review* in May 2013, "the problem is pervasive, and the other side, despite its professed care for women, has stridently opposed every piece of legislation directed at the problem, and thwarted efforts at enforcement when such laws are passed (as happened in Pennsylvania)."

The Illinois safeguards were completely repealed by abortion activists in the Illinois General Assembly in the spring of 2019.

The Second Round: From *Webster* to *Casey*

Webster illustrated that much of the Court was willing to question *Roe*, and it launched what became a three-year strategy to create a showdown on *Roe*. *Webster*, as one federal judge put it, "altered the constitutional landscape."[112]

In addition to *Ragsdale*, the Court decided to hear abortion cases from Ohio and Minnesota on July 3, 1989: *Ohio v. Akron Center for Reproductive Health* and *Hodgson v. Minnesota*. It looked as though the Court's majority—comprising Rehnquist, White, O'Connor, Scalia, and Kennedy—was signaling its willingness to continue sifting through the Court's abortion doctrine, possibly even moving to decide a series of abortion cases that would address *Roe* head on. With the Court agreeing the same day to hear the euthanasia case, *Cruzan v. Missouri Department of Health*, AUL was suddenly engulfed in briefing four Supreme Court cases.

The Court decided the Ohio and Minnesota cases in June 1990. In *Akron II*, it upheld Ohio's one-parent–notice statute. The decision in *Hodgson* applied a more deferential standard toward abortion legislation and upheld one-parent notice for abortion but struck down two-parent notice. It was the first abortion regulation found unconstitutional by

Justice O'Connor, thereby showing the limits of her willingness to completely reverse *Roe*.

After *Akron II* and *Hodgson*, the Court took up yet another abortion case, *Rust*. The case involved a court challenge to the Reagan and George H.W. Bush Administration's regulations prohibiting abortion counseling or abortion referral by programs receiving federal family planning funds under Title X of the Public Health Service Act. The Court agreed to hear *Rust* on May 29, 1990, it was argued at the end of October, and the Court upheld the federal regulations in 1991.[113] AUL represented the Association of American Physicians and Surgeons (AAPS) as *amicus curiae* in support of the administration's policy.

During this time, AUL was cautious about the direction O'Connor seemed to be headed with the Court's abortion doctrine. Forsythe published a 1991 analysis of the Court's abortion cases, questioning whether O'Connor's opinions in *Akron*, *Thornburgh*, and *Webster* signaled that she was willing to overturn *Roe* and emphasizing the uncertainty of the contemporary outlook for abortion litigation:

> [H]ow far will she go in upholding substantive prohibitions on abortion in the first trimester when ninety percent of all abortions are performed? Will she attempt to avoid a direct confrontation? If pushed too far by a direct conflict, could her vote be lost to the Blackmun minority? What would be the political impact of such a loss, given Justice O'Connor's position as a Reagan appointee and as the only woman justice to this point? At the same time, the judicial standard for abortion that O'Connor espoused as of 1991 was ambiguous. "The 'undue burden' standard allows judges great subjectivity to determine what burdens are 'undue' and what state interests are 'compelling' or 'legitimate.' ... In short, it is far from clear that Justice O'Connor will join with a majority if the Court decides to overturn *Roe v. Wade*.[114]

Forsythe also pointed out that "Justice Souter's views on abortion are a big question mark. He does not demonstrate—either in his writing or in his public comments—that he is either philosophically or emotionally committed to the principle of the sanctity of human life."[115]

Given that the Court in *Webster* had granted the states more deference, AUL moved to "nationalize" its state legislative strategy. In November 1989, AUL sponsored its first national Legislators Educational Conference (LEC) to educate state legislators on pro-life public policy. More than 100 state legislators attended in Chicago. Around the same time, AUL published several articles challenging the Court's abortion doctrine and advising states on the best way to legislate in the uncertain climate.[116]

Webster prompted three jurisdictions—Louisiana, Utah, and the territory of Guam—to pass strong limits on abortion based on changing expectations that the Court might be moving to overturn *Roe*. Utah considered abortion prohibitions in reaction to the *Webster* decision, and asked AUL to testify in favor of them. Forsythe flew to Salt Lake City to testify in support of the Utah bill (S.B. 23) on January 24, 1991, and spoke to both the House Republican and House Democratic caucuses. Governor Norman Bangerter signed the bill on January 25, 1991, launching a 60-day process to prepare for inevitable litigation.

On March 19, 1990, Guam passed a law prohibiting virtually all abortions, except in cases of ectopic pregnancy and in cases when two physicians found that "there is a substantial risk that continuance of the pregnancy would endanger the life of the mother or gravely impair her health."[117] Crucial test cases were on the their way to the Court.

What Might Have Been

The nomination of David Souter to replace Justice William Brennan on July 25, 1990 came as a great disappointment. President George H. W. Bush interviewed Fifth Circuit judge Edith Jones for the spot at the same time. Michael Stokes Paulsen worked at the time in the Justice Department's Office of Legal Counsel, assigned to the Supreme Court nomination, and was able to witness the contrast between Souter and Jones. Paulsen favored Jones and believed Souter would have a negative effect on the Court's balance on *Roe*, but he was bound to confidentiality and couldn't alert a friend at AUL before the nomination was final.[118]

The Supreme Court would have been markedly different had Judge

Jones been nominated and confirmed. She would have been a pro-life and conservative presence on the Court, and she might well have been the fifth vote and encouragement to Anthony Kennedy to overturn *Roe* in *Casey* in 1992. Had *Roe* not been overturned in *Casey*, Jones would have been present to counter Justice O'Connor's turn in favor of legal abortion and Ruth Bader Ginsburg's aggressive pro-abortion posture after 1993. The Bush Administration's message to pro-life groups about the Souter nomination was to ignore the facts and rather "trust and obey." The subsequent nomination of Judge Clarence Thomas to replace Justice Thurgood Marshall the following year, in July 1991, was encouraging—but even that couldn't erase the disappointment of Souter's confirmation.

The Showdown in *Casey*

Meanwhile, AUL was closely monitoring the lower court litigation against Pennsylvania governor Robert Casey, who signed into law multiple abortion limits, passed in response to *Webster*. The litigation made its way to the federal appeals court in Philadelphia, which upheld each part of the policy except for the spousal-notice requirement, a provision which AUL had *not* supported in the legislature.[119]

Late in the Court's term for scheduling oral argument, the Justices decided on January 21, 1992, that it would hear *Planned Parenthood of Southeastern Pennsylvania v. Casey*[120] but initially limited its review only to the constitutionality of the Pennsylvania statutory provisions.[121] Since the Court expressly declined in January 1992 to review *Roe* itself, as requested by Governor Casey, AUL did not expect *Casey* to involve a direct confrontation of *Roe*. At the time it seemed that *Ada v. Guam Society of Obstetricians and. Gynecologists* might be a more likely vehicle, since Guam had passed a stronger limit on abortion.

Casey was scheduled for oral argument on April 22, 1992, and AUL organized the *amicus* briefing effort. AUL staff counsel Kevin Todd filed a brief with Professor Albert Blaustein (1921-1994) of Rutgers Law School, a renowned scholar of judicial precedent, urging the Supreme Court to overrule *Roe*. They filed the brief on behalf of three U.S. senators and 38 members of the House of Representatives, including nine Democrats.

In a detailed and scholarly brief of 30 pages, Todd and Blaustein examined the factors of *stare decisis* that weighed in favor of overturning *Roe*. They demonstrated that *Roe* was unsettled, "an impaired decision," wrongly decided as a constitutional matter, and "demonstrably unworkable." They urged the Court to return the abortion issue to the democratic process: "*Roe* is constitutional error of the most radical variety, and the traditions of this Court call for such error to be dispatched without ambiguity or equivocation."

The *Casey* decision of June 29, 1992, was a tremendous disappointment, though not a devastating shock; AUL had had doubts that O'Connor or Souter would vote to overturn *Roe*.[122] A three-judge plurality of O'Connor, Kennedy, and Souter wrote a lengthy joint opinion preserving the right to abortion. The AUL team learned of the decision in the group's Chicago office, and they watched the network coverage on the Supreme Court steps. The decision left AUL team reeling for a day or two, but after reading the decision and holding a press conference, they remained determined to move forward.

Despite the defeat, AUL's work in *Casey* was instrumental in the Court's gradual movement against *Roe*, as it altered the substance of that decision without undoing it. Four justices had supported overruling *Roe* outright. Abortion activists complained that *Casey* left them with "half a loaf." The Court approved state informed-consent laws for the first time and reiterated that parental-consent statutes were constitutional. It provided a rough road map for the states in the 1990s and began the continuous and dramatic decline in the U.S. abortion rate, thanks in large part to the possibility that states could regulate and restrict abortion more after *Casey*.

Taking Guam to the Supreme Court

AUL was left wondering what should be done with Guam's appeal in the wake of *Casey*. On July 1, AUL chairman Victor Rosenblum met with AUL attorneys to discuss the group's defense of Guam's abortion prohibition, and they decided to recommend an appeal to the Supreme Court.

In 1990, Governor Joseph Ada and his counsel asked AUL to represent Guam in defense of the law, and four AUL attorneys were appointed special assistant attorneys general for Guam, along with Maura Quinlan who had moved from AUL to private practice in Harrisburg, Pennsylvania. Linton and Forsythe met in Agana with Katherine Maraman, counsel to the governor, to discuss the litigation strategy.

Abortionists in Guam filed a facial challenge to the law, arguing that it was completely invalid as to any abortion at any point in pregnancy, and the district court invalidated the law in a summary judgment on August 23, 1990. Linton and AUL's staff counsel Leanne McCoy drafted AUL's brief for Guam in the Ninth Circuit Court of Appeals in January 1991, and Linton argued the appeal before the Ninth Circuit in Honolulu on November 4, 1991. The Ninth Circuit struck down Guam's statute.[123]

Despite the *Casey* decision, Governor Ada wanted to fight all the way to the Supreme Court, so AUL filed an appeal in July 1992, two weeks after the ruling in *Casey*, pressing the case that the Guam statute could be constitutionally applied to at least some abortions, especially after fetal viability.

Unfortunately, the Supreme Court refused to hear Guam's appeal at the end of November 1992, effectively confirming that the Court would not hear cases after *Casey* with statutes as protective as Guam's, which prohibited abortion except to save the life of the mother or to prevent severe impairment of her physical health. This sparked a dissent from Justice Scalia, joined by Rehnquist and White, the two original dissenters in *Roe*.[124]

Even if lawyers might have believed that the appeal had little chance, Justice Scalia used the opportunity to highlight one of the "abortion distortion" factors in the Supreme Court's abortion doctrine.[125] In other areas of law, the Court would rule that a facial challenge—to the entirety of a law—"must be rejected unless there exists *no set of circumstances* in which the statute can constitutionally be applied." Virtually the only exception to this rule was a challenge to a law infringing on free-speech, a right ratified in the text of the First Amendment.

Justice Scalia pointed out the damage to self-government from judicial overreach through facial challenges: "Facial invalidation based on overbreadth impermissibly interferes with the state process of refining and limiting—through judicial decision or enforcement discretion—statutes that cannot be constitutionally applied in all cases covered by their language."

Scalia agreed with AUL's petition on behalf of Guam, writing, "I see no reason why the Guam law would not be constitutional at least in its application to abortions conducted after the point at which the child may live outside the womb."[126] The Court needed to address the issue, in his view, because the U.S. Court of Appeals for the Fifth Circuit had used the same facial-challenge weapon against Louisiana's law as the Ninth Circuit had against Guam.

Scalia's 1992 dissent in *Ada* highlighted the unprecedented way in which the Court allowed the abortion industry to distort abortion litigation, enabling abortionists to escape the burden of presenting facts in court and enabling federal judges to avoid having to discern facts about abortion. This didn't just occur with facial challenges, which essentially render facts irrelevant, but also with third-party standing, by which abortionists appear in court to "represent the interests" of women and tell judges that women don't need, for instance, health-and-safety standards for abortion.

Only First Amendment liberties are entitled to such measures, and the fact that they were permitted in cases dealing with abortion elevated abortion to the level of the First Amendment. Without ever giving a constitutional reason, the Court started to treat abortion like free speech and exempted abortion from the facial challenge rule.[127] Indeed, even after the Court downgraded abortion in *Casey*, and no longer treated abortion as a "fundamental right," the Court exempted abortion from the facial challenge rule. The Court never gave a reasoned explanation for how abortion, a judicially created right, was "deeply rooted" in American law and tradition. For reasons of truth-seeking and constitutional authority, the Court's allowance of such evasions defied reason.

The states took *Casey* as a sign to attempt to enact common-sense abortion limits for the next 25 years. But, since the Court failed to clarify the law in *Casey* or Guam, abortionists started to use facial challenges routinely against state abortion laws, making it harder for states to pass and enforce any limits on abortion, even after the prenatal child is viable. That would be the trend for the next three decades, during which the closely-divided Court would flip back and forth between deference and harsh scrutiny of state abortion limits.

Chapter 4 Endnotes

1   Forsythe, Abuse of Discretion, *supra* ch.2 note 46; Clarke D. Forsythe & Bradley N.
     Kehr, *A Road Map Through the Supreme Court's Back Alley*, 57 Vill. L. Rev. 45 (2012).

2   Wynn v. Scott, 448 F. Supp. 997 (N.D. Ill. 1978), *aff'd,* Wynn v. Carey, 582 F.2d 1375
     (7th Cir. 1978) (parental consent law of 1977); Wynn v. Scott, 449 F. Supp. 1302 (N.D.
     Ill. 1978) (addressing the constitutionality of the 1975 Illinois statute), *aff'd,* Wynn v.
     Carey, 599 F.2d 193 (7th Cir. 1979).

3   Bundesverfassungsgericht [BVerfG] [Federal Constitutional Court] Feb. 25, 1975, 39
     Entscheidungen des Bundesverfassungsgerichts [BVerfGE] 1 (Ger.). *See* Benda, *supra*
     ch. 2 note 75. *See also* Jonas, *supra* ch. 2 note 74 (providing an English translation of
     the decision).

4   Life, Liberty, & Law, *Patrick Trueman on the Early Days of Americans United for Life,*
     Its Visionary Approach to Human Rights, and What's Next, Ams.United for Life (Sep-
     tember 14, 2020). https://podcasts.apple.com/us/podcast/patrick-trueman-on-the-ear-
     ly-days-of-americans/id1472791329?i=1000491184144 (Patrick Trueman recalling the
     significance of the translation); Life, Liberty, & Law, *Patrick Trueman on the Early*
     Days of Americans United for Life, supra ch. 2 note 56 (Jack Gorby discussing the
     translation).

5   John D. Gorby, *Introduction to the Translation of the Abortion Decision of the Feder-*
     al Constitutional Court of the Federal Republic of Germany West German Abortion
     Decision: A Contrast to Roe v. Wade*: Introduction,* 9 John Marshall J. Prac. & Proc.
     557, 561 (1976); Interview with John D. Gorby, Professor, John Marshall Law School
     (Sept. 2015) (on file with author).

6   Gorby, *Introduction to the Translation of the Abortion Decision, supra* ch. 4 note 5,
     at 577 (emphasis added).

7   Interview of Jack Gorby, *supra* ch. 4 note 5. *See also* Gorby, *Introduction to the*
     Translation of the Abortion Decision, supra ch. 4 note 5, at 577 n.73. Jonas, *West*
     German Abortion Decision, supra ch. 2 note 74 (providing and English translation of
     the decision).

8   *Danforth*, 428 U.S. at 91.

9   Forsythe, *A Road Map Through the Supreme Court's Back Alley, supra* note 1. *See*
     also Forsythe, Abuse of Discretion, *supra* note ch. 2 note 46, at 233–34 (detailing an
     exchange between Justices Brennan, Powell, and Blackmun, refusing to publicly
     acknowledge the substandard conditions in abortion clinics).

10   428 U.S. 106 (1976).

11   On the point of third-party standing, only four justices joined Part II-B of Justice
     Blackmun's opinion. Justice Stevens, in his first term on the Court, pointedly did
     not join Part II-B because he supported the standing of abortionists in the case only

because their own financial interest was alleged and they alleged their own constitutional rights were at stake, *Id*. at 121–22 (Stevens, J., concurring in part).

12   *Id*. at 122. (Powell, J., concurring in part and dissenting in part).

13   140 S. Ct. 2103, 2146 (2020).

14   Horan, *supra* ch. 1 note 30, at 76.

15   *See* Pierce v. Soc'y of Sisters, 268 U.S. 510, 534–35 (1925); Meyer v. Nebraska, 262 U.S. 390 (1923).

16   *Wynn*, 582 F.2d 1375; *see* Motion and Brief, Amici Curiae of Americans United for Life, Inc. and Eugene F. Diamond, M.D. in Support of Appellants Francis X. Bellotti and Jane Hunerwadel, Bellotti v. Baird, 443 U.S. 622 (1979) (No. 78-329), *available at* https://aul.org/wp-content/uploads/2018/10/1978-Bellotti-v.-Baird.pdf.

17   Bellotti, 443 U.S. 622.

18   450 U.S. 398 (1981); *see* Brief Amicus Curiae of Americans United for Life in Support of Appellees, Scott m. Matheson, et al., *Matheson,* 350 U.S. 398 (No. 79-5903), *available at* https://aul.org/wp-content/uploads/2018/10/H_L_vMatheson.pdf.

19   Clarke D. Forsythe & Regina Maitlen, *Stare Decisis, Settled Precedent &* Roe v. Wade, 34 Regent U. L. Rev. 385 (2022).

20   *Wynn*, 449 F. Supp. 1302, *aff'd, Wynn*, 599 F.2d 193 (addressing both the 1975 Act and 1977 Act).

21   Carey v. Wynn, 439 U.S. 8 (1978).

22   Motion and Brief, Amicus Curiae of Americans United for Life, inc. in Support of Appellants Beal, et al., Colautti v. Franklin, 439 U.S. 379 (1979) (No. 77-891), *available at* https://aul.org/wp-content/uploads/2018/10/1978-Beal-v.-Franklin.pdf.

23   439 U.S. 379.

24   *Id*. at 391–93.

25   Forsythe, Abuse of Discretion, *supra* ch. 2 note 46, at 49–50, 125–53.

26   Commonwealth v. Edelin, 359 N.E.2d 4 (Mass. 1976). *See also* Floyd v. Anders, 440 F. Supp. 535 (D.S.C. 1977), *vacated and remanded*, Anders v. Floyd, 440 U.S. 445 (1979). *See generally* Nancy K. Rhoden, *The New Neonatal Dilemma: Live Births from Late Abortions*, 72 Geo. L. J. 1451 (1984).

27   Dennis J. Horan, *Viability, Values and the Vast Cosmos*, 22 Catholic Law. 1, 28–29 (1976).

28   Linda A. Bartlett et al., *Risk Factors for Legal Induced Abortion-Related Mortality in the United States*, 103 Obstetrics & Gynecology 729, 729 (2004) ("Compared with women whose abortions were performed at or before 8 weeks of gestation, women whose abortions were performed in the second trimester were significantly more likely to die of abortion-related causes.").

29   Pub. L. No. 107-207, 116 Stat. 926, (2002) (codified as 1 U.S.C. § 8).

30   A 2019 law review article by former AUL attorneys Paul Linton and Maura Quinlan compiled recent medical evidence to show that the Court's viability rule made even less sense in 2019 than it did in 1973. Paul Benjamin Linton & Maura K. Quinlan, *Does Stare Decisis Preclude Reconsideration of* Roe v. Wade?: *A Critique of* Planned Parenthood v. Casey, 70 Case W. Rsrv. L. Rev. 283 (2019).

31   Tom Marzen also contributed to this brief while a law student at Illinois Institute of Technology Chicago-Kent college of Law; *see* Motion and Brief, Amicus Curiae of Americans United for Life, Inc. In Support of Petitioner John H Poelker, Poelker v. Doe, 432 U.S. 519 (1977) (No. 75-442), *available at* https://aul.org/wp-content/uploads/2018/10/1976-Poelker-v.-Doe.pdf.

32   432 U.S. 519.

33   432 U.S. 464 (1977).

34   432 U.S. 438 (1977).

35   408 F. Supp. 660, 662–63 (D. Conn. 1975). The three-judge district court held that Connecticut's limit violated the Equal Protection Clause in an opinion by Judge Jon O. Newman, the judge who had written an opinion in 1972 espousing viability as a dividing line for legal abortion that so influenced the majority in *Roe*. *See* Forsythe, Abuse of Discretion, *supra* ch. 2 note 46, at 129–37.

36   432 U.S. 438 (No. 75-554). On the brief were Horan, Gorby, Rosenblum, and Dolores Horan.

37   Shortly after those decisions, Horan and Marzen retailed their brief into an article entitled *The Moral Interest of the State in Abortion Funding: A Comment on* Beal, Maher, *and* Poelker. 22 St. Louis U. L.J. 566 (1979).

38   Harris v. McRae, 448 U.S. 297, 325 n.27 (1980).

39   Life, Liberty, & Law, *Patrick Trueman on the Early Days of Americans United for Life*, *supra* ch. 4 note 4.

40   McRae v. Califano, 491 F. Supp. 630 (E.D.N.Y. 1980).

41   McRae v. Mathews, 421 F. Supp. 533 (E.D.N.Y. 1976).

42   Califano v. McRae, 433 U.S. 916 (1977).

43   *McRae*, 491 F. Supp. 630.

44   Zbaraz v. Quern, 469 F. Supp. 1212 (N.D. Ill. 1979).

45   Harris v. McRae, 444 U.S. 1069 (1980). Rosenblum, Horan, Gorby, Anderson, Trueman, Marzen and Destro were on the briefing. *See* Brief of Intervening Defendants-Appellees James L. Buckley, Jesse A. Helms, Henry J. Hyde, and Isabella Pernicone in Support of Appellant Harris, *Harris*, 448 U.S. 297 (No. 79-1268), *available at* https://aul.org/wp-content/uploads/2018/10/1980-Harris-v.-McRae.compressed.pdf *and* Reply Brief of Intervening Defendants-Appellees James L. Buckley, Jesse A. Helms, Henry J. Hyde, and Isabella Pernicone in Support of Appellant Harris, *Harris*, 448 U.S. 297 (No. 79-1268), *available at* https://aul.org/wp-content/up-

loads/2019/03/1980-Harris-v.-McRae-Reply-Brief.pdf.

46   *Harris*, 448 U.S. 297; Williams v. Zbaraz, 448 U.S. 358 (1980). AUL's briefing in *Williams* is available online. Jurisdictional Statement, *Williams*, 448 U.S. 358 (No. 79-4), *available at* https://aul.org/wp-content/uploads/2019/07/1979-Williams-v.-Zbaraz-jurisdictional-statement.pdf *and* Reply Brief of Intervening Defendants-Appellants, *Williams*, 448 U.S. 358 (No. 79-4), *available at* https://aul.org/wp-content/uploads/2019/07/1979-Williams-v.-Zbaraz-on-behalf-of-Intervening-Defendants-Appellants-Dr.-Jasper-F.-Williams-and-Dr.-Eugene-F.-Diamond.pdf.

47   See Michael J. New, *Hyde @ 40: Analyzing the Impact of the Hyde Amendment*, Charlotte Lozier Inst. (Sept. 27, 2016), https://lozierinstitute.org/hydeat40/ *and* Michael J. New, *Addendum to Hyde @ 40: Analyzing the Impact of the Hyde Amendment*, Charlotte Lozier Inst. (July 21, 2020), https://lozierinstitute.org/addendum-to-hyde-40-analyzing-the-impact-of-the-hyde-amendment/.

48   Dennis J. Horan & Thomas H. Marzen, *The Supreme Court on Abortion Funding: The Second Time Around*, 25 St. Louis U. L.J. 411 (1981).

49   *Id.* at 412.

50   *Id.* at 426.

51   *Cf. Roe*, 410 U.S. at 152–53 *with id.* at 159.

52   448 U.S. at 325.

53   *Id.*

54   *Norton*, 408 F. Supp. at 663 n.3 (Newman, J.). Justice Brennan said it more starkly in *Beal*, 432 U.S. at 449 (Brennan, J., dissenting) (citing *Norton*, 408 F. Supp. at 663 n.3) (alteration in original) ("[A]bortion and childbirth, when stripped of the sensitive moral arguments surrounding the abortion controversy, are simply two alternative medical methods of dealing with pregnancy … .").

55   Horan, *The Supreme Court on Abortion Funding, supra* ch.4 note 48, at 426.

56   On this assumption, the justices would conclude that public funding for abortion is required under the equal-protection rationale for abortion rights, which the late Justice Ruth Bader Ginsburg later espoused in her 2007 dissent in *Gonzales*, 550 U.S. at 172 (Ginsburg, J., dissenting) ("[L]egal challenges to undue restrictions on abortion procedures do not seek to vindicate some generalized notion of privacy; rather, they center on a woman's autonomy to determine her life's course, and thus to enjoy equal citizenship stature.").

57   476 U.S. 747 (1986).

58   Clarke D. Forsythe, *A Legal Strategy to Overturn* Roe v. Wade *After Webster: Some Lessons from Lincoln*, 1991 BYU. L. Rev. 519 (1991).

59   530 U.S. 914 (2000).

60   462 U.S. 416.

61   On the brief were Horan, Rosenblum, Trueman, Marzen and AUL Staff Counsel Maura

Quinlan. Brief, Amicus Curiae of Americans United for Life in Support of Petitioner City of Akron, *Akron*, 462 U.S. 416 (No. 81-746), *available at* https://aul.org/wp-content/uploads/2018/10/1982-Akron-v.-Reproductive-Healthcare-Clinic.pdf.

62   *Akron v. Akron Center For Reproductive Health*, Oyez, https://www.oyez.org/cases/1982/81-746 (last visited May 26, 2022).

63   Motion for Leave to File Brief Amicus Curiae of Americans United for Life in Support of Petitioners, Planned Parenthood Ass'n of Kan. City, Mo., Inc. v. Ashcroft, 462 U.S. 476 (1983) (No. 81-1255), *available at* https://aul.org/wp-content/uploads/2018/10/1983-Ashcroft-v.-PP.pdf.

64   462 U.S. at 426 n.9; *see* Brief Amicus Curiae of Americans United for Life in Support of Appellee, Commonwealth of Virginia, Simopoulos v. Virginia, 462 U.S. 506 (1983) (No. 81-185), *available at* https://aul.org/wp-content/uploads/2018/10/1982-Simopoulos-v.-Commonwealth-of-VA.pdf.

65   Paige Comstock Cunningham et al., *Where Are We Now: The Supreme Court Decisions Ten Years After* Roe v. Wade *in* AUL Studies in Law and Medicine (Ams. United for Life, Ser. No. 17).

66   462 U.S. at 488 n.12. This was a very muted version of what Justice Powell actually concluded about the conditions in abortion clinics. Forsythe, Abuse of Discretion, *Supra* ch. 2 note 46, at 233–34.

67   *Id.*

68   139 S. Ct. 1780 (2019).

69   Clarke D. Forsythe, *Homicide of the Unborn Child: The Born Alive Rule and Other Legal Anachronisms*, 21 Val. U. L. Rev. 563 (1987).

70   462 U.S. at 452.

71   *See* Presser & Forsythe, *Restoring Self-Government on Abortion, supra* ch. 3 note 23 at 330.

72   Horan, *Abortion and the Conscience Clause, supra* ch. 2 note 65, at 293.

73   Lee Epstein, Conservatives in Court 163 (1985).

74   *Id.* at 97.

75   *Id.* at 115.

76   *Id.* at 164.

77   No. 84 C 5602, 1984 U.S. Dist. Lexis 15313 (N.D. Ill. 1984).

78   764 F.2d 1265 (7th Cir. 1985), *cert. denied*, 474 U.S. 980 (1985).

79   476 U.S. 54 (1986).

80   Amended by S.B. 47, 81st Gen. Assemb. (1979) (enacted); H.B. 666, 83d Gen Assemb. (1983) (enacted); H.B. 1399, 83d Gen. Assemb. (1984) (enacted).

81   Charles v. Carey, 579 F. Supp. 464 (N.D. Ill. 1983), *aff'd sub nom.*, Charles v. Daley, 749 F.2d 452 (7th Cir. 1984), *appeal dismissed sub nom.*, Diamond v. Charles, 476

U.S. 54 (1986).

82   471 U.S. 1115 (1985).

83   476 U.S. 54. With him on the briefs were Victor Rosenblum, Ed Grant, Maura Quin-lan, Paige Cunningham, and Clarke Forsythe.

84   *Id.*

85   Charles v. Daley, 846 F.2d 1057 (7th Cir. 1988), *cert. denied*, 492 U.S. 905 (1989). *See also* Flight Attendants v. Zipes, 491 U.S. 754 (1989) (holding district courts may award Title VII attorney's fees against intervenors-defendants only where the intervention is frivolous, unreasonable, or without foundation).

86   476 U.S. 747.

87   *Id.* at 783–85 (citation omitted).

88   In the wake of the *Thornburgh* decision, Horan, Grant, and Forsythe used the opportunity to critique the opinions and analyze the debate between Stevens and White in their separate *Thornburgh* opinions, and compiled a long list of scholarly critiques of the *Roe* decision. Dennis Horan, Clarke Forsythe & Edward Grant, *Two Ships Passing in the Night: An Interprativist Review of the White-Stevens Colloquy on* Roe v. Wade, 6 St. Louis U. Pub. L. Rev. 229 (1987).

89   487 U.S. 589 (1988).

90   Reproductive Health Services v. Webster, 851 F.2d 1071 (8th Cir. 1988).

91   *Id.* The law was co-authored by Missouri attorney Andrew Puzder. Marlan C. Walker & Andrew F. Puzder, *State Protection of the Unborn After* Roe v. Wade*: A Legislative Proposal*, 13 Stetson L. Rev. 237 (1984).

92   Paul Reidinger, *Will* Roe v. Wade *Be Overruled?*, ABA J., July 1, 1988, at 66.

93   Andrea Sachs, *Law: Abortion on the Ropes: Is the Historic* Roe v. Wade *Ruling About to Be Overturned?*, Time Mag. (Nov. 30, 1988), https://content.time.com/time/subscriber/article/0,33009,956422,00.html.

94   Letter from William Webster, Attorney General, State of Missouri, to Americans United for Life (Jan. 31, 1989) (on file with author) (thanking AUL for help with the jurisdictional statement).

95   492 U.S. 490.

96   *Id.* at 530 (O'Connor, concurring in part and concurring in the judgment). *See* Brief of the American Association of Prolife Obstetricians and Gynecologists (AAPLOG) and the American Association of Pro-life Pediatricians (AAPLP) as *Amici Curiae* in Support of Appellants, *Webster,* 492 U.S. 490 (No. 88-605), *available at* https://aul.org/wp-content/uploads/2019/03/1988-Webster-v.-Reproductive-Health-Services.pdf.

97   Anthony Kennedy Papers, Library of Congress (on file with author).

98   Dellapenna, Dispelling the Myths, *supra* ch. 1 note 3, at 543–75, 624, 673; Forsythe, *The Effective Enforcement of Abortion Law Before* Roe v. Wade, *supra* ch. 3. note 6.

99   James Davison Hunter, Before the Shooting Begins: Searching for Democracy in America's

CULTURE WAR (1994).

100   Friendship Med. Ctr. v. Chi. Bd. of Health, 505 F.2d 1141 (7th Cir. 1974), *cert. denied*, 420 U.S. 997 (1975). *See also* Forsythe, *A Road Map Through the Supreme Court's Back Alley, supra* ch. 4 note 1.

101   *See* HUSH (Mighty Truth Productions, Inc. 2015).

102   *See* Justin L. Mack, *Probe Completed into Dead Indiana Abortion Doctor with Thousands of Fetal Remains at Home,* INDIANAPOLIS STAR (Dec. 30, 2020), https://www.indystar.com/story/news/local/indianapolis/2020/12/30/ulrich-klopfer-investiga-tion-into-doctor-fetal-remains-ends/4085822001/.

103   Ragsdale v. Turnock, 625 F. Supp. 1212 (N.D. Ill. 1985).

104   *Id.*

105   Ragsdale v. Turnock, 841 F.2d 1358 (7th Cir. 1988).

106   492 U.S. 916 (1989).

107   Brief of Certain Illinois Senators and Representatives as *Amici Curiae* in Support of Appellants, *Turnock,* 492 U.S. 916 (No. 88-790), *available at* https://aul.org/wp-con-tent/uploads/2018/10/1989-Turnock-v.-Ragsdale.pdf.

108   734 F. Supp. 1457 (N.D. Ill. 1990).

109   Ragsdale v. Turnock, 941 F.2d 501, 511 (7th Cir. 1991) (Flaum, J., concurring in part, dissenting in part).

110   Turnock v. Ragsdale, 493 U.S. 987 (1989).

111   Turnock v. Ragsdale, 503 U.S. 916 (1992); Thomas Hardy, *Abortion Case marks Hartigan,* CHI. TRIB. (Nov. 24, 1989), https://www.chicagotribune.com/news/ct-xpm-1989-11-24-8903120419-story.html.

112   941 F.2d at 511 (Flaum, J., concurring in part, dissenting in part).

113   Rust v. Sullivan, 500 U.S. 173 (1991). AUL's brief in *Rust* is available online. Brief of the Association of American Physicians and Surgeons as *Amicus Curiae* In Support of Respondent, *Rust,* 400 U.S. 173 (No. 89-1391), *available at* https://aul.org/wp-con-tent/uploads/2018/10/1990-Rust-v.-Sullivan.pdf.

114   Forsythe, *A Legal Strategy to Overturn* Roe v. Wade *After Webster, supra* ch. 4 note 58, at 540.

115   *Id.* at 541

116   *See* Linton, *Enforcement of State Abortion Statutes after* Roe, *supra* ch. 2 note 57; Susan Oliver Renfer et al., *The Woman's Right to Know: A Model Approach to the Informed Consent of Abortion,* 22 LOY. U. CHI. L.J. 409 (1991).

117   Guam Pub. L. 20-134 (1990).

118   Michael Stokes Paulsen, *Hell, Handbaskets, and Government Lawyers: The Duty of Loyalty and Its Limits,* 61 L. & CONTEMP. PROBS. 83 (1998).

119   Planned Parenthood v. Casey, 947 F.2d 682 (3d Cir. 1991).

120 502 U.S. 1056 (1992).

121 *Id.* University of Chicago Law Professor Dennis Hutchinson, in his biography of Justice Byron White, reported that Justice David Souter played a decisive role in persuading the Justices in January 1992 to limit the grant of review in *Casey* to the specific provisions of the Pennsylvania law and not review the question of overruling *Roe.* DENNIS J. HUTCHINSON, THE MAN WHO ONCE WAS WHIZZER WHITE: A PORTRAIT OF JUSTICE BYRON R. WHITE 428 (1998).

122 Forsythe, *A Legal Strategy to Overturn* Roe v. Wade *After Webster, supra* ch. 4 note 58.

123 Guam Soc'y of Obstetricians & Gynecologists v. Ada, 962 F.2d 1366 (9th Cir. 1992).

124 Ada v. Guam Soc'y of Obstetricians & Gynecologists, 506 U.S. 1011 (1992).

125 *Danforth,* 428 U.S. at 98 (White, J., concurring in part and dissenting in part) ("I am not yet prepared to accept the notion that normal rules of law, procedure, and constitutional adjudication suddenly become irrelevant solely because a case touches on the subject of abortion.").

126 Ada, 506 U.S. at 1011–1012 (Scalia, J., dissenting).

127 *See* Kevin Martin, *Stranger in a Strange Land: The Use of Overbreadth in Abortion Jurisprudence,* 99 COLUM. L. REV. 173 (1999).

CHAPTER 5

The Battle of Ideas

The case against *Roe v. Wade* between 1973 and the *Planned Parenthood of Southeastern Pennsylvania v. Casey* decision illustrated the power of ideas and their influence on law—demonstrated, for instance, by the dissents from Justices White, Rehnquist, O'Connor, and Scalia during those years.

Ideas drive change in law, society, and culture. For example, many of the writings of C.S. Lewis, Oxford and Cambridge scholar of the mid-20th century, engaged in the battle of ideas. "In his academic work, as well as in his popular writings, Lewis paid close attention to ideas. In approaching his scholarship on English literature, Lewis always took particular interest in the *ideas* the author was communicating."[1] The teachings of Jesus Christ founded a movement that captured the Roman Empire in less than 300 years. The words of Winston Churchill inspired the entire British nation at a time of world war. The sermons, speeches, and writings of Martin Luther King, Jr., spurred the civil-rights movement in America.

But even the best ideas require support and development. They may lie fallow for years, undeveloped, until they are discovered and elevated. The laws of nature weren't understood in even an elementary way until pre-Socratic Greek philosophers outlined them. The importance of markets in the efficient distribution of human goods and as a vehicle for human prosperity was not widely understood until the 18th century, assisted by Adam Smith's 1776 book *An Inquiry into the Nature and Causes of the Wealth of Nations.*

It is a common notion that "the truth always wins out," but the constraints and obstacles of this fallen world should make it clear that this is often false. Human weakness and error have long obstructed the victory of truth in human affairs. What is true is that ideas require support because there will always be opposition to the truth and because human understanding and the human will are weak.

Life in a democratic society frequently requires defending the truth in the face of majority opinion. As early as the 1830s, Alexis de Tocqueville captured this reality in *Democracy in America*:

> In America, the majority draws a formidable circle around thought. Inside those limits, the writer is free; but unhappiness awaits him if he dares to leave them. It is not that he has to fear an auto-da-fe, but he is the butt of mortifications of all kinds and of persecutions every day. A political career is closed to him; he has offended the only power that has the capacity to open it up … [Thus,] he yields, and finally he bends under the effort of each day and returns to silence as if he felt remorse for having spoken the truth.[2]

Bad ideas can have significant influence if they receive sufficient support. When powerful people back a destructive idea—such as anti-Semitism—it may take considerable time before its failure or negative effect is recognized, or it may wane only to simmer below the surface and be revived in some future day.

Ideas are at the center of law and public policy and are incorporated into proposals that become legislation. Ideas are at the center of judicial opinions that decide cases and render a verdict on legislation and governmental policy. Cultural and legal change are, at the root, a battle of ideas.

Lawyers use ideas and arguments—reasoned explanation—to persuade powerful public officials, especially judges and lawmakers. Arguments are at the heart of criticizing and thereby altering the law. Legal practice and the evolution of the law are founded on arguments from briefs and oral arguments. The foundational disciplines of bioethics, law, and medicine, are susceptible to the critiques of reason and argument.

Antonin Scalia's judicial opinions, especially his dissents, involved debating legal ideas. Scalia wrote that dissents "will not be cited, and will not be remembered, unless some quality of thought or of expression commends them to later generations." His audience was future generations of law students.[3]

This has been a key reason for AUL's work in the courts and legislatures, including its filing of *amicus curiae* briefs when it was not representing parties in litigation, because briefs can add to the parties' arguments and judicial deliberation in appeals. They may contribute additional arguments or data, frame the case in new ways, or present important context to the implications of a case. They may bring expertise or experience of important authorities and organizations. Their essential purpose is to persuade, and the authors may later develop the arguments in additional venues: law-school debates, law reviews, the media, or future cases. Though evidence that they have been read is best indicated by judicial citation of the briefs—Justices Powell, O'Connor, and Alito have cited AUL's briefs in various cases—the authors always attempt to wield persuasive power.

Abstract conceptualizing may go nowhere without a concrete proposal. In the United States, the opening salvo for legalized abortion was one such concrete proposal: the American Law Institute's Model Penal Code (MPC) for abortion in 1962, which advocated broad exceptions in abortion law. That idea instigated the debate; it was the "first significant step in the U.S. towards 'abortion liberalization'" and "completion of the Code touched off a growing debate and agitation for reform."[4] The AMA announced public support for the Model Penal Code proposal in 1967 and the American College of Obstetricians and Gynecologists (ACOG) followed in 1968. Thirteen states passed a version of the MPC between 1967 and 1970.

As the MPC example shows, effective engagement in the battle of ideas requires that lawyers, scholars, activists, and commentators engage leaders in the academy or the profession, including high-ranking lawyers, scholars and jurists, as well as Supreme Court justices. By engaging with them intelligently and persuasively, the author rises to that level, raises their profile, and may gain a platform for future debate. It's important to battle the titans.

Consequently, because of the framework of the American legal system, ideas and arguments were at the heart of *Roe* and necessary for any effective strategy to overrule it. Criticism of *Roe* was conducted in the Supreme Court through dissenting and separate opinions by the justices. The two dissents in *Roe* continued and gained influence as the Court and the country experienced *Roe*. Justice White continued dissenting from *Roe* until he retired in 1993; his most telling line—that *Roe* was "an exercise of raw judicial power"—is still frequently cited.[5] O'Connor wrote two withering critiques of *Roe* in her 1983 opinion in *City of Akron v. Akron Center for Reproductive Health* and in her 1986 dissent in *Thornburgh v. American College of Obstetricians and Gynecologists*. Scalia joined the criticism of *Roe* in 1989 in his separate opinion in *Webster v. Reproductive Health Services*, and then Justice Thomas joined Scalia's dissent in *Casey*, and wrote his own in *Stenberg v. Carhart* in 2000, *Whole Woman's Health v. Hellerstedt* in 2016, and *June Medical Services, LLC v. Russo* in 2020.

The case against *Roe* also has been conducted in books, law reviews, popular commentaries, editorial pages, websites, and podcasts. This criticism was necessary to create understanding of the facts, sustain opposition, and keep *Roe* unsettled.[6] This was an approach encouraged by AUL's board in the earliest years. *Abortion and Social Justice* was their opening salvo.

After *Abortion and Social Justice*, AUL continued to publish or sponsor numerous other books integrating legal, medical, and ethical arguments that involve affirmative protection for the prenatal human being, limits on abortion and suicide by physician, embryo protection, and critiques of judicial opinions and legislative proposals.

Through his briefs, articles, and books, Dennis Horan launched the battle of ideas over legal abortion and bioethics and began AUL's tradition of pursuing scholarship in defending the right to life. The February 1971 legal–medical conference at Loyola University Medical Center in Chicago, focusing on the status of abortion in the courts and legislatures, and Horan's writings on abortion and other bioethical issues, illustrated Horan's commitment to engaging the legal and medical community with arguments about evolving bioethical issues. Horan, David Mall, Tom Marzen, and Ed Grant launched and sustained AUL's scholarship in the 1970s and 1980s. Marzen, Thomas (Burke) Balch, and Grant co-authored articles with Horan and enabled AUL to turn briefs into legal publications. As former AUL president Ed Grant recalled:

> Dennis certainly wanted things written and published—he was extremely keen on that, both at AUL and at [the law firm he led] Hinshaw (his practitioners' treatise on legal malpractice law, among the first if not the first to be published). He saw this as essential in light of how the courts had used Cyril Means to find a right to abortion [in *Roe*]. By getting things published (both at AUL and in his legal practice), he believed that people would turn to the authors as leaders in the field, and also influence the outcome of court cases, legislation, etc. A good way of putting this would be "scholarship in action." I can think of many examples, but one that immediately comes to mind is the Marzen, O'Dowd, Crone, Balch article on Suicide—Dennis was quite emphatic, to put it mildly, that this get published, and of course he was right, as it wound up being cited by the Supreme Court.[7]

Prudence requires discernment and deliberation. Research, scholarship, and analysis enable advocates to implement those virtues more effectively. Scholarship—reflecting thorough research, objectivity, investigation, analysis, and publication in reputable journals—is needed to accurately understand reality, an essential end of prudence. Zeal, passion, and bias can derail our understanding of reality, which is necessary to comprehend the opportunities for and obstacles to success. Horan's early publications were grounded in his legal training and prudential perspective.

Horan's critique of *Roe*'s viability doctrine started in his May 1974 speech to the diocesan attorneys and continued in September 1975 in a paper "originally presented as a conference paper at the inter-disci-plinary conference on abortion conducted by the State University of New York at Buffalo School of Law, September 19–20, 1975." It was subsequently published as "Viability, Values, and the Vast Cosmos".[8] The primary purpose was "to shed light on the growing importance of the concept of viability through a discussion of cases which have arisen since [*Roe*]." Horan highlighted numerous bioethical questions opened up by the Supreme Court's decisions in *Roe* and *Doe*.

He examined the 1975 West German and 1975 Canadian decisions on abortion, four state Supreme Court decisions, and the prosecution of Dr. Kenneth Edelin for allowing a child born alive after abortion to die without care, then pending in Massachusetts, along with medical devel-opments in caring for premature infants. Horan noted: "It is apparent from a review of this material that the medical literature, using survival of the neonatal period as the definition of viability, accepts 20 weeks as the lower end of the viability spectrum."[9]

By the end of the 1970s, the movement needed a new review of abor-tion and its effects, and AUL sponsored the publication of *New Perspec-tives on Human Abortion* in 1981, edited by David Mall and Dr. Thomas Hilgers. Later, AUL resident scholar, Marvin Olasky, Ph.D., published *Abortion Rites: A Social History of Abortion in America.*

To determine whether public policies are effective and whether they have a positive or negative effect, research and scholarship are need-ed for an empirical investigation. In a certain sense, research gathers the data, and scholarship evaluates it. In 1991, AUL collaborated with Wheaton College professor James Rogers, Ph.D., a quantitative research analyst. He published a landmark article in the *American Journal of Public Health* in 1991, finding that Minnesota's parental-notice law reduced teenage-pregnancy and teenage-abortion rates. These data were presented to the Supreme Court in *Hodgson v. Minnesota*, which upheld Minnesota's parental-notice law. Rogers's research also showed the fallacies in O'Connor's position striking down the two-parent–notice provision, with no judicial bypass, on a mere facial challenge without an analysis of the law's effects. Contrary to wide-spread assumptions that limiting teen abortion would increase teen births, Rogers' study found that teen abortions *and* births declined during the enforcement of the Minnesota law, *suggesting that the law reduced abortions and births by reducing teen pregnancies.*

In 1977, AUL also launched a series of monographs, *Studies in Law and Medicine.* For two decades, the series featured original articles and reprinted other commentaries on legal, bioethical, and medical ethics issues. They addressed topics such as *Euthanasia and Brain Death: Ethical and Legal Considerations, Redefining the Issues in Fetal Experimentation*, and abortion and the Fourteenth Amendment.

AUL later sponsored Clarke Forsythe's book, *Politics for the Greatest Good: The Case for Prudence in the Public Square*, published by InterVarsity Press. The book presented a prudential and natural-law approach to public policy in a representative democracy, grounded in the Founding Fathers' natural-law philosophy and the prudential tradition of Thomas Aquinas. It rebutted a "perfectionistic" approach to law and policy that misinterprets the cardinal virtues, as well as the ethical teaching of the Catholic Church. It sought to dispel the myth that an "all or nothing" approach is the only moral option and to give legislators and activists a coherent way to think through the prudential questions and a confidence that "all or something" is morally sound. With chapters on William Wilberforce and the slave trade in England and Abraham Lincoln and American slavery, it described successful prudential strategies as a guide for lawyers and legislators.

Anticipating the 40th anniversary of *Roe* in 2013, AUL sponsored the research and publication of Forsythe's second book, *Abuse of Discretion: The Inside Story of Roe v. Wade*, which involved a review of the personal papers of eight of the nine justices who voted in *Roe*. Those personal papers tell a completely different story about the two years of deliberations inside the Court leading up to the release of the ruling in January 1973. They confirm that the deliberations and writing of the *Roe* opinion were even more arbitrary and capricious than the public had previously known. Due to the content of those personal papers, *Abuse of Discretion* may be the most important book written about *Roe* since *Roe*. The 40th anniversary of the decision featured a number of legal conferences, including scholarly criticism of *Roe*. In September 2013, Encounter Books published *Abuse of Discretion* with an October 2013 launch at the National Press Club hosted by then–AUL president Charmaine Yoest. Forsythe spoke on his book at legal conferences at Stanford Law School that March and at Washington and Lee University School of Law School in November. A favorable book review by Professor Jeffrey Rosen, later the President of the National Constitution Center, was featured in the Saturday edition of the *Wall Street Journal* on October 11, 2013. *Encounter Books* sponsored a talk by Forsythe, and public discussion of the book by Mollie Hemingway and Charmaine Yoest, in Manhattan in November 2014. All of these were an effort to disseminate the book's findings and conclusions.

In 2020, during the pandemic, AUL's team produced two major publications: an expanded edition of *Unsafe* and *Defending Life 2021*, the 16th and final print edition.[10]

Many legal and political factors needed to come together to change abortion law in America, including changes in leadership and in the Supreme Court justices. What is also important, perhaps more important than counting heads on the Court, is the battle of ideas, including effective criticisms of *Roe*. Judge Robert Bork wrote in 1982:

> Absent a constitutional amendment, a general means to ensure that courts stay within the limits the Constitution provides for them can only be intellectual and moral. That may seem a weak control. It does not seem so to me. Intellectual criticism in the short run may be quite ineffective. In the long run, ideas will be decisive. That is particularly true with respect to courts, more so perhaps than with any other branch of government.[11]

The powerful criticisms directed at *Roe* for 20 years—by anti-*Roe* justices, the Justice Department, and numerous legal scholars—hit *Roe* like a hurricane in *Webster* and *Casey*.[12] The house of *Roe* was lifted off of its original foundations, weak as they were, and came to rest on increasingly shifting sands.

The criticisms that Justice White initiated in *Roe* were carried on by Justices Rehnquist, Scalia, and Thomas. As AUL board member and the late Judge John Noonan wrote, by "the lessons of experience and the force of better reasoning" *Roe* will ultimately "answer to reason."[13]

That would require a persistent effort to maintain a spirited and inspired campaign for the battle of ideas—on abortion, as well as assisted suicide and the bioethical challenges to the equal dignity of human beings.

Chapter 5 Endnotes

1   Dyer & Watson, C.S. Lewis on Politics and the Natural Law, *supra* ch. 2 note 33, at 135.

2   Thomas L. Krannawitter, Vindicating Lincoln: Defending the Politics of Our Greatest President 31 (2008) (citing Alexis de Tocqueville, Democracy in America).

3   Antonin Scalia, *Dissents*, OAH Mag. Hist., Fall 1998, at 18.

4   Dellapenna, Dispelling the Myths, *supra* ch. 1 note 3, at 587, 595–99, 790, 600, 635.

5   *Doe*, 410 U.S. at 222 (White, J., dissenting) ("As an exercise of raw judicial power, the Court perhaps has authority to do what it does today; but in my view its judgment is an improvident and extravagant exercise of the power of judicial review that the Constitution extends to this Court.").

6   *See* Forsythe & Maitlen, *Stare Decisis, Settled Precedent &* Roe v. Wade, *supra* ch. 4 note 19.

7   Interview with Edward R. Grant, *supra* ch. 2 note 67.

8   Horan, *Viability, Values and the Vast Cosmos, supra* ch. 4 note 27.

9   *Id.* at 27.

10   *See* Ams. United for Life, Unsafe: America's Abortion Industry Endangers Women: A 50-State Investigative Report on the Dirty and Dangerous Abortion Industry (3d ed., 2021).

11   Patrick B. McGuigan, *The Court, the Judges, the Law*, Oklahoman (June 6, 1991), https://oklahoman.com/story/news/1991/06/06/the-court-the-judges-the-law/62525905007/ (referencing Robert Bork's writings for the 1982 Free Congress Foundation conference).

12   *See* Forsythe, *A Survey of Judicial and Scholarly Criticism of* Roe v. Wade *Since 1973: Legal Criticism and Unsettled Precedent, supra* ch. 3 note 1.

13   Noonan, A Private Choice, *supra* ch. 3 note 12; John T. Noonan, Jr., *The Root and Branch of* Roe v. Wade, 63 Neb. L. Rev. 668 (1984).

CHAPTER 6

Federalism and the States

In the American constitutional system of federalism, authority to protect human life—at all stages and from all threats—resides first and foremost in the states, not in the courts and not in Congress. The states have general legislative authority, while the federal government has only enumerated powers. The states exercised that general legislative authority from colonial times, before the U.S. Constitution was drafted and ratified.[1] The Constitution preserved that general legislative authority in the states, and the states maintain general legislative authority to regulate the professions, including the medical profession.[2]

This reality was on display during the pandemic of 2020. Though plenty of media commentary focused on how the Trump Administration managed the ongoing situation, most constitutional authority for public health and safety was located in the states. And, when President Biden issued a vaccine mandate through OSHA, lawyers David Rivkin and Robert Alt pointed out that the American constitutional order leaves considerable emergency powers to the states: "The states have plenary police power to regulate health and safety. Congress has only those limited powers enumerated in the Constitution."[3] The federal government does not have the "police power" of the states.

And, there is a further division of authority between state and local governments. When New York City Mayor Bill De Blasio suggested on March 19, 2020, that he might issue an order for residents to shelter in place within 48 hours, then-New York governor Andrew Cuomo reminded the public, and the mayor, that such an order was the governor's call, that of the state, not the mayor's or the city's.

In *Roe*, the Supreme Court created a unique disaster, a radical departure from this federalist framework. The justices announced a vague and sweeping right to abortion, removing the issue from the people and their elected representatives, and centralizing control in the Court, thereby assuming a self-appointed role as a sort of national abortion control board.

Judicial creation of a constitutional right implies that states cannot limit that right. An immediate concern on first reading of *Roe* was that the Court could expand the vague right of "privacy" and declare constitutional "rights" to assisted suicide, fetal experimentation, in vitro fertilization, or genetic engineering. That didn't happen, and some scholars believe that was because of the immediate backlash to *Roe*.

When the Court had the opportunity to expand *Roe* into a national right to assisted suicide in 1997, it refused to do so. The threat that the Court would expand a "right to privacy" into other bioethical areas, traditionally the province of state law, has almost certainly receded with the current Court majority. As with assisted suicide, virtually all bioethical issues are decided by democratic means through the state legislation process.

The Roberts Court is likely to reinforce the federalist structure outlined in the Constitution, as suggested by the Court's 2012 decision in *National Federation of Independent Businesses v. Sebelius*,[4] in which a majority of the justices, including Roberts, Scalia, and Thomas, held that Congress had no authority under the Commerce Clause to impose an individual mandate requiring individuals to buy insurance under the Affordable Care Act. (The mandate nevertheless survived because Chief

Justice Roberts provided the fifth vote to uphold the mandate, identifying it as a tax.[5])

In *Gonzales v. Carhart*,[6] Thomas wrote a separate opinion, emphasizing that he would not consider a Commerce Clause claim against the federal Partial Birth Abortion Ban Act (PBABA) because no one had raised the issue.[7] It suggested that Thomas, who is among the most anti-*Roe* justices, was unsure of Congress's constitutional authority to enact the PBABA.

Unfortunately, many overlook the fact that the federalist structure of the U.S. Constitution has strengthened the cause for life since the 1960s. Though 13 states expanded access to legal abortion during the decade leading up to *Roe*, 31 states debated abortion in the decade before *Roe* and yet retained their prohibitions of abortion, except to save the life of the mother, at the time of *Roe*. Despite its disastrous reasoning and impact, *Roe* did recognize that the states had an interest in regulating abortion.

Since *Roe*, it has been the states more than Congress that have been the forum for legislative and political action on abortion. They have been the source of legislative limits, political action, and test cases in courts for two primary reasons: States have the constitutional authority to legislate, and the diversity and flexibility in the states enable action even when congressional gridlock grinds progress to a halt. The number of states with pro-life governors and pro-life working majorities in the legislatures has grown significantly since 1973.[8]

Certainly, the federal government has acted to enlarge its powers since the Founding, and the Supreme Court approved that expansion during the New Deal. But even today, judges and legal scholars recognize that the federal government's power is constitutionally limited and that states retain primary authority in the areas of criminal law, police power, and public health.

As Cato Institute senior fellow Walter Olson has written, "In America's constitutional design, while federal law is supreme, the national government is confined to enumerated powers. It has no general authority to dictate to state governments. Many of the powers government holds, in particular the 'police power' invoked to counter epidemics, are exercised by state governments and the cities to which states delegate power."[9]

One of the self-inflicted wounds of *Roe* is that the Court overlooked the dynamics of federalism. The Court invalidated every existing state abortion law but overlooked the fact that the states retained other means of protecting prenatal human beings from conception, such as in prenatal-injury law, wrongful-death law, and fetal-homicide law.[10]

There's substantial evidence that right-to-life movements are stronger and more vital in countries with federalist systems and weaker in countries with parliamentary systems. This has been clear for a long time. When William Wilberforce pursued his anti-slavery strategy in the 1780s and 1790s, he worked through Parliament, the only legislative authority in Great Britain. But when Parliament refused to consider an anti-slavery proposal during a given year, Wilberforce and his allies had no means to act legislatively until the next parliamentary session.

AUL's strategy has always recognized the wisdom of relying on state law, because of the constitutional authority of the states and the diversity among them. The notion that the Supreme Court or Congress can solve a problem by one ruling or one statute is largely an illusion.

So, the states will continue to be an essential place to develop pro-life policy for several major reasons: the Constitution is federalist, and the states have general legislative authority; a body of state law already protects life, and those laws can be expanded; overturning *Roe* will return authority to the states; and pro-life movements in countries with federalist structures, in contrast to parliamentary structures, are more effective.

For this reason, state policy is a wise area to focus when it comes to future issues in bioethics. The moral skepticism of the U.S. judicial class, and the experience with state and federal judges since the 1960s—as in cases such as *Byrn*—should give Americans pause about relying on judges to legally protect human life unless express constitutional or statutory authority is available. To the extent that originalist judges join state and federal courts in the future, they, too, will look to constitutional and statutory text for their rulings and defer to state power if there is no express federal power that overrides it. Either scenario reinforces the importance of state law for protecting human life in the realm of bioethics.

Building Early Fences around *Roe* (1973-1989)

Illinois Legislation and Test Cases

When *Roe* was decided, AUL recognized the significance of the federalist structure of the U.S. Constitution. Even as Congress debated constitutional amendments in the first years following *Roe*, many states placed legislative limits on abortion that attempted to determine the practical meaning of *Roe* and the Supreme Court's dictates. By the end of 1976, nearly three dozen states had passed new abortion laws.[11] Out of these efforts came the test cases on abortion that reached the courts in the years between *Roe* and *Casey*.

Only one state, Rhode Island, mounted an attempt in 1973 to repudiate *Roe* by reenacting an outright prohibition on abortion, except to save the life of the mother. In response to the passage in Justice Blackmun's opinion in *Roe* that stated "we need not resolve the difficult question of when life begins," Rhode Island added findings about prenatal development and declarations that human life began at conception. That law was quickly enjoined, struck down by the federal district court, and affirmed by the U.S. Court of Appeals for the First Circuit. The Supreme Court refused to hear the case, *Doe v. Israel*, on May 13, 1974.[12] In effect, the Court's majority was saying that those issues had already been addressed in *Roe*. Neither of the two dissenters in *Roe* dissented from the decision not to hear the Rhode Island case, sending the signal that it was not a fruitful strategy.[13]

The Rhode Island case showed that the Court was not going to revisit *Roe* for the foreseeable future. Justice Blackmun's musings on human life were not an invitation to repudiate the Court's decision, especially while the majority remained the same. Blackmun reacted emotionally and negatively to the public response to *Roe* and dug in his heals on an ideological level. Despite being a nearly life-long Republican, he retired in April 1994, during the Clinton Aadministration, enabling the Democrat president to replace him with pro-*Roe* justice, Stephen Breyer, who retired in 2022.

At AUL, Dennis Horan understood that continued litigation would not be possible using cases such as Rhode Island's. A lower court would quickly issue an injunction, the law would be invalidated, and the Supreme Court would refuse to review. Within a few years, it became clear that if the state lost, federal law would require the losing state to pay the attorneys for the abortion activists. Continued litigation was only possible with laws that sought to impose limits on abortion not foreclosed in *Roe, Doe,* or subsequent decisions. *Roe*'s practical constraints became clearer with each test case.

In the aftermath of the Rhode Island setback, alternative strategies were needed. Test cases to challenge *Roe* depended on passing unique types of state legislation. AUL supported state statutes that did not directly contradict *Roe* but that would highlight aspects of abortion law that remained unclear.

AUL's lawyers had to explore every nook and cranny of *Roe*, uncovering its fault lines and opportunities it offered. Tom Marzen began a nine-year tenure with AUL in 1975, while still a law student in Chicago. His pro-life contacts referred him to Horan, and Marzen considered volunteering for "the pro-life law firm." He visited the AUL office, met Pat Trueman and John Gorby, and began work.

In the spring of 1977, before the Supreme Court issued its decisions in *Beal, Maher,* and *Poelker,* Marzen wrote a 22-page memo outlining "a scheme for the regulation of abortion practices within the Supreme Court decisions of" *Roe, Doe, Danforth,* and *Bellotti I.* He emphasized "mandatory pre-abortion counseling," independent of the counseling a woman might otherwise receive from the abortionist.

During the 1970s, situated in Illinois and with limited resources, AUL focused its legislative work on its own state. Illinois was the center of AUL's "pilot project" for abortion legislation and litigation. The strategic response to *Roe* and *Doe* was exemplified by the Illinois Abortion Law of 1975, which Horan substantially drafted. An Illinois lobbyist, Ralph Rivera, brought Horan a draft bill in 1974, and Horan developed amendments, drafted the preamble, and added several provisions. Rivera took Horan's draft, shared it with his colleagues, and found sponsors in the Illinois House and Senate, where it was introduced in 1975.

The Illinois Act eventually contained 14 sections, including informed-consent requirements, a hospital requirement for abortions after the first trimester, limits on and a standard of care for abortions of viable fetuses, a prohibition on fetal experimentation, requirements for the protection of infants born alive after abortion, a prohibition on saline abortion after the first trimester, abortion-data reporting requirements, a requirement for a pathology report, conscience protections for individuals and institutions, and a severability clause.

The Illinois law reflected AUL's strategy. The first goal was to establish important principles in the law and see them enforced. But it was quickly understood in 1973 and 1974, after Florida, Minnesota, Missouri, Utah, and other states passed abortion limits, that virtually any limits would be challenged in court using *Roe* as a sword.[14] (AUL and the states could not initiate litigation. That depended on abortion activists filing suit.) AUL sought to shape legal issues in anticipation of test-case litigation, issues that, unlike the Rhode Island approach, were not foreclosed by *Roe*, thereby attempting to create a test case and induce the Court to explain what *Roe* meant or to determine what enforcement the Court would allow. With each decision, the Court defined *Roe* for purposes of politics and public debate, and each time the Court struck down state regulations the extreme scope of *Roe* became clearer.

In hindsight, the Illinois law probably attempted to achieve too much in one bill; it certainly made test-case litigation complex. It was immediately challenged in federal court in Illinois. The purpose of the Illinois Abortion Act of 1975 was not to "regulate" abortion—in the sense of "managing" the industry—but to limit abortion, to protect pre-existing principles such as parental rights for the care of minors, to create a test case, and to reveal the scope of *Roe*.

In the 1970s, pro-life organizations in Springfield, Illinois, could pass virtually anything they wanted and override the governor's veto. The 1975 act was amended several times during the 1970s, in hopes of altering the wording enough that federal courts would uphold it. AUL helped to defend these bills, but the cases never went to the Supreme Court and, after years of litigation, they sputtered out. Simultaneously, other states were exploring similar questions, and their test cases answered some of the outstanding legal questions about *Roe*.

Continued litigation was also important because it provided an opportunity for continued dissent among the Supreme Court justices. If states ceased passing laws, the justices would have no further chance to disagree with *Roe*, and *Roe* would have become settled.

In December 1975, nearly three years after *Roe*, Justice White, who had dissented in *Roe*, dissented with Chief Justice Burger from the Court's denial of review in *Greco v. Orange Memorial Hospital Corporation*.[15] *Greco* was one of the first cases to reach the Supreme Court after *Roe*, considering whether a quasi-public-private hospital could constitutionally "refuse to perform elective abortions." White wrote, "The task of policing this Court's decisions in *Roe v. Wade* and *Doe v. Bolton* is a difficult one; but having exercised its power as it did, the Court has a responsibility to resolve the problems arising in the wake of those decisions." This must have been a not-so-subtle challenge to justices who wanted to avoid the issue. After *Greco*, countless cases headed to the Court, which, with time, would demonstrate that the Court remained divided and *Roe* remained unsettled.

Prenatal Children in the Law Outside the Context of Abortion

State legislation also enabled AUL to initiate proposals enhancing legal protection for the unborn child as a human being in the womb. AUL worked outside the context of abortion, on issues that wouldn't be thwarted by *Roe* or the Court's abortion doctrine.

The common law historically had protected the prenatal human being to the greatest extent possible given existing medical knowledge and technology. Before modern medical technology, for example, doctors and midwives relied on quickening—or the maternal experience of fetal movement which can occur between 16 and 18 weeks of pregnancy—for evidence of prenatal life. Before then, there was little reliable evidence that a prenatal child was alive. (The stethoscope wasn't invented until 1808.) As medical science developed, and it became clear that quickening did not signify the beginning of prenatal life and that the life of a human being begins at conception, the law could protect the prenatal child from conception. In 1969, Louisell wrote of "the law's steady progress toward recognition of the dignity, value and essential equality of human life."[16]

Abortion isn't the only way a prenatal human being can die. State courts from the 1940s through 1960s were willing to expand legal protection for the prenatal human being in prenatal-injury law and wrongful-death law, as medical science and the knowledge of prenatal development advanced.[17]

But *judicial* expansion of legal protection for the unborn slowed after *Roe*, likely because the judicial class, federal and state, took their cues from the Supreme Court. *Roe* signaled to the American judiciary that judicial protection of "fetal rights," even apart from abortion, wasn't politically correct.

The fact that our country permits abortion on demand even now after *Roe* but legally recognizes other prenatal injury seems schizophrenic to many. That schizophrenia is the result of *Roe*. Though *Roe* was broad in its sweeping control of the abortion issue, it focused narrowly on abortion, the right to "terminate pregnancy," as the Court put it.

What did *Roe* say about a state's protection of prenatal human beings *outside* the context of abortion? In the short term, it was unclear. *Roe* did not provide a definitive answer but left a crack in the door, allowing legislatures to protect the prenatal child in other contexts.

After *Roe*, states courts questioned these attempts to protect prenatal children, and judges cited the dictum in Blackmun's opinion that the state could not "adopt one theory of life."[18] But that took Blackmun's words out of context. What Blackmun actually said was that the state couldn't "adopt one theory of life" to "override the rights of the pregnant woman."[19] That didn't apply in the case of an assault against a woman that resulted in a fetal homicide.

AUL first became involved in the issue of prenatal protection outside the context of abortion in 1975 in Chicago, shortly after the group moved to Chicago and the Legal Defense Fund was founded. AUL attorneys, led by Jack Gorby, drafted a legal memo urging the Cook County State's Attorney to prosecute a case of fetal homicide involving a viable prenatal child. The prosecution was unsuccessful, but Illinois eventually passed an explicit fetal homicide law in 1986, which had been drafted by AUL.

AUL filed briefs in several state fetal-homicide cases in the 1970s and 1980s, but they were mostly unsuccessful, for one of two reasons. First, courts would apply Blackmun's words in *Roe* to hold that states could not protect the prenatal human, even in the non-abortion context. Other courts, meanwhile, held that general homicide laws could not be applied to the killing of a prenatal child without clear, explicit language in the statute.[20]

The solution was for states to pass explicit fetal-homicide legislation, and AUL shifted to a legislative focus. In 1987, Forsythe published "Homicide of the Unborn Child" in the Valparaiso Law Review, with a model bill drafted by AUL staff counsel Maura Quinlan.[21]

By the 1980s, state courts began to recognize that *Roe* didn't apply to state protection of the prenatal child outside the context of abortion, and states became free to enact such legislation. Even the California Supreme Court reached that conclusion in 1994 in *People v. Davis*,[22] interpreting the California fetal homicide law of 1970 to protect the prenatal child outside the context of abortion at 8-10 weeks gestation.

Since its work in the Cook County case, AUL has championed state fetal-homicide legislation in many states, often called "unborn victims of violence" laws. As of 2022, 31 states have enacted fetal-homicide legislation protecting the unborn from *conception*; almost all of those laws have been passed in the years following *Roe*. These laws reflect public sentiment and represent a significant public counter to the Supreme Court's abortion doctrine. Passing them required an enormous effort in state legislatures and in state and federal courts, where the legislation faced the threat of judicial invalidation by an unjustified expansion of the Court's abortion doctrine.

Legal Protection of the Embryonic Human Being

Roe opened the door to experimentation on the prenatal human being because the Court's egregious historical misinterpretation declared that the common law never protected the prenatal human while in the womb, only after delivery (birth).[23] But the same legal logic that allowed fetal-homicide statutes and prenatal-injury suits also allowed legal protection by statute of the embryonic human being from human experimentation, whether inside or outside the womb.

In 1975, David Louisell was appointed to serve on the National Commission for the Protection of Human Subjects of Biomedical and Behavioral Research, which addressed human embryo research. Louisell had published studies in the 1960s on bioethical issues, including organ transplantation. When the Commission's report came out in May 1975,

Louisell dissented in part.[24] The subsequent year, Horan and Louisell, along with Professor Robert Destro, published papers in a symposium issue of the Villanova Law Review, reviewing the commission's recommendations and existing federal regulations.[25]

The status and custody of frozen, or cryopreserved, human embryos garnered national attention in *Davis v. Davis*.[26] A Tennessee state trial court, after a lengthy evidentiary hearing, understood that the embryos were embryonic human beings and awarded custody to the mother who wanted to care for them. The court of appeals overruled that decision and held that the embryos were to be treated as *property*. AUL's brief in the case, written by staff counsel Kevin Todd on behalf of the American Academy of Medical Ethics and filed in the Tennessee Supreme Court, argued that the lower courts had erred in treating the cryopreserved human embryos as property, that *Roe* and other federal "privacy" cases could not be the source of a paternal right to destroy embryos and did not prohibit legal protection of embryonic human beings, and that Tennessee's common and statutory law supported their protection. But the Tennessee Supreme Court effectively treated the embryos as property, and the U.S. Supreme Court refused to hear the case in February 1993.[27]

In August 2001, President George W. Bush addressed the nation on the use of embryonic stem cells, outlining a federal policy for limited use of embryonic stem cells. His administration followed this policy, but it was rescinded by the Obama Administration in December 2009. The Bush policy recognized the embryo as a human being and limited the federal government's use of them, but the states needed to provide legislative protection for these human beings.

As Paul Linton pointed out in *Abortion Under State Constitutions*, states lacked "any statutory or common law authority to guide state courts in resolving disputes over the proper disposition" of embryonic human beings.[28] Until IVF embryos became a biological reality in the late 1970s, there was no law specifically addressing their status. In that moral and legal vacuum, courts in at least seven states treated embryonic humans as property. In 2001, AUL developed model legislation for states that would ban human cloning and destructive human-embryo research.

This emphasis continued with AUL's model legislation on embryo custody published in *Defending Life 2020*.

These issues are not going away. In 2020, former AUL president Paige Cunningham, was appointed chairman of the National Institutes for Health Human Fetal Tissue Research Ethics advisory board, which held its first meeting on July 31, 2020.[29] During that meeting, the panel approved one of 13 proposals for regulating the use of fetal tissue. Media criticism of the panel's action show that these issues, and the use of fetal tissue, are still alive.

Like many bioethical issues, the protection of human beings from conception to natural death remains first and foremost an issue for states to regulate. The state legislative progress over decades has revealed that the states are a vital arena for momentum, a striking contrast to parliamentary systems—and success in the U.S. is an example to countries around the world.

Chapter 6 Endnotes

1   *See* Dellapenna, Dispelling the Myths, *supra* ch. 1 note 3.

2   At least one early American colony prohibited midwives from performing abortions. Several states adopted and enforced English common law prohibitions on abortion. *Id.*

3   David B. Rivkin, Jr., & Robert Alt, Opinion, *Biden's Lawless Vaccine Mandate*, Wall St. J. (Sept. 28, 2021), http://www.wsj.com/articles/biden-lawless-vaccine-mandate-constitution-occupational-safety-11632841737?.

4   Nat'l Fed'n of Indep. Bus. v. Sebelius, 567 U.S. 519 (2012).

5   *Id. See e.g.*, Randy E. Barnett, Our Republican Constitution; Securing the Liberty and Sovereignty of We the People (2016).

6   550 U.S. 124.

7   *Id.* at 169.

8   *See* Paul Benjamin Linton, *Overruling* Roe v. Wade*: Lessons from the Death Penalty*, 48 Pepp. L. Rev. 261 (2021).

9   Walter Olson, Opinion, *Federalism and the Coronavirus Lockdown*, Wall St. J. (Mar. 30, 2020), https://www.wsj.com/articles/federalism-and-the-coronavirus-lockdown-11585609012.

10   Paul Benjamin Linton, *The Legal Status of the Unborn Child under State Law*, 6 U. St. Thomas J.L. & Pub. Pol'y. 141 (2011).

11   Joseph P. Witherspoon, *The New Pro-Life Legislation: Patterns and Recommendations*, 7 St. Mary's L.J. 637 (1976).

12   *Doe v. Israel*, 358 F. Supp. 1193 (D.R.I. 1973), *aff'd*, 482 F.2d 156 (1st Cir. 1973), *cert. denied,* Israel v. Doe, 416 U.S. 993 (1974).

13   A similar case was filed in state court in Rhode Island in 1975, where the plaintiffs, the Constitutional Right to Life Committee, presented medical evidence by a team of doctors that included Drs. Thomas Hilgers and Joseph Stanton. While the Rhode Island Supreme Court acknowledged that "[t]here is no disagreement that the evidence presented to the trial court conclusively established that human life commences from the moment of conception," the Court held that *Roe* superseded any state interests. Const. Right to Life Comm. v. Cannon, 363 A.2d 215, 219 (1976).

14   Early litigation included Coe v. Gerstein, 376 F. Supp. 695, (S.D. Fla. 1973), *cert. denied*, 417 U.S. 279 (1974) (per curiam); Doe v. Rampton, 366 F. Supp. 189 (D. Utah 1973), *vacated and remanded*, 410 U.S. 950 (1973); Doe v. Hale Hosp., 500 F.2d 144 (1st Cir. 1974), *cert. denied*, 420 U.S. 907 (1975). At least thirty-two states passed legislation in first few years: Ariz. Rev. Stat. Ann. § 36-2301 (Supp. 1976); Ark. Stat. Ann. § 41-304 (Supp. 1975); Cal. Health & Safety Code § 25955 (Deering 1975); Ga.

CODE ANN. § 26-1201 (Supp. 1975); IDAHO CODE ANN. § 18-605 (Supp. 1975); ILL. REV. STAT. ch. 38, § 81-11 (1976); IND. ANN. STAT. § 10-108 (1975); KY. REV. STAT. § 311.710 (Supp. 1974); LA. REV. STAT. § 40:1299.31 (Supp. 1975); ME. REV. STAT. ANN. tit. 22, § 1575 (Supp. 1975); MD. ANN. CODE art. 43, § 129A (Supp. 1975); MASS. GEN. LAWS ANN. ch. 112, § 121 (1975); MICH. STAT. ANN. § 47.57 (51) (Supp. 1975); MINN. STAT. § 145.412 (Supp. 1976); MO. REV. STAT. § 188.010 (Supp. 1976); MONT. REV. CODES ANN. § 94-5-613 (1974); NEV. REV. STAT. § 442.250 (1973); N.J. REV. STAT. § 2A:65A-1 (Supp. 1976); N.Y. PENAL LAW § 125.40 (McKinney 1975); N.C. GEN. STAT. § 14-45.1 (Supp. 1975); N.D. CENT. CODE § 14-02.1 (Supp. 1975); OHIO REV. CODE ANN. § 4731.91 (1973); PA. STAT. ANN. tit. 35, § 6001 (Supp. 1976); R.I. GEN. LAWS ANN. §11-23-5 (Supp. 1975); S.C. CODE ANN. § 32-682 (Supp. 1974); S.D. CODE § 34-23A-1 (Supp. 1975); TENN. CODE ANN. § 39-301 (1975); UTAH CODE ANN. § 76-7-302 (Supp. 1974); VA. CODE ANN. § 18.1-62 (Supp. 1975); WIS. STAT. § 441.06(6) (1974); WYO. STAT. ANN. § 6-77.2 (Supp. 1975).

15 423 U.S. 1000 (1975).

16 David W. Louisell, *Abortion, the Practice of Medicine and the Due Process of Law*, 16 UCLA L. REV. 233, 253 (1969).

17 WILLIAM L. PROSSER, HANDBOOK OF THE LAW OF TORTS 336 (4th ed. 1971) ("So far as duty is concerned, if existence at the time is necessary, medical authority has recognized long since that the child is in existence from the moment of conception, and for many purposes its existence is recognized by the law.").

18 *Roe,* 410 U.S. at 162.

19 410 U.S. at 162.

20 *See e.g.*, People v. Guthrie, 293 N.W.2d 775 (Mich. Ct. App.1980).

21 Forsythe, *Homicide of the Unborn Child, supra* ch. 4 note 69.

22 872 P.2d 591 (Cal. 1994).

23 Joseph W. Dellapenna exhaustively criticizes this misinterpretation. Dellapenna, DISPELLING THE MYTHS, *supra* ch. 1 note 3.

24 Harold M. Schmeck, Jr., *Member of Fetal Research Panel Objects to Some Proposal,* N.Y. TIMES (May 21, 1975), https://www.nytimes.com/1975/05/21/archives/member-of-fetal-research-panel-objects-to-some-proposals.html.

25 Dennis J. Horan, *Fetal Experimentation and Federal Regulation, 22* VILL. L. REV. 325 (1976); David W. Louisell, *National Commission for the Protection of Human Subjects of Biomedical and Behavioral Research: Research on the Fetus,* 22 VILL. L. REV. 315 (1976) (republishing Louisell's dissenting statement to the Commission's report); Robert A. Destro, *On the Report and Recommendations of the National Commission for the Protection of Human Subjects of Biomedical and Behavioral Research—Research on the Fetus—Introduction, 22* VILL. L. REV. 297 (1976).

26 842 S.W.2d 588 (Tenn. 1992), *cert. denied sub nom.*, Stowe v. Davis, 507 U.S. 911

(1993).

27   *Stowe,* 507 U.S. 911.

28   Paul Benjamin Linton, Abortion Under State Constitutions: A State-by-State Analysis 490 (1st ed., 2008).

29   Office of Science Policy, *Archives of the NIH Human Fetal Tissue Research Ethics Advisory Board - FY2020,* Nat'l Inst. Health, https://osp.od.nih.gov/biotechnology/ nih-human-fetal-tissue-research-ethics-advisory-board/#members (last visited May 31, 2022).

CHAPTER 7

Death, Dying, and Euthanasia

Technology and culture in the 1960s did much to alter traditional attitudes toward death and care for the dying, raising difficult ethical and legal issues and challenging the simpler standards provided by common law.

Before 20th-century statutes, the common law allowed a doctor to make a judgment of death based on "the total stoppage of the circulation of the blood and a cessation of the animal and the vital functions consequent therein, such as respiration, pulsation, etc."[1]

With the founding of the AUL Legal Defense Fund in 1974, Dennis Horan and the team quickly became involved in end-of-life issues, including the withdrawal of life-sustaining treatment, living wills, nutrition and hydration, euthanasia, and care for infants born with Down syndrome. Euthanasia in particular was of natural interest to Horan, due to his medical-malpractice expertise. At the time, AUL's work was the only pro-life legal effort in the nation focused on euthanasia.

Horan spearheaded the publication of *Death, Dying, and Euthanasia*,[2] a compendium of more than 800 pages addressing seven salient bio-ethical issues: the definition of death, the treatment of the handicapped newborn, euthanasia, suicide and the right to reject medical treatment, the legal aspects of mercy killing, medical and social perspectives on dying, and legalizing euthanasia. The book contained 35 original and reprinted essays on end-of-life issues from a range of perspectives, by authors including Alexander Capron, Dr. Vincent Collins, Leon Kass, Eugene Diamond, John Robertson, Dennis Horan, Stanley Hauerwas, Pope Pius XII, Joseph Fletcher, Paul Ramsey, C. Everett Koop, Arthur Dyck, Rev. Kevin O'Rourke, David Louisell, Yale Kamisar, Leo Alexander, Glanville Williams, Robert Byrn, and Germain Grisez.

Death, Dying, and Euthanasia reprinted the landmark decision by the New Jersey Supreme Court in the case of Karen Ann Quinlan[3] and added commentary from Horan, who aptly described the medical and legal landscape in 1976:

> For many years the problem of defining death was basically one of a simple medical judgment made by a physician at the deathbed in a home or in a hospital. The criteria for determining when death occurred were medical criteria easily applied by physicians and seldom, if ever, questioned by the public. There existed no statutory definitions of death, and the common law considered the issue only in relation to the distribution of property or in determining whether a person who had been the victim of an assault died within a year and a day. The common law defined death as a moment when life had ceased, "defined by physicians as a total stoppage of the circulation of the blood and a cessation of the animal and vital functions consequent therein, such as respiration, pulsation, etc." Any more was not necessary, and so no more was undertaken. Then, two advancing areas of medicine converged on the deathbed to create one of our current problems. The first of these was the increasing ability of medicine to resuscitate dying patients and to maintain those patients on sophisticated

machinery. The second was the ability of medicine to transplant organs from one person to another. Both of these advances depended upon a myriad of factors ... related to the tremendous growth in medical technology of recent years.[4]

At the time, AUL was skeptical about new legislation in the states to regulate care for the chronically and terminally ill. Horan and Dr. Joseph Stanton were confident that the common law and Hippocratic medicine, as well as legal prohibitions against suicide or assisted suicide, had established a workable legal and ethical system for protecting human life, and that physicians could be trusted to make ethical end-of-life decisions.

After the publication of *Death, Dying, and Euthanasia*, Horan and Tom Marzen continued to publish on the subject until 1984.[5] When Marzen died in 2007, Dave Andrusko, editor of National Right to Life News, wrote of him in an obituary:

Unquestionably, he was one of the nation's foremost authorities on euthanasia in general, assisted suicide in particular. A mutual friend, Richard Doerflinger, tellingly observed that "Tom became a linchpin figure in promoting mutual understanding and collaboration between the pro-life and disability rights movements in defending vulnerable human life. The entire movement against legalized euthanasia and assisted suicide would today be an incomparably weaker and poorer influence in our society if not for the work he did and the coalitions he helped build."[6]

AUL sponsored the research and writing by Marzen, Burke, Balch and other co-authors, which was eventually published in 1985 as "Suicide: A Constitutional Right?" in the Duquesne Law Review. The Supreme Court eventually cited the article eleven times in its landmark 1997 decision in *Washington v. Glucksberg*[7] and once again in *Vacco v. Quill*.[8]

After *Quinlan*, AUL was directly involved in a series of landmark medical-treatment cases involving the withdrawal of food and fluids, including in Illinois, New Jersey, Maine, Massachusetts, Missouri, and New York. The initial aim was to persuade state courts to look to common law and statutory sources for legal guidance, including the common-law right to refuse life-sustaining medical treatment, rather than apply *Roe v. Wade* or sweep treatment for the terminally ill into the constitutional "right of privacy."

AUL's litigation began in New York in 1979 with the case of Brother Joseph Fox, who lapsed into a coma after surgery and was placed on a respirator. The case dealt not only with the question whether the respirator could be withdrawn but also with the scope of the decision and the rationale used by New York courts. Would the court base its decision on a "constitutional right of privacy"—vesting its standards largely in the courts and empowering the judiciary to make such decisions—or base its decision on common law and statutory law, allowing the state legislature to address the issue and allowing citizens to retain authority through their representatives?

The New York Supreme Court in Nassau County, New York, rightly found that:

> there is a common-law right to bodily self-determination, which includes the right of a competent adult to refuse life-sustaining medical treatment. This general right is, however, subject to being overridden by State interests in appropriate circumstances. Among the State interests which must be weighed are interests in the protection of third parties, such as minor children, the maintenance of latitude for physicians and hospitals to fulfill their ethical obligations and, by far the most important, the preservation of all human life.[9]

It was fortunate that Ed Grant became executive director of AUL as these cases were heating up in the courts. After working for AUL while at Northwestern Law School, Grant moved to Philadelphia after graduation to work for the law firm Drinker Biddle but remained connected with AUL. When Paige Cunningham took a hiatus from AUL leadership after the "Reversing *Roe*" conference in 1984, Horan and Victor Rosenblum persuaded Grant to return to AUL as executive director and general counsel in October 1984. Even before Grant rejoined, he worked with Horan on legal publications addressing death and dying.[10] Grant continued to publish with Horan while litigating death and dying cases between 1984 and 1988.[11]

Grant also worked with Dr. C. Everett Koop, while he was U.S. surgeon general, to publish on the legal issues. Koop presented a major speech at the University of Notre Dame, and Grant worked with him to convert the speech into an article.[12]

As AUL general counsel, Grant was involved in numerous cases across the country involving the withdrawal of nutrition and hydration, including trial and appellate litigation in the *Conroy* case in New Jersey, involving a nursing-home resident, decided in 1985.[13] The issue hit the Illinois courts in 1988, when Horan, Grant, Forsythe, and Ann-Louise Lohr filed a brief in the Illinois Appellate Court in the *Prange* case,[14] in which AUL briefed the appeal along with the National Legal Center for the Medically-Dependent and Disabled, founded by James Bopp, Jr., an energetic and innovative pioneer in the law protecting human life.

Then the Supreme Court case of Nancy Cruzan intervened. On July 3, 1989, the same day that the Supreme Court issued its decision in *Webster*, the Court agreed to hear *Cruzan*, from Missouri. AUL worked with the National Legal Center to organize the *amicus* briefs in *Cruzan*.

The Court, in a majority opinion by Chief Justice Rehnquist, did not envelop these issues within a federal constitutional "right of privacy" but held that Missouri could require "clear and convincing evidence" of an incompetent patient's desires before allowing the withdrawal of life-sustaining nutrition and hydration. In effect, the Court rightly left that issue to the states.

Back in Illinois, AUL's involvement in *Prange* led the Illinois Supreme Court to appoint AUL to argue against the withdrawal of food and fluids in *Greenspan*. After AUL filed its briefs, the Illinois Supreme Court considered the intervening case of *Longeway*[15] and allowed the withdrawal of nutrition and hydration from an elderly woman in a nursing home in Chicago, over the dissents of Justices Daniel Ward and William Clark. The majority emphasized the lack of specific legislative guidance on the matter.

On January 25, 1989, Forsythe argued *Greenspan* before the Illinois Supreme Court in Springfield, contending that the relevant Illinois statutes, including the Illinois Living Will Act, did not authorize the Cook

County public guardian to withdraw nutrition and hydration from the elderly patient. On July 9, 1990, in a 4-2 decision, the Illinois Supreme Court held that Illinois statutes did not prevent the withdrawal of nutrition and hydration by the public guardian when the family supported it.[16]

As AUL feared, the withdrawal of artificial (tube) feeding inevitably expanded to cover a wider class of disabled patients. In 1991, AUL filed a brief, written by Grant, in the Missouri case of Christine Busalacchi on behalf of a group of renowned doctors and bioethicists in the United States, including Leon Kass, Edmund Pellegrino, Mark Siegler, and Fred Rosner.[17]

Later, AUL sponsored the publication of Forsythe's article, "Protecting Unconscious, Medically-Dependent Persons after *Wendland* and *Schiavo*." In light of the two decisions by the California and Florida courts, Forsythe proposed some state legislative amendments:

> In light of what *Wendland* and *Schiavo* revealed about the inadequacy of state statutes and judicial procedures, the states should consider legislation that (1) enhances the educational value of advance directives, (2) adopts presumptions in favor of sustaining the lives of the unconscious patients if they do not execute advance directives, (3) enhances judicial evaluation of conflicts of interests by guardians, (4) ensures that guardians are exercising informed consent, and (5) clarifies procedures to ensure efficient resolution when the guardian's decision is challenged by family members.[18]

AUL's legal work in the courts and legislatures throughout the 1970s and 1980s eventually shaped the Supreme Court's consideration of the withdrawal of life-sustaining treatment in *Cruzan* in 1990, as well as the Court's rejection of a national right to assisted suicide in 1997.

Baby Doe and the Care of Vulnerable Newborns

The language, ambiguity, and assertion of expansive judicial power in *Roe* cast a shadow over the value of all vulnerable human lives. The Court referred to prenatal human beings as "potential life" even while it acknowledged that they were growing week by week. It denied that they were persons, though they were protected as persons by state tort and criminal law. By failing to recognize that they were protected by state homicide law, the Court implied that they were not even human beings. It legislated a private right to kill prenatal human beings.

Roe created a right to abortion up to the point of fetal viability and beyond, indeed at any point before prenatal human beings were delivered fully outside the womb. And Justice Byron White issued a memorable dissent: "As an exercise of raw judicial power, the Court perhaps has authority to do what it does today; but in my view its judgment is an improvident and extravagant exercise of the power of judicial review that the Constitution extends to this Court."[19] State and federal laws were necessary to protect human lives that the Court had threatened with its broad and ambiguous opinion in *Roe*.

Infanticide was on the horizon. Academics held it out as an ethical option. As a practical and ethical matter, some saw infanticide as a simple extension of *Roe*, an "abortion ex utero." None knew this better than Dr. C. Everett Koop, who, before becoming surgeon general in the Reagan a\Administration, had been a surgeon in the 1970s, operating to save the lives of infants born with Down syndrome who had a blockage in their esophagus.[20]

AUL worked hard to prevent a right to infanticide by providing legal protection for handicapped newborns in the decade between 1975 and the federal Infant Doe regulations in 1985 and 1986. In 1975, Horan published "Euthanasia, Medical Treatment and the Mongoloid Child" in the Baylor Law Review.[21] In 1980, AUL organized and sponsored an International Conference on Infanticide and the Handicapped Newborn. The collection of papers was published in 1982 as *Infanticide and the Handicapped Newborn*, edited by Horan and Melinda Delahoyde. With an introduction by Paul Ramsey, the book featured articles by lawyers, including Horan, Valentine, and Rosenblum, and John A. Robertson, and doctors including Koop and Dr. Jerome LeJeune. In February 1982, Horan and Marianne Guerrini published "The Order to Treat: Judicial Intervention in Benign Neglect of Defective Infants" in the *Linacre Quarterly*.[22]

The case of "Infant Doe" in Bloomington, Indiana, in April 1982 drew national attention and spurred federal legislation. The infant in question was born with Down syndrome and a blockage between its esophagus and stomach, making feeding impossible, but the issue was surgically repairable. The parents decided to deny permission for a surgical correction. The case was taken to court, which denied relief for the child, and the state appealed to the Supreme Court, an appeal in which AUL assisted the local county attorney. The Supreme Court denied review in 1983.[23]

After the Bloomington case, AUL was involved in the formulation of the Infant Doe regulations under section 504 of the federal Rehabilitation Act of 1973, implementing the federal Child Abuse Amendments of 1984, which were challenged in federal court. AUL convened a meeting of attorneys in Chicago to organize briefs for the Supreme Court, and AUL attorneys Horan, Rosenblum, Grant, Quinlan, and Forsythe filed a brief on behalf of medical specialists, including Drs. David McLone and Siegfried Pueschel.

AUL was disappointed by the Supreme Court's divided decision in *Bowen v. American Hospital Association* on June 9, 1986,[24] holding that regulations from the Reagan Administration—creating standards for the provision of healthcare to handicapped infants—could not be enforced under Section 504 of the Rehabilitation Act of 1973. The Court's 4-1-3 decision, with a plurality opinion by Stevens, joined by Marshall, Blackman, and Powell, invalidated the Infant Doe regulations. Burger concurred in the judgment only, not in Stevens's opinion, but he issued no opinion of his own. White dissented in an opinion joined in its entirety by Brennan and in part by O'Connor. In the aftermath, Rosenblum and Grant published "The Legal Response to Babies Doe: An Analytical Prognosis."[25]

The Infant Doe regulations were re-established and clarified in the 1988 update to the Child Abuse Prevention and Treatment Act (CAPTA).[26] This version of the rule was published in the Code of Federal Regulations in 1990[27] and finally secured the Infant Doe regulations a place in federal law, but only temporarily.[28] These regulations were affirmed in 2010 by Congress and the Obama Administration when CAPTA was reauthorized,[29] and they remained in effect until March 30, 2015, when HHS removed the regulations to bring the code into conformity with the Affordable Care Act (ACA).[30] While the ACA's framework did away with the regulations, it is unclear whether they were intentionally re-pealed or simply overlooked in the regulatory overhaul.

Preventing the Spread of Assisted Suicide and Euthanasia

The national debate over the withdrawal of medical treatment resulted in important state legislation to clarify the doctor-patient relationship and improve the decision-making process. But it also spurred a popular movement to legalize assisted suicide, which achieved its first signifi-cant success when Oregon adopted by ballot initiative the Death with Dignity Act in 1994 by a slim 51-49 margin.

In a strategy that resembled the abortion issue of the 1960s, proponents took the issue into the courts, challenging state prohibitions on assisted suicide and seeking a national constitutional right to assisted suicide. In 1997, the U.S. Supreme Court decided the landmark cases of *Vacco*[31] and *Glucksberg*.[32] Many observers believe that the Court's deliberations in these cases were influenced by the backlash to *Roe*. The majority cer-tainly seemed disabused of the notion that the courts should take over, control and fix the issue under the guise of constitutional interpretation. The Court in *Vacco* held that the Due Process clause of the Constitution did not protect a right to assisted suicide, and held in *Glucksberg* that the Equal Protection clause of the Constitution did not protect a right to assisted suicide. So, the Justices left the issue to the people and their elected representatives in the states.

Consequently, the states were free, as they had been for the two previ-ous centuries, to decide on their own whether physician-assisted sui-cide would be legal. Since the Court left the issue to states, campaigns have been launched to legalize assisted suicide by legislation or ballot initiative in the states.

Michigan was threatened by a campaign to legalize assisted suicide in 1998 (Proposal B), and AUL partnered with Right to Life of Michigan to write and produce an ad entitled "Troubling Questions." Created by Hanon-McKendry of Grand Rapids, Michigan, the ad raised questions about the practical implications of legalizing assisted suicide. It was broadcast in Michigan and won a Telly Award. Proposal B was defeated 71.1 percent to 29.8 percent in November 1998.[33]

Tragically, as of 2023, nine states and the District of Columbia had le-

galized physician-assisted suicide by legislation or referendum: California, Colorado, Hawaii, Maine, New Jersey, New Mexico, Oregon, Vermont, and Washington.

Leaving the issue to the states also meant that state courts might decide
the issue under their state constitution. Four state supreme courts since
1997 have rejected the claim of a state constitutional right to assisted
suicide: Florida,[34] Alaska,[35] New Mexico,[36] and New York.[37] The courts
have rejected the challenges largely on reasoning similar to that of
Glucksberg, finding that their state constitutions do not have a guaranteed right to physician-assisted suicide.

The Montana Supreme Court has been the only state court to legalize
assisted suicide by judicial edict, holding that there was "nothing in
Montana Supreme Court precedent or Montana statutes indicating that
physician aid in dying is against public policy."[38]

Nevertheless, state campaigns to legalize assisted suicide by legislation,
referendum, or ballot initiative have picked up in the states. Consequently, there is a real threat that persistence will eventually pay off
and states will fall one by one, legalizing this form of suicide.

AUL has testified against the legalization of assisted suicide in many
states. In 2011, AUL helped Idaho pass a law specifically prohibiting
physician-assisted suicide, as well as in Georgia in 2012. In 2012, Massachusetts rejected a ballot initiative to legalize assisted suicide.

These efforts are reflected in AUL's annual legislative compendium,
Defending Life. Throughout these years, AUL published legislation
for states to address palliative care, train medical professionals in the
treatment of pain (Pain Medicine Education Act in 2011), and prohibit
assisted suicide.

Though some states have rejected assisted suicide and some have
strengthened their laws against the practice, many fear that there is
a trend in favor of legalization, domestically and internationally. With
current demographic trends and the "graying" of America, it will be
necessary to maintain a persistent opposition to the spread of assisted suicide and euthanasia in the U.S. while enhancing pain relief and
education and promoting state legislation that addresses and clarifies
legal procedures during disagreements between families and healthcare

providers over medical futility. All of this is necessary for a culture of life in America.

Chapter 7 Endnotes

1   Denis J. Horan, *Introduction* to Death, Dying, and Euthanasia (1980 ed.) xi, *supra* ch. 1 note 30.

2   Death, Dying, and Euthanasia (1977 ed.) *supra* ch. 1 note 29. A paperback edition was published in 1980.

3   In re Quinlan, 355 A.2d 647 (N.J. 1976).

4   Horan, *Introduction, supra* note 1 at xii.

5   Dennis J. Horan, *Euthanasia as a Form of Medical Management, in* Death, Dying, and Euthanasia (1980 ed.), *supra* ch. 1 note 30; Denis J. Horan, *Euthanasia and Brain Death: Ethical and Legal Considerations, 315* Annals N.Y. Acad. Sci. 363 (1978); Dennis J. Horan & Thomas J. Marzen, *Death with Dignity and the "Living Will": A Commentary on Legislative Developments, 5* J. Legis. 81 (1978).

6   David Andrusko, "Thomas J. Marzen, RIP, 34 Nat'l Right to Life News 13 (Aug. 2007), *available a*: https://www.nrlc.org/archive/news/2007/NRL08/Marzen.html.

7   521 U.S. 702 (1997).

8   521 U.S. 793 (1997).

9   In re Application of Eichner, 102 Misc.2d 184, 203 (N.Y. Sup Ct. 1979).

10 *See e.g.*, Dennis J. Horan & Edward R. Grant, *Prolonging Life and Withdrawing Treatment: Legal Issues*, 50 Linacre Q. 153 (1983).

11 Dennis J. Horan & Edward R. Grant, *The Legal Aspects of Withdrawing Nourishment*, 5 J. Legal Med. 595 (1984).

12 C. Everett Koop & Edward R. Grant, *The "Small Beginnings" of Euthanasia: Examining the Erosion in Legal Prohibitions Against Mercy-Killing*," 2 Notre Dame J.L. Ethics & Pub. Pol'y. 585 (1987).

13 *In re Conroy,* 486 A.2d 1209 (N.J. 1985).

14 In re Estate of Prange, 520 N.E.2d 946 (Ill. App. Ct. 1988), *vacated,* 527 N.E.2d 303 (Ill.) (vacating the appellate decision after the death of the patient and dismissing the appeal), *cert. denied sub nom.* Murphy v. Benson, 488 U.S. 892 (1988).

15 In re Estate of Longeway, 549 N.E.2d 292 (Ill. 1989).

16 In re Estate of Greenspan, 558 N.E.2d 1194 (Ill. 1990).

17 Brief of Edmund Pellegrino, M.D., Leon R. Kass, M.D., Mark A Siegler, M.D., Fred Rosner, M.D., William J Burke, M.D., Leslie Steven Rothenberg, J.D., In re Christine Busalacchi v. Busalacchi, No. 59582 (Mo. Ct. App. May 5, 1991), *available at* https://aul.org/wp-content/uploads/2019/03/1991-In-re-Christine-Busalacchi-v.-Busalacchi.pdf.

18 Clarke D. Forsythe, *Protecting Unconscious, Medically-Dependent Persons after*

Wendland *and* Schiavo, 22 Const. Comment 475, 477 (2005).

19   *Roe,* 410 U.S. at 222 (White, J., dissenting).

20   C. Everett Koop, *Life and Death and the Handicapped Newborn*, 5 Issues L. & Med. 101 (1989) (making the case for the protection of infants with disabilities).

21   Horan, *Euthanasia, Medical Treatment and the Mongoloid Child, supra* ch. 1 note 28.

22   Dennis J. Horan & Marianne E. Guerrini, *The order to Treat: Judicial Intervention in Benign Neglect of Defective Infants,* 49 Linacre Q. 42 (1982).

23   In re Treatment and Care of Infant Doe, No. GU 8204-004A, slip op. at 2 (Ind. Cir. Ct. Apr. 12, 1983), *petition for writ of mandamus and prohibition denied sub nom.* State of Indiana ex rel Infant Doe v. Monroe Circuit Court, No. 482 S 140 (Ind. Apr. 14, 1982), *appeal dismissed sub nom.* In re Guardianship of Infant Doe, No. 1-782A 157 (Ind. Ct. App. Feb. 3, 1983), *petition for transfer denied*, No. 1-782 A 157 (Ind. June 15, 1983), *cert. denied sub nom.* Infant Doe v. Bloomington Hosp., 464 U.S. 961 (1983). AUL's petition for a writ of certiorari is available online. Petition for a Writ of Certiorari, Infant Doe, 464 U.S. 961 (No. 83-437). *available at* https://aul. org/wp-content/uploads/2018/10/1983-Infant-Doe-v.-Bloomington-Hospital.pdf.

24   476 U.S. 610 (1986). AUL's *amicus* brief is available online. Brief *Amicus Curiae* of David G. McLone, M.D., Ph.D., Siegried Pueschel, M.P.H., Ph.D., Margaret Mahon, R.N., M.S.N., Lawrence J. Brodeur, J.D., in Support of Petitioner, Margaret H. Heckler, Bowen, 476 U.S.610 (No. 84-1529), *available at* https://aul.org/wp-content/up-loads/2018/10/1985-Heckler-v.-American-Hospital-Assoc.pdf.

25   Victor G. Rosenblum & Edward R. Grant, *The Legal Response to Babies Doe: An Analytical Prognosis,* 5 Issues in L. & Med. 391 (1986).

26   *Id.*

27   Services and Treatment for Disabled Infants, 45 C.F.R. 1340.15 (subsequently repealed 8- Fed. Reg. 16577 (Mar. 30, 2015)).

28   45 CFRE 1340.15 - *Services and Treatment for Disabled Infants*, U.S. Gov't Publ'g Off., https://www.govinfo.gov/app/details/CFR-1996-title45-vol3/CFR-1996-title45-vol3-sec1340-15/summary.

29   Joel Beckwith, *A Cry for Help: Preventing Passive Euthanasia Decision-Making for Neonates with Non-Fatal Congenital Defects*, 34 J. Legal Med. 273, 274 (2013).

30   80 Fed. Reg. 16577.

31   521 U.S. 793.

32   521 U.S. 702.

33   *Michigan Proposal B, Physician-Assisted Death Initiative (1998),* Ballotpedia, https:// ballotpedia.org/Michigan_Proposal_B,_Physician-Assisted_Death_Initiative_(1998) (last visited June 1, 2022).

34   Krischer v. McIver, 697 So. 2d 97, 100 (Fla 1997) ("…[I]t is clear that the public policy

of this state as expressed by the legislature is opposed to assisted suicide.").

35   Sampson v. State, 31 P.3d 88 (Alaska 2001) ("Thus, we reject Sampson and Doe's contention that physician-assisted suicide is a fundamental right within the core meaning of the Alaska Constitution's privacy and liberty clauses.").

36   Morris v. Brandenburg, 376 P.3d 836, 857 (N.M. 2016) ("If we were to recognize an absolute, fundamental right to physician aid in dying, constitutional questions would abound ... .").

37   Myers v. Schneiderman, 85 N.E.3d 57, 60 (N.Y. 2017) ("Although New York has long recognized a competent adult's right to forgo life-saving medical care, we reject plaintiffs' argument that an individual has a fundamental right to aid-in-dying as the define it.").

38   Baxter v. State, 354 Mont. 234, 250 (Mont. 2009).

CHAPTER 8

Protecting Free Speech and Freedom of Conscience

The Justices in *Roe v Wade* had a short-sighted understanding of the social, political and constitutional implications of their decision. Millions of Americans dissented from the proposition that prenatal children could be killed by abortion, and the unintended consequences of the decision provoked wider dissent. In addition, the *Roe* decision threatened the conscience rights of doctors, medical professionals, and millions of American taxpayers.

The ambiguity of *Roe* threatened to create a situation in which doctors would be compelled to perform abortions. An immediate need in the aftermath of the case was to protect doctors and hospitals who refused to be complicit in abortion, which meant protecting pro-life influence in the medical profession and in the public square.

It immediately became clear that abortion activists were willing to force abortion on Americans and compel their support. Abortion advocates quickly sued public hospitals to compel them to facilitate abortion.

Within five months of the *Roe* decision, Congress moved to pass the first of several federal conscience statutes, the Church amendment.[1]

Dennis Horan sounded the alarm in a talk at the tenth national meeting of diocesan attorneys in Washington, D.C., framing it as a right not to be involved in abortion:

> The abortion controversy is currently in the coercive stage. The hard core proponents of legalized abortion are now busy opposing abortion legislation that keeps abortion in the criminal code, or that seeks to regulate abortion other than through the medical practice act. Their aim is the psychological satisfaction of making abortion not only legal, but morally acceptable to all but the cranky Catholics. Part of the plan includes opposition of conscience clauses. Obviously, this latter stance smacks of a betrayal of their promise that their wish was only freedom now...
>
> The initial campaign is aimed at the public hospital. ... In the hands of the lower courts, the woman's constitutional right to decide is translated into the public hospital's obligation to provide and perform, on the theory that a refusal constitutes state interference. ... However, this fight may not be over, since there is a direct conflict for the conscientious administrator of these funds who is also compelled by the Social Security Act to provide aid for the unborn child. ... This, of course, represents a conflict on the part of the person administering the same funds since he must provide the funds to destroy the child, and he must provide the funds for the child's benefit. ...
>
> The conscience clause is also the target of litigation. The twist here is an attempt through the courts to limit the conscience clause only to individuals and exclude any entity or institution. In the three-judge court case now pending in Minnesota the plaintiffs have argued the unconstitutionality of the corporate conscience clause in both the Minnesota statute and the "Church Amendment."[2]

Overlooked by abortion activists was the fact that the Supreme Court, in *Roe*'s companion case, *Doe v. Bolton*, had unanimously left standing Georgia's conscience rights statute.[3]

Expanding Conscience Protection

The First Amendment protects the free exercise of religion and freedom of speech, but it does not provide protection unless governmental (state) action is involved. The First Amendment provides no protection against *private* organizational or corporate action. Private organizations and institutions—such as private hospitals and corporations—may coerce individuals under threat of losing employment. Since the First Amendment doesn't provide legal protection, state and federal legislation were needed to protect conscience rights in the private marketplace.

The Court's decision in *Roe* sparked approximately 45 states to pass conscience-rights legislation within a year or two, protecting physicians from being coerced into participating in abortion—a remarkable response and achievement.[4]

But, over time, it became clear that those early laws were too limited in scope—too limited in the people they protected, the action they insulated, and the medical procedures they covered.

Decades after *Roe*, the conscience rights of medical professionals are still under assault, and their livelihoods are threatened by abortion advocates. In 2004, realizing the limited scope of the protection provided through state conscience laws enacted in 1973 and 1974, AUL published comprehensive model legislative protection that would expand the personnel protected, enlarge the scope of action protected, and enlarge the scope of procedures included under the protection. Mississippi was one of the first to pass a comprehensive Healthcare Rights of Conscience Law.

Thankfully, Illinois was one of the earliest states to see the need for comprehensive protection of conscience. In April 2005, Illinois governor Rod Blagojevich issued an executive order compelling Illinois pharmacists to stock and prescribe abortion-inducing drugs. AUL counsel Ed Martin sued Blagojevich on behalf of an Illinois pharmacist. After several years of litigation, the Illinois Supreme Court, in an appeal argued by

Professor Mark Rienzi, invalidated the executive order as a violation of Illinois law.[5]

Medical technology, cultural change, and corporate agendas will continue to create ethical conflicts for individuals, associations, religious organizations, and medical professionals in America. There are more laws today protecting conscience rights, but the issue has never been completely settled because abortion activists strongly resist these policies. The threat continues, as today abortion activists attempt to force professionals either to perform or refer for abortions or to leave their profession. But abortion is obviously not the only medical or scientific development that will challenge the conscience of Americans. As Americans witnessed during the pandemic of 2020-2022, medical professionals who don't toe the line dictated by cultural elites will continue to be challenged by cultural and medical trends and developments.

The Battle to Shut Down Abortion Protest

Backlash against *Roe* led to grassroots efforts to protest abortion and to block abortion clinics across the country. Joseph Scheidler was a leader in that grassroots mobilization, and in 1985 he published *Closed: 99 Ways to Stop Abortion*, outlining his strategies and tactics.

The next year, the National Organization for Women (NOW) filed suit in federal district court against national leaders of abortion-clinic protests, including Scheidler and the Pro-Life Action League of Chicago, under federal antitrust laws. Scheidler asked Horan and AUL executive director Ed Grant to defend him.

Grant brought to AUL litigation experience, a sharp mind and pen, a capacity to juggle legislation, litigation, and scholarship, and a heart for the full range of the bioethical issues that AUL addressed. Between 1984 and 1987, Grant played a major role in editing the 1984 conference papers into the 1987 book *Abortion and the Constitution: Reversing Roe v. Wade Through the Courts*. But his interest was always to return to private practice and to pursue Horan's model of private practice as his main professional focus while staying involved in pro-life policy on the side.[6]

AUL represented Scheidler and his colleagues in *NOW v. Scheidler* to eliminate the threat that antitrust laws—and later the Racketeer-Influenced, Corrupt Organizations Act (RICO) law—posed to pro-life advocates and organizations.

After the federal courts initially refused to dismiss the antitrust case against Scheidler, NOW spent the years between 1986 and 1991 conducting an extensive and harassing investigation into Scheidler's work, activities, and finances. Originally filed as an antitrust case, it morphed into a case brought under the federal RICO law, drafted by pro-life Notre Dame Law professor Robert Blakey in the 1970s. It was an intentionally broad law, designed to be a powerful tool against organized crime, not against political protests.

In February 1989, NOW filed a new complaint, alleging a violation of RICO and seeking to consider hundreds or even thousands of pro-life Americans as "co-conspirators." NOW claimed that Scheidler's actions fell within RICO because he committed "extortion." But NOW never claimed the essential element under federal RICO law: "extortion" required that Scheidler obtained, or attempted to obtain, property from any abortion clinic, provider, or patient. AUL sought to highlight that critical legal defect and have the RICO case against Scheidler thrown out.

In 1991, NOW filed a statement arguing that the case against Scheidler was a RICO case. AUL coordinated a meeting of defense attorneys aimed at beating this argument, with a discussion led by Blakey. After five years of intense and expensive litigation, the federal district court threw out both the antitrust case and the RICO case on May 28, 1991, on the unfortunate rationale that RICO required an "economic motive."[7] NOW lost in the U.S. Court of Appeals, which handed down its 3-0 decision on June 29, 1992—the same day that the Supreme Court decided *Planned Parenthood v. Casey*—agreeing that RICO required an economic motive.[8]

NOW filed a petition to the Supreme Court in November 1992, asking for further review. In May 1993, Clinton Administration Solicitor General Drew Days urged the Court to hear the case and restore the antitrust and RICO claims against Scheidler and clinic protesters. Paul Linton and Clarke Forsythe drafted a response in May and June, working with Jay Sekulow and Walter Weber of the American Center for Law and Justice (ACLJ). It was filed in early June on behalf of Scheidler, Operation Rescue, and its founder Randall Terry. AUL staff counsel Ann-Louise Lohr carried much of the burden of the *NOW* litigation during these years.

On June 14, 1993, the same day that President Clinton nominated Ruth Bader Ginsburg to the Supreme Court, the Court agreed to hear NOW's appeal, *limited to the RICO claim,* thereby ending the antitrust claims.[9] The defense counsel, including the ACLJ's Vince McCarthy and Pat Monaghan, met with Blakey at AUL's office in Chicago on Friday, July 9, to discuss the appeal and decide who should argue; they agreed on Blakey. AUL attorneys proceeded to draft the brief with Blakey in July and August.

Shortly after Justice Ginsburg joined the Supreme Court in 1993, AUL and allies briefed the first appeal to the Court. AUL pressed the key legal defect in the RICO case: that the RICO case must be dismissed because there was no federal extortion alleged or implicated by pro-life protest, even if it diminished the business of an abortion clinic. Blakey argued the appeal at the Supreme Court on Wednesday, December 8, 1993, before Justices Rehnquist, Blackmun, O'Connor, Kennedy, Thomas, Stevens, Scalia, Souter, and Ginsburg.

On Monday, January 24, 1994, the Supreme Court stunned AUL with a unanimous decision holding that RICO did not require proof that either the racketeering enterprise or the predicate acts of racketeering were "motivated by an economic purpose." The justices failed to address the federal extortion issue.[10] They sent the RICO case, without the antitrust claim, back to the district court for more litigation.

In October 1994, AUL filed a second petition hoping to short-circuit the oppressive litigation, urging the Supreme Court to throw out the case on the specific legal basis that there was no valid RICO case because there was no valid Hobbs Act extortion claim. NOW had never alleged that Scheidler and his group *obtained any property* from the business, its employees, or its customers, as required to prove extortion. Shortly before Christmas, the Supreme Court refused to hear the appeal, sending it back to the district court for nine more years of litigation.[11]

In 1995, Chicago commercial litigator Thomas Brejcha assumed the defense of Scheidler and his group. Brejcha persevered for years to ensure that RICO could no longer be used against abortion protesters.

After another eight years of litigation, and another appeal, the Supreme

Court in February 2003 threw out the litigation for the exact same legal reason that AUL raised back in 1994: NOW could not allege extortion because Scheidler and other defendants never *obtained property* from the clinics as required by the Hobbs Act.[12] After 18 years of litigation that practically bankrupted Joe Scheidler, his colleagues, his family, and his attorneys, the Court ruled 8-1, with a majority opinion by Chief Justice Rehnquist, that there was no underlying RICO violation because there was no Hobbs Act extortion. Only Justice Stevens dissented.

The lower courts, however, still refused to throw out the case. Brejcha continued to fight the issue and returned to the Supreme Court for a fourth time in 2005. AUL filed a brief in support of Scheidler and his colleagues in August 2005, and Scheidler won a unanimous victory in the Supreme Court in February 2006, with the Court directing the lower court to enter judgment for Scheidler.[13] Eight more years of litigation occurred before Scheidler was able to recover costs and fees from NOW. Federal appeals judge Frank Easterbrook, in the final opinion, concluded:

> This suit began 28 years ago and has been to the Supreme Court three times ... All defendants who stuck it out to the end (some settled) prevailed across the board ... This litigation has lasted far too long. At last it is over.[14]

Twenty-eight years of litigation to establish the simple fact that the abortion protesters had never violated RICO. Brejcha eventually formed the Thomas More Society in Chicago, an organization that has zealously defended the rights of Americans in the courts from coast to coast.

Freedom of speech and conscience continue to be essential rights in witnessing to the truth of the dignity of human life. They are crucial in public life and in the medical profession and to participate in the electoral and legislative processes. Yet they remain under assault, as the cancel culture has shown, and protecting them in the future will require vigilance and perseverance.

These bioethical principles—the sanctity of human life at all stages of development, the care for the chronically and terminally ill, freedom of conscience—are essential to defend and protect in their own right. But AUL also knew that faltering in these areas would threaten public support for the campaign against abortion and the legal strategy against *Roe*. If Americans were not vigilant in protecting human life at all stages of development, AUL feared that support for the prenatal human being might diminish. There would always be a need to protect human life in the law at every stage of development.

Chapter 8 Endnotes

1   Pub. L. No. 93-45, tit. IV, § 401(b) to (c), 87 Stat. 91, 95–96 (codified at 42 U.S.C. § 300a-7). *See* Office for Civil Rights, *Conscience Protections for Health Care Providers*, U.S. Dep't of Health & Hum. Servs. (Sept. 14, 2021), https://www.hhs.gov/conscience/conscience-protections/index.html.

2   Horan, *Abortion and the Conscience Clause, supra* ch. 2 note 65, at 289–291.

3   Doe, 410 U.S. at 197–98, 205 (discussing Georgia's statutory conscience protections)

4   Lynn D. Wardle, *Protection of Health-Care Providers' Rights of Conscience in American Law: Present, Past, and Future*, 9 Ave Maria L. Rev. 1 (2011); Lynn D. Wardle, *A Matter of Conscience: Legal Protection for the Rights of Conscience of Health Care Providers*, 2 Cambridge Q. Healthcare Ethics 529 (1993); Lynn D. Wardle, *Protecting the Rights of Conscience of Health Care Providers*, 14 J. Legal Med. 177 (1993). *See also* Mark L. Rienzi, *The Constitutional Right Not to Participate in Abortions: Roe, Casey, and the Fourteenth Amendment Rights of Healthcare Providers*, 87 Notre Dame L. Rev. 1 (2011).

5   Morr-Fitz, Inc v. Blagojevich, 910 N.E.2d 373 (Ill. 2008). *See also* Francis J. Manion, *Protecting Conscience through Litigation: Lessons Learned in the Land of Blagojevich*, 24 Regent U.L. Rev. 369 (2012).

6   After he joined Hinshaw, Grant addressed the Interprofessional Symposium by the Illinois State Bar association, which Grant later published. Edward R. Grant, *What in the World Is Going On? A Consideration of the California Euthanasia Proposal*, 57 Linacre Q. 58 (1990).

7   Nat'l Org. for Women v. Scheidler, 765 F. Supp. 937 (N.D. Ill. 1991).

8   Nat'l Org. for Women v. Scheidler, 968 F.2d 612 (7th Cir. 1992).

9   Nat'l Org. for Women v. Scheidler, 508 U.S. 971 (1993).

10   Nat'l Org. for Women v. Scheidler, 510 U.S. 249 (1994) (hereinafter NOW I).

11   Scheidler v. Del. Women's Health Org., 513 U.S. 1058 (1994) (hereinafter NOW II).

12   Scheidler v. Nat'l Org. for Women, Inc., 537 U.S. 393 (2003) (hereinafter NOW III). AUL's *amicus curiae* brief is available online. Brief of *Amicus Curiae* Americans United for Life in Support of Petitioners, NOW III (No. 01-1118), *available at* https://aul.org/wp-content/uploads/2019/03/2002-Scheidler-v.-NOW-and-Operation-Rescue-v.-NOW.pdf.

13   Scheidler v. Nat'l Org. for Women, Inc., 547 U.S. 9 (2006) (hereinafter NOW IV). AUL's *amicus curiae* brief is available online. Brief of *Amicus Curiae* Americans United for Life in Support of Petitioners, NOW IV (No. 04-1244), *available at* https://aul.org/wp-content/uploads/2019/03/2005-Scheidler-et-al-v.-NOW-and-Operation-Rescue-v.-NOW.pdf.

14   Nat'l Org. for Women, Inc. v. Scheidler, 750 F.3d 696, 697, 700 (7th Cir. 2014).

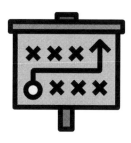

CHAPTER 9

Back to the Drawing Board After *Casey*

The Supreme Court's decision in *Planned Parenthood v. Casey* in June 1992 was a setback so disappointing that it provoked some to entirely relinquish the goal of overturning *Roe v. Wade* through the courts. Others concluded that all that could be done was to "change hearts and minds," abandoning the realm of public policy altogether. This attitude was so wide-spread that Charles Krauthammer broadcast it in an op-ed in the *Washington Post* at the end of 1992 after Bill Clinton won the presidency.

Instead, in the aftermath of *Casey*, AUL reviewed its strategy for the reversal of *Roe*, focusing on revised legislation that could be enacted at the state level. This plan necessitated a detailed review of *Roe* and *Casey*, as well as the ways in which the decision in *Casey* had altered the holding in *Roe*. AUL held another national legislative conference in Chicago that summer, recognizing how important the 1992 presidential election would be.

The *Casey* decision, like *Roe*, contained the seeds of its own destruction. A plurality of three justices, O'Connor, Souter and Kennedy, jerry-rigged an opinion that was simply incoherent. The plurality emphasized *stare decisis* but expressly overruled two previous abortion decisions, *Akron* and *Thornburgh*.[1] They refused to overrule *Roe* in the face of political pressure, but failed to acknowledge the political pressure on both sides.[2] They suggested that abortion was "*sui generis*,"[3] even though there is a long Anglo-American tradition protecting prenatal life, which has only grown through state protection in prenatal injury, wrongful death, and fetal homicide law in the 20th century.[4] The plurality talked about a "covenant"[5] but not the Anglo-American legal protection for the prenatal human that historically paralleled that covenant. The plurality "call[ed] the contending sides ... to end their national division by accepting a common mandate rooted in the Constitution,"[6] but never explained how an abortion "right" was "rooted in the Constitution."[7] They only justified the "right" by repeating the *ipse dixit* of *Eisenstadt v. Baird* ("If the right of privacy means anything, it is the right ...").[8] And the famous "mystery" passage in their opinion, espousing expressive individualism, necessarily ignored the reality that state legal protection specifically protects the prenatal human *as a human being*.[9] *Casey* did not "reaffirm" *Roe* on the merits but on *stare decisis*—because it was once decided.[10] *Casey* did not provide a constitutional foundation for *Roe* in the text, history, or structure of the Constitution.[11] Then, there are several ambiguous recitations of *Roe*'s analysis.[12] Finally, there is the vague "mystery" passage.[13] *Casey* failed its own test: "a decision without principled justification would be no judicial act at all."[14]

But *Casey*'s weaknesses were not as apparent in 1992. *Casey* sparked a fruitful reexamination and debate over pro-life strategy in the courts and legislatures. Critics complained that the litigation strategy that led to *Casey* was the problem and that the goal should be a federal constitutional personhood ruling, not a federalism decision that would return the issue of abortion to the states. AUL was compelled to examine the question: What had 20 years of state abortion legislation and litigation produced?

The decision forced AUL to review the fundamentals. While politics and culture inevitably shape the abortion debate, *Roe* was a legal problem that required an effective legal solution.

Despite five justices reaffirming *Roe* in *Casey*, the Court upheld, by a 7-2 vote, key regulations on abortion passed by Pennsylvania in 1989 in the aftermath of *Webster*—informed-consent regulations (including a 24-hour waiting period), parental-consent regulations, and abortion-data-reporting requirements. Abortion-reporting requirements are necessary for accurately understanding the short-term and long-terms risks of abortion and, thus, for fully informed consent for women. The policy is designed to assess the effects of *Roe* and legal abortion and to protect maternal health by gathering evidence of the morbidity (injuries) and mortality (death) from abortion. The Court issued *Roe* in 1973 without any reliable national system of abortion reporting, collection, and analysis—and none exists today.

AUL's post-*Casey* strategy focused on new publications, legislation, and litigation, including the publication "The Good News About *Planned Parenthood v. Casey*." Among other themes, it urged states to enact detailed informed consent for abortion legislation, which would require that women get detailed information about the nature and risks of abortion, as well as abortion alternatives.

Some critics contended that the *Casey* decision "show[ed] the uselessness of present pro-life strategy," meaning that any "incremental strategy" was "useless" unless it was designed to achieve a constitutional personhood ruling from the Court. They did not advocate a new campaign for a constitutional personhood amendment but a campaign for a personhood ruling from the Supreme Court.

The distinction here relates to the two principal rulings by the Supreme Court in *Roe*: that abortion was subsumed within the "fundamental right of privacy" under the liberty clause of the Fourteenth Amendment and that unborn children were not "persons" within that same Amendment.

Overturning the first holding of *Roe*—that abortion is a constitutional right—would allow states to adopt their own abortion policies. Some refer to this as a "states' rights" ruling, but it would be more accurately called a federalist ruling, because it involves state constitutional authority, not rights. Overruling the second holding of *Roe* would be entirely different; it would affirmatively prevent states from enacting policies to legalize abortion. *Casey* reaffirmed that the four dissenting justices, including Scalia and Thomas, would never issue a "personhood ruling" for textual and institutional reasons. They had said as much in their opinions in *Casey* and in previous opinions on abortion. However difficult it would be to secure a federalist ruling from the Court, a personhood ruling would be even harder.

Because the Constitution's text is silent about abortion, the states exercised authority before 1973 to prohibit abortion or, as 13 states did by statute between 1967 and 1970, loosen legal protection for women and unborn children under the law. Before *Roe*, no court, whether state or federal, had ever invalidated a state's authority to do so. Although a personhood ruling remained a pro-life aspiration, a federalist ruling has the benefit of returning authority to the states to prohibit abortion.

The "incremental" strategy wasn't a detriment to possibly achieving a personhood ruling, because the two strategies could be compatible. In briefs and at oral argument, lawyers could still argue in favor of a personhood ruling as a legal interpretation of the Fourteenth Amendment. It is not a fact-laden strategy requiring a trial but an interpretation of constitutional text.

A personhood ruling has long been a hope, but not appeared a strong practical possibility. No sitting justice since *United States v. Vuitch*, the first abortion case addressed by the Court in the modern era, has supported the proposition that the prenatal human being is a "person" within the protection of the Fourteenth Amendment. The two original dissenters to *Roe* in 1973—Rehnquist and White—espoused a federalist approach to abortion, denying that there was any constitutional right to abortion. They held that view until they retired.

Scalia, who joined the Court in 1986, and Thomas, who joined in 1991, urged overruling on federalist grounds. This was the view that the four dissenters advanced in *Casey*: "The States may, if they wish, permit abortion on demand, but the Constitution does not require them to do so."[15] They may have believed that an unborn child should be a person under state tort or criminal law—statutory personhood—but they held simply that *Roe* should be overturned and abortion policy returned to the states because there is no constitutional right to abortion.

Abortion legislation that created test cases in the courts did not preclude or prevent a personhood ruling from the Supreme Court. A personhood ruling is a rationale for the decision to overrule *Roe*. State legislation had not precluded such a rationale. Strategy focusing on discrete issues, such as informed consent, parental notice, or a 20-week limit, hasn't undermined the possibility of a personhood ruling.

Even in the context of a case involving state abortion legislation, legal advocates can, and still do, urge a personhood ruling by the Court. In virtually every Supreme Court case, from *Roe*—including Charles Rice's brief on behalf of AUL—to the 2021 *Dobbs* case from Mississippi, pro-life advocates and organizations have filed briefs urging the Court to adopt a personhood ruling based on the Fourteenth Amendment. Over the past half century, the Court has not lacked for briefs or arguments making such a case.[16]

According to Justices Scalia and Thomas, there were two good reasons why abortion should remain a state issue rather than a federal issue decided by judges through a particular reading of the Fourteenth Amendment. First, they argued that there was no textual reason to be certain that the framers of the Fourteenth Amendment meant to remove issue from the states, enough to justify the Supreme Court taking over the issue.[17] Second, there was an institutional reason for leaving the issue to states. The Court had caused a self-inflicted wound by centralizing and controlling the abortion issue, a fear borne out by the confirmation hearings for Robert Bork, Clarence Thomas, Samuel Alito, and Brett Kavanaugh. Scalia said that the Court should get out of the "abortion-umpiring business."[18] The Court would not extricate itself but mire itself more deeply in the "abortion-umpiring business" if it stopped deciding whether abortion laws were too *strict* under *Roe* and started deciding whether abortion laws were too *loose* through a constitutional "personhood" ruling.

Thomas agreed with Scalia, and the originalist justices who have joined the Court since Scalia and Thomas—Roberts, Alito, Gorsuch, Kavanaugh, and Barrett—and who have seen the effects of the "abortion-umpiring business" on the Court, apparently agree that the Court should leave abortion to the states rather than control it as a Fourteenth Amendment issue. During the arguments in the Supreme Court in *Dobbs* in December 2021, the Solicitor General for Mississippi, under questioning from Justice Kavanaugh, confirmed that Mississippi was only asking the Court to overturn *Roe* on a federalist basis. The Court's final decision in *Dobbs*, leaked in May 2022, confirmed that *Roe* would be overruled on a federalist rationale.

The contention that a personhood ruling was the only plausible or legitimate way to overrule *Roe* failed to grapple with the clear rationale of the four *Casey* dissenters for a federalist overruling. Their rationale addressed the institutional role of the Court in American democracy. Scalia, joined by Rehnquist, White, and Thomas, urged that the Court leave behind its role as "the national abortion umpire":

> [B]y foreclosing all democratic outlet for the deep passions this issue arouses, by banishing the issue from the political forum that gives all participants, even the losers, the satisfaction of a fair hearing and an honest fight, by continuing the imposition of a rigid national rule instead of allowing for regional differences, the Court merely prolongs and intensifies the anguish. We should get out of this area, where we have no right to be, and where we do neither ourselves nor the country any good by remaining.[19]

This rationale has a good deal of statesmanlike wisdom in it, and the institutional argument against a personhood ruling is well-nigh impregnable, given current cultural, political, and judicial constraints.

A federalist overruling of *Roe* does not prevent the states from treating the prenatal child as a person in state law. Indeed, many states treat the unborn child—at all stages of pregnancy—as a person for purposes of tort or criminal law, outside the context of abortion. It was the Court in *Roe* which created a situation in which states can treat unborn children as persons in the case of a vehicular homicide but not in the case of abortion. The rationale for new state abortion laws now that *Roe* is overturned is precisely that unborn children are persons.

Casey was clearly a disappointment. When the Court seemed poised to overturn *Roe*, and when many commentators were predicting that it would be overturned, the Court's upholding four state abortion regulations seemed like a small step indeed. But the disappointment of subjective hopes could not obscure the objective gains.

The litigation campaign was one of the pro-life movement's most successful means of keeping the practice of abortion prominently before the eyes of the nation. Every abortion case at the Supreme Court received pervasive media coverage, providing vital public education on the issue. The strategy created more than 30 test cases and compelled the Court to apply *Roe*'s standards to new, discrete legal issues. Because of this continual application of *Roe* to new statutes in new cases, *Roe* remained as unsettled as ever, despite an enormous effort by legacy media, abortion-advocacy organizations, billionaires, wealthy foundations, and the Democratic party to settle it.

State legislation, meanwhile, has been the democratic means of securing legitimacy for abortion limits in the law. The dissenters in *Casey* were convinced, and accurately predicted, that the standards applied in *Casey* were inherently arbitrary and unworkable. As expected, state abortion limits meaningfully cut back abortion rates and reduced the harms to women and children after *Casey*. Since *Casey*, the U.S. has seen a dramatic drop in the abortion rate, more than 50 percent, and the statistical research of Dr. Michael New has attributed a substantial amount of that decrease to state limits on abortion.[20]

In the aftermath of *Casey*, respected scholars and public intellectuals severely criticized the joint opinion by O'Connor, Kennedy, and Souter preserving *Roe*. George Weigel wrote that the opinion "was symptomatic of a court in deep intellectual crisis." Harvard Law professor Mary Ann Glendon pointed out that American abortion law remained the most permissive in the western world. Stanford Law School professor Michael McConnell said on the "MacNeil/Lehrer NewsHour" that it would be "a recipe for disaster" if the Court were to "dig in its heels" in such a ruling. In the *Chicago Tribune*, McConnell concluded that the Court had "poured gasoline on the abortion controversy." George Will called *Casey* an "arrogant" opinion. Richard John Neuhaus called the decision "the *Dred Scott* of our time," and Charles Krauthammer concluded that the decision was "appalling constitutional law" and that "the damage it does to the Constitution in its zeal to legislate correct abortion policy is profound." "By short-circuiting the democratic process,"

Krauthammer wrote, "the court prolongs and inflames the abortion debate."

The prudential strategy of litigation unsettled *Roe* between 1973 and 1992. It is often overlooked that *Casey* was the first time that four justices publicly concluded that *Roe* should be explicitly overturned. Justices Rehnquist, White, Scalia, and Thomas took this position in *Casey*, insisting on the essential unconstitutionality of *Roe*. The four dissenters encouraged a continued campaign against *Roe*.

The joint opinion made more frank concessions about the nature of abortion practice than the Court had ever made. The plurality confessed that abortion is mostly practiced as an unplanned form of birth control[21] and acknowledged that there are only "rare circumstances in which the pregnancy is itself a danger to [the mother's] own life or health, or is the result of rape or incest."[22] What's more, the opinion recognized that women may suffer adverse psychological consequences from abortion.[23]

Consequently, AUL concluded that *Casey* contained the seeds of its own destruction *if* AUL persevered in the courts and legislatures. The *Casey* decision opened new opportunities for state legislation. After some deliberation, AUL tackled those opportunities in the states with zeal for the rest of the 1990s.

Chapter 9 Endnotes

1   Planned Parenthood of Se. Pa. v. Casey, 505 U.S. 833, 870, 882 (1992).

2   *Id.* at 867.

3   *Id.* at 857.

4   Dellapenna, Dispelling the Myths, *supra* ch. 1 note 3; Linton, *The Legal Status of the Unborn Child Under State Law, supra* ch. 6 note 10.

5   *Casey*, 505 U.S. at 901.

6   *Id.* at 867 (alteration in original),

7   *Id.*

8   *Id.* at 896 (citing *Eisenstadt*, 405 U.S. at 453).

9   Linton, *The Legal Status of the Unborn Child Under State Law, supra* ch. 6 note 10.

10 *Casey*, 505 U.S. at 854–69. *See also* Dellapenna, Dispelling the Myths, *supra* ch. 1 note 3, at 853 (The plurality "contented themselves with standing on the rule of stare decisis without an original examination of the relevant history and tradition.").

11 McDonald v. City of Chicago, 561 U.S. 742, 767 (citing Glucksberg, 521 U.S. at 721) ("[W]e must decide whether the right to keep and bear arms is fundamental to *our* scheme of ordered liberty … or as we have said in a related context, whether this right is 'deeply rooted in this Nation's history and tradition.'" (emphasis in original)). *See Casey*, 505 U.S. at 982 (Scalia J., concurring in judgment in part and dissenting in part) ("The authors of the joint opinion, of course, do not squarely contend that *Roe v. Wade* was a correct application of 'reasoned judgment'; merely that it must be followed, because of *stare decisis*.").

12 *Casey*, 505 U.S. at 848 ("[T]he Constitution places limits on a State's right to interfere with a person's most basic decisions about family and parenthood … as well as bodily integrity."); *id.* at 851 ("Our law affords constitutional protection to personal decisions relating to marriage, procreation, contraception, family relationships, child rearing, and education."); *id.* at 853 ("[I]ts holding invoked the reasoning and the tradition of the precedents we have discussed, granting protection to substantive liberties of the person."); *id.* at 869 ("[T]he basic decision in Roe was based on a constitutional analysis which we cannot now repudiate.")

13 *Id.* at 851 ("At the heart of liberty is the right to define one's own concept of existence, of meaning, of the universe, and of the mystery of human life.").

14 *Id.* at 865. *Cf.* Citizens United v. Fed. Election Comm'n, 558 U.S. 310, 384 (2010) (Roberts, C.J., concurring) ("*Stare decisis* is a doctrine of preservation, not transformation … There is … no basis for the Court to give precedential sway to reasoning that it has never accepted, simply because that reasoning happens to support a conclusion

reached on different grounds that have since been abandoned or discredited.").

15 505 U.S. at 979 (Scalia, J., concurring in the judgment in part and dissenting in part, joined by Rehnquist, CJ., and White and Thomas, JJ.).

16 *See* Clarke D. Forsythe & Keith Arago, Roe v. Wade & *the Legal Implications of State Constitutional "Personhood" Amendments*, 30 Notre Dame J.L., Ethics & Pub. Pol'y 273 (2016).

17 Justice Rehnquist made that point in his dissent in *Roe*, 410 U.S. at 177.

18 *Casey*, 505 U.S. at 996 (Scalia, J., concurring in the judgment in part and dissenting in part). He reiterated this in his dissent in *Stenberg*, 530 U.S. at 956.

19 *Casey*, 505 U.S. at 1002. *See also Stenberg*, 530 U.S. at 956 (Scalia, J., dissenting) ("If only for the sake of its own preservation, the Court should return this matter to the people — where the Constitution, by its silence on the subject, left it — and let *them* decide, State by State, whether this practice should be allowed. *Casey* must be overruled." (emphasis in original))

20 Michael J. New, *Analyzing the Effect of Anti-Abortion U.S. State Legislation in the Post*-Casey *Era*, 11 State Pol. & Pol'y Q. 28 (2011); Michael J. New, *Analyzing the Impact of U.S. Antiabortion Legislation in the Post*-Casey *Era: A Reassessment*, 14 *State Pol. & Pol'y Q.* 228 (2014).

21 505 U.S. at 856.

22 *Id.* at 850–51.

23 *Id.* at 882.

CHAPTER 10

Adaptation and Resilience During the Most Pro-Abortion Presidency Yet

T he *Casey* defeat in June 1992 was followed by an electoral defeat in November. The Clinton presidency virtually guaranteed that *Roe* could not be effectively defeated for four or eight more years. The political obstacles to changing the Court were raised to their highest level by the first president since *Roe* who was openly committed to nominating pro-*Roe* Justices. So, the Clinton presidency was a turning point in the fight against *Roe* since 1973—the first president to aggressively push abortion—as the administration's campaign to bring RU-486 abortion pills to the U.S. market would show—and the first to have a pro-abortion litmus test for Justices and lower court judges. Because *Roe* centralized the issue in the Court, and presidents nominate justices, the prospects for the fight against *Roe* were inhibited or enhanced by each presidential administration.

After *Casey*, a direct challenge to *Roe* through test cases was, for the time being, on hold. Clinton's election halted the drive to change the

Court that had made progress during the Reagan and Bush presidencies, an obstacle that forced AUL to revise its strategy.

And yet, by working strategically in the states and courts, the pro-life movement still managed to make progress by the end of Clinton's presidency. Those years were a time of strategic opportunity amid limitations, an important era for AUL to adjust its strategy while continuing to fight for the same principles it always had.

Contrary to what Charles Krauthammer wrote in his column on *Casey* at the end of 1992, the path forward was not a choice between "hearts and minds" or public policy goals. It was a "both-and" strategy.

Overturning a Supreme Court decision supported by a major political party and dozens of foundations and billionaires depended on establishing certain political conditions. The president nominates new justices, and the Senate either confirms or denies those nominations. In some circumstances, the Senate majority declines to consider the nomination, as in the wake of Justice Scalia's death in February 2016. That is consistent with both the Senate's constitutional role and precedent.

In response to the Supreme Court's 1857 decision in *Dred Scott v. Sanford*, anti-slavery leaders such as Abraham Lincoln and William Seward forthrightly announced that they were determined to overrule *Dred Scott* through the means afforded by the Constitution—the election of an anti-slavery president and appropriate Supreme Court nominations. Even if the Civil War had not come, it is possible that Lincoln would have achieved the overruling of *Dred Scott* through his nomination of anti-slavery justices to the Court, though perhaps with great difficulty if Southern senators had blocked such nominees. The strategy for overruling *Roe* depended on the same constitutional and political conditions, which had to be adapted according to obstacles and opportunities.

Adaptation also meant persevering with AUL's mission during a time of transition in board and team leadership, something that has happened several times during AUL's 50 years. At the end of 1992, AUL president Guy Condon left AUL and became the leader of CareNet, where he accomplished much in seven years, building the pregnancy-care network in the U.S., before his tragic death in a car accident in November 2000 at the age of 46.

Paige Cunningham returned to AUL to succeed Condon as president.

AUL considered beginning an initiative to legally defend pregnancy-care centers but decided against it for strategic and financial reasons. Tom Murray, a steady financial and administrative hand, led AUL's administration as the organization entered a difficult year. Karol Emmerich joined the AUL board and offered serious, experienced counsel and advice in organizational management for a decade, along with Thomas J. Donnelly, a generous and prudent lawyer and business leader from Pittsburgh.

Immediate Challenges from the Clinton Administration

In 1993 and 1994, the Clinton Administration aggressively pushed a series of pro-abortion initiatives. The threats during those first two years of his presidency came from Clinton's efforts to change the composition of the courts through pro-*Roe* nominees, from threatened congressional action on the Freedom of Choice Act (FOCA), and from an aggressive push to bring the French abortifacient, RU-486 (mifepristone), to the U.S. market as quickly as possible.[1] FOCA attempted to federalize abortion by statute and eliminate state abortion regulations across the country, a significant threat to legislative progress at the state level.[2]

But the Clinton Administration was unable to get FOCA through Congress before Democrats lost the House in the 1994 midterms. AUL educated grassroots organizations about the legal significance of FOCA and the effects it would have on state abortion limits. In addition, AUL disseminated a FOCA litigation memo outlining potential legal challenges to the law, including an attack based on Section Five of the Fourteenth Amendment.[3] (The experience fighting FOCA during the Clinton years would be useful when then–Senator Barack Obama endorsed FOCA in 2007 and 2008.)

The spring of 1993 brought two additional blows compounding the problems caused by *Casey* and Clinton. On March 19, 1993, Justice Byron White, one of the original dissenters in *Roe*, announced his retirement, decreasing the number of anti-*Roe* justices from four to three. AUL knew it was a setback, though it wasn't a surprise—White was a life-long Democrat who chose to retire during a Democratic presidency. David Savage wrote that White's "departure would allow the first high court appointee by a Democratic president in quarter of a century" and "could mark the start of a gradual shift toward the left." Clinton would

nominate only pro-*Roe* justices, and he proceeded to do so with the se-
lections of Ruth Bader Ginsburg to replace White in 1993 and Stephen
Breyer to replace Harry Blackmun in 1994.

Sen. Orrin Hatch (R-UT)'s quick endorsement of Judge Ginsburg enabled her nomination to appear more moderate than she was, under-
cutting AUL's ability to oppose her.[4] Nevertheless, AUL president Paige
Cunningham opposed the Ginsburg nomination before the Senate
Judiciary Committee on July 23, 1993. Cunningham rebutted the notion
of women's "reliance interests" in abortion and reviewed the negative
effects of abortion on women, backed by her recent publication with
Forsythe, "Is Abortion the 'First Right' for Women?"[5] Ginsburg's zealous pro-abortion judicial votes and opinions over the next 27 years—
through *Stenberg v. Carhart, Gonzales v. Carhart, Whole Woman's
Health v. Hellerstedt*, and *June Medical Services v. Russo*—more than
justified AUL's opposition. The following year, Justice Blackmun retired,
enabling President Clinton to name his successor, Stephen Breyer. Cunningham also testified against his nomination before the Senate Judiciary Committee.

What AUL knew of both nominees proved true. They proved to be
staunch abortion-rights supporters, Breyer in a detailed, methodical
way, and Ginsburg in an aggressive, zealous way. Both justices voted to
strike down any and every limit on abortion that they encountered: 31
state prohibitions on partial-birth abortion in 2000, the federal Partial-Birth Abortion Ban Act (PBABA) in 2007, credentialing and emergency room transfer laws in 2016, and Louisiana's admitting-privileges
law in 2020. They would tolerate no limits on abortion and they would
not defer to "state interests," as the *Roe* Court called them, in maternal
health or the life of the prenatal child. Throughout those years, neither
ever offered a constitutional rationale for *Roe* or *Casey* that was deeply
rooted in our nation's law, history, or tradition.

At the end of June 1993, the U.S. House weakened the Hyde Amendment, which had been in place since 1976 and upheld in its strictest
form by the Court in *Harris v. McRae* in 1980. The House permitted
federal taxpayer funding for abortions in cases of rape and incest,
approved by a 256-171 vote. The pro-life movement was split over
whether to support a modified Hyde Amendment with rape and incest
exceptions added or to back no Hyde Amendment at all. Congressman

Henry Hyde supported the modified version, and AUL saw no reason not to support his judgment. The Hyde Amendment remains an annual rider to congressional appropriation bills, rather than its own permanent legislation. In 2016, the Democratic party platform for the first time advocated removing Hyde protections entirely, and in his 2020 presidential campaign, Joe Biden flip-flopped on the issue and went on to support taxpayer-funded abortion as president.

The Next Stage of Abortion Litigation

The prediction of Chief Justice Rehnquist in his *Casey* dissent that the "undue burden" standard is "not built to last" could be realized only through test cases involving abortion legislation. These would reveal the arbitrary and unworkable nature of the new standard adopted in *Casey*.[6]

Significant hurdles arose in the 1990s, burdening these necessary test cases. *Casey* was a great disappointment, signaling that Justice O'Connor would never overturn *Roe*. But in April 1993, in an abortion case from Fargo, North Dakota, she slipped even further in a pro-abortion direction. Joined by Justice Souter, Justice O'Connor increased the burden on states to defend any state abortion law by creating an ambiguous standard for what states had to prove. Henceforth, states could not put an "undue burden" on a "large fraction" of a "relevant" group of women. What constituted a "large fraction"? Which group of women were "relevant"? This "large faction" and "relevant" group test was an additional hurdle not spelled out in *Casey*, and it meant that a majority of justices were returning to the "strict scrutiny" of state abortion legislation that they had rejected 10 months earlier in *Casey*. The Court's majority didn't abandon the "large fraction" test until *June Medical* in 2020, and then only implicitly.

In Illinois, AUL's 20-year abortion-litigation campaign came to an end, as the political obstacles became higher, and the opportunities in other states became more attractive. In January 1993, the *Herbst* case in federal court in Illinois was in settlement negotiations, and AUL's General Counsel Paul Linton was involved in discussions to help Illinois state's attorneys defend the state's abortion clinic regulations. AUL's senior legislative counsel, Denise Mackura, a zealous and creative lawyer, was heading up AUL's state-legislation work in the difficult first year of the

Clinton Administration. She was working on a parental-notice law in Illinois, and AUL met with Governor Jim Edgar's legislative aide in late April. A parental-notice law eventually passed but was burdened by opposing litigation from the ACLU for decades.[7] Despite the many hurdles, between 1993 and 1995, AUL worked with more than one-third of state attorneys general nationwide on pro-life litigation.

In addition to Cunningham's and Forsythe's report, "Is Abortion the 'First Right' for Women?", AUL published one of the first comprehensive legal critiques of the *Casey* decision, Linton's "*Planned Parenthood v. Casey: The Flight from Reason in the Supreme Court*," a major rebuttal of *Casey* and its flawed *stare decisis* analysis. The piece was lauded by Pennsylvania governor Robert Casey at an AUL banquet.[8] The Court's new rationale for abortion—women's "reliance interest" in abortion as a back-up to failed contraception—was a primary focus of criticism.

In September 1993, Cunningham spoke at Wheaton College for the conference "Is There a Future for the Prolife Movement?" along with James Davison Hunter, who was completing his book *Before the Shooting Begins: The Search for Democracy in America's Culture Wars*, and with former surgeon general and AUL board member C. Everett Koop, and bioethicist Nigel Cameron.

AUL's Stand Against Abortion Clinic Violence

In March 1993, when abortionist David Gunn was shot in Pensacola, Florida, AUL drew a clear and public line against clinic violence of any kind. Myrna Gutierrez, a bright, experienced, clear-sighted public-relations expert, was in charge of AUL's public-affairs work at the time and led the creation of a unified statement from AUL and major pro-life organizations condemning the shooting and clinic violence. AUL's public statement drew a strong moral line, effectively marginalizing anyone who defended such violence. After 1994, there were few shootings at U.S. abortion clinics; the last in Colorado Springs in 2015.[9]

Fully Informed Consent for Women

Though *Casey* opened the door for more effective state limits on abortion, virtually every one was aggressively opposed in the courts by abortionists. The most effective in reducing abortions included informed-consent laws based on a woman's right to know, parental notice or consent policies, and limits on public funding of abortion to reduce abortion rates.[10] Fully informed consent has been a pillar of American law for a century. The law imposes a high standard on doctors. Except when it comes to abortion.

For 20 years after *Roe*, the Supreme Court prevented states from enacting detailed informed-consent laws, requiring states to defer to abortion providers, thereby preventing women from receiving detailed information about the nature of abortion, including information about fetal development, and the short-term and long-term risks. Fully informed consent is especially needed in the case of an elective abortion that is not medically-indicated.

AUL made this legislation an immediate priority after *Casey*, conducting an exploratory trip in 1993 to study the effects of Mississippi's informed-consent law. In April 1994, AUL won a huge victory when a federal appeals court upheld the North Dakota informed-consent law in a 2-1 vote. AUL was the only pro-life firm to file an *amicus* brief, and the court largely followed the rationale that AUL had presented. A number of states enacted similar laws between 1993 and 2000, and AUL assisted with several, including Mississippi's. These efforts eventually led to ultrasound informed-consent laws, which include viewing an ultrasound as part of the informed-consent process prior to an elective abortion.

By allowing state informed-consent laws, *Casey* enabled states to highlight a contradiction between abortion on demand and the new "undue burden" standard, the same contradiction that *Casey*'s dissenters had identified: How much persuasive information about the nature of abortion, fetal development, and alternatives—leading to reduced abortions—constitutes an "undue burden" on the "right" to abortion?

AUL believed that enhancing state laws such as these would create a slate of compassionate state policies, effectively reducing abortion rates and encouraging the Court, through the litigation that abortionists would inevitably instigate, to examine its own handiwork and the nature of the abortion industry. Even litigation involving these regulations could reveal the contradictions in *Casey* and the abortion policy the Court had imposed on the nation.

By supporting these laws, AUL worked to enhance the information that women would receive, especially as medical progress revealed the short- and long-term risks of abortion for women. During 1995 and 1996, AUL worked to include information on the association between abortion and breast cancer in informed-consent laws. Attorney John Kindley had demonstrated this relationship in a law review article published in the Wisconsin Law Review in 1998.[11] Later, a 2014 article by Forsythe in the Washington and Lee Law Review cited more than 30 international peer-reviewed medical studies finding an increased risk for breast cancer after abortion.[12]

AUL focused on expanding state regulation of abortion from 1992 to 2000, the desert years of the two terms of the Clinton Administration between *Casey* and *Stenberg v. Carhart*. In the wake of pro-life victories in the 1994 midterms, AUL provided legislative counsel and support to 43 states and Puerto Rico. In August 1995, Forsythe published a *Wall Street Journal* article highlighting the state legislative gains since the *Casey* decision.

Partial-Birth Abortion and Changing Public Opinion

After Republicans took over the House for the first time in 40 years in 1994 and Congressman Newt Gingrich (R-GA) became House Speaker, the National Right to Life Committee launched a brilliant campaign to bring partial-birth abortion to national attention with a federal bill and congressional hearings.

Partial-birth abortion is a procedure in which labor is induced and the child is partially delivered, her skull punctured and emptied, and her body removed piece by piece from the mother. During hearings over the bill, late-term abortionist Warren Hern described the procedure in detail and admitted that abortionists used it. To this day, not one medical professional or institution has highlighted a single instance in which such a procedure is "medically necessary."

During the effort to ban this procedure at the federal level, President Clinton twice vetoed federal partial-birth–abortion prohibitions, once in April 1996 and again in October 1997. But many states, viewing partial-birth abortion as an important issue that demonstrated the scope of *Roe* and humanized the unborn child, began working to pass their own prohibitions on the procedure. Between 1995 and 2000, 31 states passed prohibitions, which were eventually challenged in federal court by Planned Parenthood and the American Civil Liberties Union.[13]

It was fortunate that Nik Nikas joined AUL as general counsel in 1996. Nikas hired two new staff counsels, oversaw AUL's litigation and legislative work, and hired and oversaw summer legal interns. He served as an excellent ambassador for the organization, developing strong relationships with legislators, constituents, and donors, and became a national expert in bioethics law.

In his first year, Nikas came up to speed quickly, contributing to AUL's litigation and legislation work. Under Nikas, AUL became involved in significant litigation in Arizona and around the country, and he personally tried the defense of a pro-life Arizona law against a constitutional challenge.

Nikas arrived just in time to lead AUL's defense of partial-birth abortion bans, and between 1997 and 2000, AUL worked with two-thirds of the state attorneys general nationwide to defend these policies. Nikas assisted with the briefing strategy in *Stenberg v. Carhart*,[14] which dealt with Nebraska's partial-birth ban, and filed a brief for AUL. He advised Nebraska attorney general Don Stenberg and participated in a moot court with Stenberg before his Supreme Court argument in the case.

Unfortunately, the Supreme Court struck down bans on partial-birth abortion enacted by Nebraska and 30 other states in a 5-4 vote. Nevertheless, the decision in *Stenberg* prepared Congress to pass the federal Partial Birth Abortion Ban Act enacted during the presidency of George W. Bush. That law led to the landmark case, *Gonzales v. Carhart*,[15] in which the Court upheld the federal ban and implicitly overturned its 2000 decision in *Stenberg*, again in a 5-4 vote.

In 2000, two additional attorneys joined AUL: Dorinda Bordlee from New Orleans and Denise Burke from San Antonio. Bordlee brought significant legislative experience and Burke brought significant litigation experience—and each has had a lasting, positive effect on pro-life litigation and legislation across the country for more than two decades.

State Courts and Self-Government

In the American constitutional system, the federal Constitution is the supreme law of the land, and states and state judges are bound by the

Supremacy Clause to obey it.[16] But state constitutions independently grant powers to state governments, limit those powers, and protect individual rights. State courts can be as activist in construing their state constitutions as the U.S. Supreme Court was in *Roe*, creating unprecedented constitutional rights and removing abortion and other bioethical issues from the state legislative and executive branches, the branches that are accountable to the people through regular elections.[17] Activist state courts can, in essence, nullify the right to self-government.

Beginning in the late 1960s, several state courts created a "right" to abortion under state constitutions, much as the Supreme Court had done in *Roe*.[18] The same courts applying those decisions could expand them to create a right to assisted suicide.

AUL sought to limit state constitutional rights to abortion and preserve state legislative authority to protect human life. In the 1990s, AUL worked on this issue with the Michigan attorney general[19] and in New York in the abortion-funding case, *Hope v. Perales*.[20] AUL sought to preserve state prohibitions on assisted suicide and prevent courts from creating a state constitutional right to assisted suicide.

To correct these activist decisions, it may be necessary to pass a new state constitutional amendment. AUL supported a Florida constitutional amendment to overturn the activist state court decision that had created a state constitutional right to abortion.

Forsythe and Linton worked with former California State Supreme Court justice William P. Clark to file a brief on behalf of members of the California state legislature in the California Supreme Court in *American Academy of Pediatrics v. Lungren*, an attempt to preserve the California parental-consent for abortion law.[21] Instead, in August 1997, the state Supreme Court delivered a 4-3 decision stripping California voters and their elected representatives of their influence over the vital issue of parental involvement. Efforts to pass a state constitutional amendment to overturn that decision have never been successful.

After the Tennessee Supreme Court created a state constitutional right to abortion, pro-life leaders in Tennessee went through a multi-year process to get a state constitutional amendment on the ballot. State pro-life leaders finally passed Amendment 1 in 2014, enabling Tennessee to pass several pro-life laws in subsequent years.

Pro-life leaders in Alabama and West Virginia followed, with state constitutional amendments in 2018 that denied a right to abortion under the state constitutions. Linton was involved in many state cases, and after leaving AUL in 1995 published *Abortion Under State Constitutions: A State-by-State Analysis*. The third edition was published in 2020, and is a resource for attorneys, judges, and scholars across the nation.

This work in the State Supreme Courts inspired AUL's State Supreme Court Project, led by Denise Burke, who organized and managed the collection and writing of reports on decisions on life issues by the highest court in every state.

The threat from activist State Supreme Courts continues. In 2019, AUL supported state constitutional amendments to overturn Supreme Court decisions in Iowa and Kansas that created a constitutional right to abortion. There remains a compelling need to overturn these decisions and preserve state governmental authority to protect prenatal human beings. Our system is one of constitutional supremacy, not judicial supremacy.

The Battle Over Assisted Suicide in the Supreme Court

The chronically sick, terminally ill, disabled, young, and elderly are all especially vulnerable, and in their vulnerable state can be susceptible to undue influence or coercion from family, friends, or medical professionals.

While the suicide of one lonely person in an apartment in Queens or in the middle of rural America may not have widespread *social* repercussions, the legalization of assisted suicide is radically different. It sends a message. It changes expectations. It resets planning and calculations. It sends a signal to the ill and the vulnerable that society *endorses* their suicide. Legalization repackages assisted suicide as a positive "right." In addition, suicide becomes the cheapest option for the chronically and terminally ill, resetting expectations of families, insurance companies, and the healthcare industry. At $150 for a pill or an injection, suicide will always be the cheapest option.

Numerous studies have examined the negative implications of legaliz-

ing assisted suicide domestically and internationally.[22] The legalization
of assisted suicide is a direct threat to medical standards and the care of
the chronically and terminally ill. Legalization shows society's endorsement. Patients will undoubtedly be pressured to accede to that endorsement. Pressure on patients and on family care-givers from prolonged
chronic or terminal illness is real. "Autonomy" may become indistin-
guishable from isolation and abandonment. Legalization inevitably
changes public expectations. It will influence medical standards and the
insurance market by creating a dramatic imbalance in costs.

If suicide becomes public policy, endorsed by society, endorsed by
courts, endorsed as a "right," and always the cheapest option, what
incentives will remain for providing cancer treatment or palliative care?
What financial incentives will remain for investing in real healthcare or
innovations in technology for treatment and pain management? How
would it affect medical standards in America?

Instead of legalizing assisted suicide, the better alternative is to put the
emphasis on pain relief, training medical professionals in the treatment
of pain, and patient and family education. Americans must resist the
legalization of assisted suicide, at the state and federal level, in order
to preserve respect for individual human lives and maintain the incen-
tive to support the chronically and terminally ill. We must prevent the
disastrous effect it would have on medical and healthcare standards if
we make death the cheapest option.[23]

The battle over assisted suicide at the Supreme Court began in the
1970s and 1980s with the idea of legalizing suicide for those who "suffer." In 1994, the pro–assisted suicide group Compassion in Dying sued
Washington State to invalidate its prohibition on "promoting a suicide
attempt." AUL worked with the National Legal Center for the Medically
Dependent and Disabled on the briefing strategy in three state and federal cases to defeat this campaign for a constitutional "right" to assisted
suicide.

Two years before the Supreme Court issued its landmark cases on
assisted suicide, Linton and Forsythe filed a brief in the Ninth Circuit
in support of the Washington State statute. The opinion by Judge John

Noonan, upholding Washington's statute positively influenced the Supreme Court's decisions.[24]

In 1997, AUL worked with the National Legal Center to convene an *amicus* conference to organize the briefs in the impending assisted-suicide cases: *Vacco v. Quill*[25] from New York and *Washington v. Glucksberg*[26] from Washington State.

In *Vacco*, the Court determined that a prohibition on assisted suicide did not violate the Equal Protection clause, based on the understanding, developed through state medical treatment cases in the 1970s and 1980s, that there was a logical, justified reason for the law to "treat assisted suicide and the refusal of lifesaving treatment differently." The Court in *Glucksberg* ruled that a prohibition on assisted suicide did not violate the Due Process clause. The Supreme Court *unanimously* held that state laws banning assisted suicide without exception do not violate the Fourteenth Amendment.

AUL directly contributed to preventing the constitutionalization of assisted suicide in the quarter century between *Roe* and *Glucksberg* in three distinct ways: the development of legal doctrine in state medical treatment cases in the 1970s and 1980s, which relied on common-law principles and left policy to state legislatures rather than judges; the continued battle to show that *Roe* was incoherent constitutional doctrine inducing the Court not to expand the "right to privacy" and declare a national right to assisted suicide; and the development of research and scholarship of the Duquesne Law Review article, "Suicide: A Constitutional Right?"[27] examining centuries of legal prohibition of suicide, on which the Court relied in *Vacco* and *Glucksberg*.

With its focus on "our Nation's history, legal traditions, and practices," *Glucksberg* left *Roe* weaker, and *Glucksberg*'s standard for unenumerated rights was reaffirmed by the Supreme Court in 2010 in the Second Amendment decision, *McDonald v. City of Chicago*,[28] which left "*Roe*'s doctrinal footings weaker than they were when *Roe* and *Casey* were decided."[29]

Abortion Pills and Their Continuing Risk to Women

A chemical form of attempted abortion has long been a threat to women and unborn children. Professor Joseph Dellapenna has chronicled this long and sorry history in *Dispelling the Myths of Abortion History.* Dellapenna noted that chemical forms of abortion were terribly dangerous to women but were almost always ineffective at producing an abortion until well into the 20th century.[30] It is a myth that there has always been some potion that women took to secretly and effectively obtain an abortion in centuries past.

But population controllers have long hoped to find such a potion, and technology in the late 20th century began to open the door to a relatively effective, less dangerous chemical abortion drug, which began with researchers in France and then came to America.

In 1994, AUL began a multi-year battle to prevent chemical abortion pills from entering the U.S. market and expanding as a method of abortion. But *Roe* controlled the legal outcome, and its contours would allow for the use of a chemical abortifacient, if a "safe and effective" drug, under federal law, came to the market. Money, technology, and testing would determine whether it could be proven "safe and effective" for women.

In February 1995, five years before the Clinton Administration approved the abortifacient RU-486 (mifepristone), AUL, working with the American Association of Pro-Life Obstetricians and Gynecologists (AAPLOG), filed a 106-page "Citizen Petition" with the Food and Drug Administration (FDA) on behalf of AUL and members of Congress, to prevent federal approval of RU-486. RU-486, a name derived from the French pharmaceutical company, Roussel-Uclaf, is actually a two-drug regime. The first, mifepristone (brand name, Mifeprex) counters the natural progesterone that promotes a pregnancy and, in effect, starves the child. The second drug, misoprostol, is a prostaglandin that causes the uterus to contract, provokes heavy bleeding, and expels the prenatal child.

The Petition detailed the likely risks of RU-486 to women and to their unborn children who might subsequently be born alive. AUL asked the FDA to "refuse to approve any New Drug Applications … for RU-486 (mifepristone) for use as a pharmaceutical abortifacient that does not contain adequate evidence that the drug has undergone nonclinical and clinical safety and effectiveness trials."[31] Although it might seem implausible that *any* children might be born alive after their mother took mifepristone and misoprostol, the science would eventually show that doctors could *reverse* the anti-progestin effect of mifepristone before misoprostol is taken with an infusion of progesterone, a technique that doctors have long used with women with low progesterone who want their pregnancies to be successful.[32]

In the final weeks of the Clinton Administration, the FDA approved RU-486 in September 2000 without having obtained necessary data on the impact of the chemical abortion on minors. The FDA circumvented the Pediatric Rule, despite the fact that adolescents would be a key demographic market for abortion pills. Tracking injuries has been difficult ever since. Neither the FDA nor the states adequately track its effects, nor has the Supreme Court, despite its self-appointed role as the national abortion control board. The Clinton FDA imposed slight post-marketing requirements on RU-486 in September 2000, despite the fact that the FDA had side-stepped the law and approved RU-486 for the US market under Subpart H of the FDA Act, which allows "accelerated approval" for drugs that treat "serious or life-threatening illnesses."[33] The FDA requires the reporting of adverse events through its FDA Adverse Event Reporting System (FAERS). For example, the *New York Times* in November 2004 reported that the FDA "has received 676 reports of problems with the drug, including 17 ectopic pregnancies, 72 cases of blood loss so severe that they required transfusions and 7 cases of serious infections." The Obama FDA eliminated some important safety requirements in 2016, including the reporting of adverse events except for death, and the Biden FDA eliminated the in-person administration requirement by doctor in December 2021, which had been in effect since September 2000.

Given the inherent risks, and the inadequate federal oversight, AUL emphasized the need for state safety requirements on chemical abortion in *Defending Life 2012*, with a major survey by AUL staff counsel Anna Franzonello. Once the medical protocol for progesterone infusion to reverse an RU-486 abortion became feasible, AUL wrote a model bill for abortion-pill reverse, based on medical protocols showing the efficacy of prostaglandin to reverse the prostaglandin-starvation effect of mifepristone.

The legal battle over chemical abortion intensified in 2020, when abortion activists sought to take advantage of the expansion of telemedicine during the COVID-19 pandemic to promote chemical abortion. They challenged in federal court the FDA's in-person physician requirement, part of the FDA's Risk Evaluation and Mitigation Strategies (REMS) conditions for chemical abortion.

The federal judge struck down the FDA in-person requirement and issued a *nationwide* injunction against it.[34] The FDA sought a stay from the federal appeals court, which rejected the stay, and the Trump Administration sought a stay from the Supreme Court, which first held the motion for a stay in abeyance, leaving in place the federal judge's decision to strike down the safety regulation.[35]

Thankfully, after the district court declined to reconsider its sweeping injunction, the Supreme Court stayed the injunction on January 12, 2021, restoring the REMS nationwide,[36] a week before the Biden Administration took office.

Working with a coalition of organizations in 2020, AUL wrote a model bill to upgrade state monitoring of chemical-abortion complications and unveiled it with a group of allied organizations in November 2020.

Despite the serious concerns that AUL had at the beginning of the Clinton Administration, the 1990s ended with more pro-life progress than had been anticipated. There were significant defeats at the federal level, with the addition of two pro-*Roe* justices to the Supreme Court and the FDA approval of RU-486, but state pro-life legislation had been strengthened and expanded in key areas. An effort to find a federal constitutional right to assisted suicide had been defeated. And the national abortion rate started its significant decline, due not to any policies under the Clinton or Obama Administrations, but thanks to pro-life work in law and culture.[37]

Chapter 10 Endnotes

1   *See* Clarke D. Forsythe & Donna Harrison, *State Regulation of Chemical Abortion After* Dobbs, 16 LIBERTY U. L. REV. (2022); STAFF OF SUBCOMM. ON CRIM. JUST., DRUG POL'Y, AND HUM. RES. OF THE H. COMM. ON GOV'T REFORM, 109TH CONG., THE FDA AND RU-486: LOWERING THE STANDARD FOR WOMEN'S HEALTH? (Oct. 2006) (hereinafter Souder Committee Report); *RU-486: Demonstrating a Low Standard for Women's Health Before the Subcomm. on Crim. Just., Drug Pol'y, and Hum. Res. of the H. Comm. on Gov't Reform,* 109th Cong. (2006); *A Judicial Watch Special Report: The Clinton RU-486 Files,* JUD. WATCH, INC. (Apr. 26, 2006), *available at* https://www.judicialwatch.org/archive/2006/jw-ru486-report.pdf (uncovering over 9,300 pages of documents).

2   *See, e.g.,* Kristen L. Burge, *When It Rains, It Pours: A Comprehensive Analysis of the Freedom of Choice Act and Its Potential Fallout on Abortion Jurisprudence and Legislation,* 40 CUMB. L. REV. 181 (2010).

3   *See, e.g.,* AMS. UNITED FOR LIFE, *Joint Resolution Opposing the Federal "Freedom of Choice Act" (FOCA), in* DEFENDING LIFE (2009 ed.).

4   *See, contra,* ERIKA BACHIOCHI, THE RIGHTS OF WOMEN: RECLAIMING A LOST VISION (2021).

5   Paige Comstock Cunningham & Clarke D. Forsythe, *Is Abortion the "First Right" for Women? Some Consequences of Legal Abortion, in* ABORTION, MEDICINE AND THE LAW (J. Douglas Butler & David F. Walbert eds., 4th ed. 1992).

6   *See* Clarke D. Forsythe & Rachel N. Morrison, *Stare Decisis, Workability, and* Roe v. Wade: *An Introduction,* 18 Ave Maria L. Rev. 48 (2020).

7   Paul Benjamin Linton, *Long Road to Justice: The Illinois Supreme Court, the Illinois Attorney General, and the Parental Notice of Abortion Act of 1995,* 41 LOY. U. CHI. L.J. 753 (2010).

8   Paul Benjamin Linton, Planned Parenthood v. Casey: *The Flight from Reason in the Supreme Court,* 13 ST. LOUIS U. PUB. L. REV. 15 (1993).

9   *See, e.g.,* Liam Stack, *A Brief History of Deadly Attacks on Abortion Providers,* N.Y. TIMES (Nov. 29, 2015), https://www.nytimes.com/interactive/2015/11/29/us/30abortion-clinic-violence.html; *Anti-abortion Violence,* Wikipedia (May 28, 2022, 4:32 PM), https://en.wikipedia.org/wiki/Anti-abortion_violence; *Colorado Springs Planned Parenthood Shooting,* Wikipedia (Apr. 23, 2022, 3:45 AM), https://en.wikipedia.org/wiki/Colorado_Springs_Planned_Parenthood_shooting; Sarah Frostenson, *40 Years of Attacks on Abortion Clinics, Mapped,* Vox (Dec. 1, 2015, 12:30 PM), https://www.vox.com/2015/12/1/9827886/abortion-clinic-attacks-mapped.

10 *See* New, *Analyzing the Effect of Anti-Abortion U.S. State Legislation in the Post-*Casey *Era, supra* ch. 9 note 20.

11 John Kindley, *The Fit Between the Elements for an Informed Consent Cause of Action and the Scientific Evidence Linking Induced Abortion with Increased Breast Cancer*

Risk, 1998 Wis. L. Rev. 1595 (1998).

12   Clarke D. Forsythe, *The Medical Assumption at the Foundation of* Roe v. Wade *and Its Implications for Women's Health*, 71 Wash. & Lee L. Rev. 827 (2014) (with three appendices citing hundreds of international, peer-reviewed medical studies); *see also* Hush, *supra* ch. 4 note 101 (a 2016 documentary reviewing the international, peer-reviewed medical studies).

13   *Stenberg,* 530 U.S. at 979 (Kennedy, J., dissenting) ("Nebraska and some 30 other states [have passed partial-birth abortion prohibitions].")); *id.* at 983 (Thomas, J., dissenting,) ("[T]he particular procedure at issue in this case, 'partial birth abortion,' so closely borders on infanticide that 30 states have attempted to ban it.").

14   530 U.S. 914. AUL's *amicus curiae* brief is available online. Brief of Amici Curiae Louisiana and Mississippi in Support of Petitioners, *Stenberg*, 530 U.S. 914 (No. 99-830), *available at* https://aul.org/wp-content/uploads/2018/10/2000-Stenberg-v.-Carhart. pdf.

15   550 U.S. 124. AUL's *amicus curiae* brief is available online. Brief of *Amici Curiae* American Association of Pro Life Obstetricians and Gynecologists (AAPLOG), Senator Tom Coburn, M.D., Congressman Charles Boustany, Jr, M.D., Congressman Michael Burgess, M.D., Congressman Phil Gingrey, M.D., Congressman Dave Weldon, M.D., C. Everett Koop, M.D., Edmund D. Pellegrino, M.D. in Support of Petitioner, *Gonzales*, 550 U.S. 124 (No. 05-380), *available at* https://aul.org/wp-content/uploads/2018/10/ GonzalesvCarhart.pdf.

16   *See generally*, Michael Stokes Paulsen & Luke Paulsen, The Constitution: An Introduction (2015) (hereinafter Paulsen & Paulsen, The Constitution).

17   The Kansas and Iowa Supreme Courts did precisely that by creating a right to abortion in their state constitutions. Hodes & Nauser, MDS, P.A. v. Schmidt, 440 P.3d 461 (Kan. 2019); Planned Parenthood of the Heartland v. Reynolds ex rel. State, 915 N.W.2d 206 (Iowa 2018).

18   *See, e.g.*, People v. Belous, 458 P.2d 194 (Cal. 1969), *cert. denied sub nom.* California v. Belous, 397 U.S. 915 (1970).

19   Mahaffey v. Attorney General, 564 N.W.2d 104 (Mich. Ct. App. 1997), *appeal denied*, 616 N.W.2d 168 (Mich. 1998).

20   634 N.E.2d 183 (N.Y. 1994).

21   940 P.2d 797 (Cal. 1997).

22   *See, e.g.*, John Keown, Euthanasia, Ethics and Public Policy: An Argument Against Legalization (2d ed. 2018); Neil M. Gorsuch, The Future of Assisted Suicide and Euthanasia (2006); Clarke D. Forsythe, *The Incentives and Disincentives Created by Legalizing Physician-Assisted Suicide*, 12 St. John's J. Legal Comment. 680 (1997); Yale Kamisar, *Against Assisted Suicide — Even a Very Limited Form*, 72 U. Detroit Mercy L. Rev. 735 (1995).

23   *See generally*, Forsythe, *The Incentives and Disincentives Created by Legalizing Physi-*

cian-Assisted Suicide, supra note 22.

24 Compassion in Dying v. Washington, 49 F. 3d 586 (9th Cir. 1995) (a 2-1 decision, with Judge Noonan writing the majority opinion), *rev'd en banc*, 79 F.3d 790 (9th Cir. 1995), *rev'd and remanded sub nom. Glucksberg*, 521 U.S. 702.

25 521 U.S. 793. AUL's *amicus brief* filed in *Vacco* and *Glucksberg* is available online. Brief *Amicus Curiae* of Members of the New York and Washington State Legislature in Support of Petitioners, *Vacco*, 521 U.S. 793 (No. 95-1858) & *Glucksberg*, 521 U.S. 702 (No. 96-110), *available at* https://aul.org/wp-content/uploads/2018/10/1996-Vacco-v.-Quill.pdf.

26 521 U.S. 702.

27 24 Duquesne L. Rev. 1 (1985).

28 561 U.S. 742.

29 Linton, *Does Stare Decisis Preclude Reconsideration of* Roe v. Wade?, *supra* ch. 4 note 30, at 318. See also Steven G. Calabresi, Substantive Due Process after Gonzales v. Carhart, 106 Mich. L. Rev. 1517 (2008).

30 Dellapenna, Dispelling the Myths, *supra* ch. 1 note 3, at 29–57.

31 Ams. United for Life, *Citizen Petition to the Food and Drug Administration*, The Free Library (Feb. 28, 1995), https://www.thefreelibrary.com/Citizen+Petition+to+the+-Food+and+Drug+Administration.-a095580039. *See also* Donna J. Harrison, Opinion, *Dangerous Medicine*, N.Y. Times (Nov. 19, 2004), https://www.nytimes.com/2004/11/19/opinion/dangerous-medicine.html; Margaret M. Gary & Donna J. Harrison, *Analysis of Severe Adverse Events Related to the Use of Mifepristone as an Abortifacient*, 40 Annals Pharmacotherapy 191 (2006).

32 *See* Forsythe, *State Regulation of Chemical Abortion After Dobbs, supra* note 1.

33 Lars Noah, *A Miscarriage in the Drug Approval Process?: Mifepristone Embroils the FDA in Abortion Politics*, 36 Wake Forest L. Rev. 571 (2001).

34 Am. Coll. of Obstetricians & Gynecologists v. U.S. Food & Drug Admin., 472 F. Supp. 3d 183 (D. Md. 2020). AUL's *amicus curiae* brief is available online. Brief *Amici Curiae* of 102 Members of Congress in Support of Defendant-Appellant FDA and Reversal of the Lower Court, *Am. Coll. of Obstetricians & Gynecologists*, 472 F. Supp. 3d 183 (No. 20-1784), *available at* https://aul.org/wp-content/uploads/2020/11/2020-11-02-ACOG-v-FDA-No-20-1784-Amicus-Brief-of-Members-of-Congress.pdf.

35 Food & Drug Admin. v. Am. Coll. of Obstetricians & Gynecologists, 141 S. Ct. 10 (2020)). Justice Alito dissented from the Court's decision to hold the motion for a stay in abeyance with an opinion joined by Justice Thomas.

36 Food & Drug Admin. v. Am. Coll. of Obstetricians & Gynecologists, 141 S. Ct. 578 (2021).

37 *See* New, *Analyzing the Effect of Anti-Abortion U.S. State Legislation in the Post-Casey Era, supra* ch. 9 note 20.

CHAPTER 11

Expanding the Cause for Life in the States

The election of George W. Bush in 2000 was a welcome relief from the Clinton Administration's aggressive pro-abortion agenda and from the threats that might have been posed had Al Gore become president. The Clinton Administration added two pro-*Roe* justices to the Supreme Court and many to the lower federal courts, but Bush presented the prospect of nominating constitutionalist judges.

Republican control of Congress in 2001 meant the end of the threat of a federal Freedom of Choice Act (FOCA), but the evenly divided Senate made it difficult to approve judges from 2001 to 2002. When Vermont Sen. Jim Jeffords, a Republican, announced in May 2001 that he would become an Independent, it shifted the majority back to Democrats. Republican Sen. Mitch McConnell, with his zealous and disciplined focus on confirming judges and his focus on the "long game," would not become majority leader for another 14 years.

AUL lawyers Clarke Forsythe, Nik Nikas, Denise Burke, and Dorinda Bordlee were immersed in a multi-day strategic planning session on the morning of September 11, 2001, when planes struck the World Trade Center in Manhattan, crashed into the Pentagon, and crashed in Shanksville, Pennsylvania. Burke was called up to active duty with the Air Force for 60 days beginning on October 1, and in late November that was extended through the end of February 2002.

With Senate majority leader Tom Daschle stonewalling progress at the start of 2002, it was all the more important to focus on progress in the states. By 2001, AUL had published 14 types of model state legislation, and it began to reemphasize a nationwide focus on the conscience rights of pro-life doctors, nurses, pharmacists, and medical students, to protect them from employment discrimination. AUL expanded its work with several legislatures and attorneys general in this developing area of law, and helped to develop a legal strategy for giving states the option to use federal money to fund abortion alternatives.

In February 2004, Peter Samuelson, an AUL board member, began a three-year tenure as AUL president, working to expand the group's work and raise its profile. In 2005, AUL published its first "State Report Cards" project, spearheaded by Samuelson, Burke, and Dan McConchie, establishing an objective standard for ranking states from most to least pro-life. During the summer of 2006, Burke spearheaded new amendments to AUL's model legislation ahead of the 2007 state legislative sessions.

It became apparent that *Casey* hadn't settled the abortion issue and that the campaign to overturn *Roe* continued. In a collection of essays entitled, *Back to the Drawing Board*, Forsythe published "Let the People Decide," an analysis of *Casey* and its implications for pro-life strategy.[1] On November 8, 2005, PBS's *Frontline* broadcast, "The Last Abortion Clinic," cast a sympathetic spotlight on the last remaining abortion clinic in Mississippi. The reporters met with the AUL legal team, and the documentary profiled AUL's work in the courts and legislatures to eliminate abortion and protect women's health.

During November 2005, AUL attorneys were interviewed by the *Wall Street Journal* in anticipation of impending arguments in the New Hampshire parental-notice case, *Ayotte v. Planned Parenthood.*[2] AUL provided legal counsel to New Hampshire legislators in drafting the law and was involved in a moot-court session to prepare attorney general and future U.S. Senator Kelly Ayotte for her successful Supreme Court argument. C-SPAN interviewed AUL's attorneys before the argument, held on November 30, 2005, the *Journal* featured AUL's work on the front page on the day of the argument, and AUL attorneys participated in a C-SPAN debate with ACLU attorney Louise Melling before the argument that morning.

In 2005, AUL helped defend U.S. Attorney General John Ashcroft's directive in *Gonzales v. Oregon.*[3] The directive sought to limit the use of drugs under the federal Controlled Substances Act to end the lives of patients. The appeal was argued in early October, just six days after John Roberts was sworn in as Chief Justice. In a 5-3 decision, Justice Kennedy wrote an opinion joining the liberal bloc of Stevens, Souter, Ginsburg, and Breyer. The Court struck down the Ashcroft directive as invalid under the Controlled Substances Act. Roberts, Scalia, and Thomas dissented.

Nikas and Bordlee departed AUL in 2005 and founded the Bioethics Defense Fund (BDF), which spearheads significant bioethical litigation and legislation. AUL and BDF collaborated in 2019 and 2020, when the Louisiana attorney general's office asked Bordlee to manage the *amicus* briefing process in *June Medical Services v. Russo.*

At the end of the Supreme Court term in 2005, Justice O'Connor announced her retirement. President Bush nominated Judge John Roberts of the District of Columbia Court of Appeals to succeed her, but Chief Justice William Rehnquist died on September 3, 2005, just three days before the Roberts confirmation hearings were set to begin. On September 5, Bush nominated Roberts to replace Rehnquist as chief justice. Roberts was confirmed by a 78-22 vote on September 29, a few days before the Court heard arguments in *Gonzales v. Oregon.* Bush next nominated White House counsel Harriet Miers for the O'Connor vacancy, provoking rancor among conservatives and resulting in the withdrawal of her nomination on October 27. Finally, Bush nominated Judge Samuel Alito of the Third Circuit Court of Appeals to fill O'Connor's seat.

The confirmation hearings for Samuel Alito began on January 9, 2006, and he was confirmed on January 31 by a 58-42 vote. With the additions of Roberts and Alito, the balance on the Court had shifted from when it decided *Stenberg* in 2000 to a Court with a more deferential perspective on state abortion limits. This development, along with corresponding political and legislative developments, altered the obstacles and opportunities and encouraged AUL to renew its focus on its strategy to reverse *Roe*.

South Dakota legislators reacted to the Supreme Court confirmations by enacting a prohibition on nearly all abortions in March 2006. Mississippi passed a similar ban. AUL was interviewed in *U.S. News & World Report,* advising caution until Roberts' and Alito's effect on the Court could be determined—in other words, at least until the impending decision on the federal partial-birth abortion ban in *Gonzales v. Carhart.*

On March 13, 2006, Victor Rosenblum died of congestive heart failure at the age of 80 after having devoted his time, talent, and financial resources to AUL for more than 30 years. The *Chicago Tribune* article reporting his death, entitled "Scholar, abortion foe," emphasized that he had worked for decades to overturn *Roe v. Wade.* The *Tribune* reported that, to liberals, Rosenblum was "something of an enigma … an avowed liberal Democrat who skillfully directed court and legislative battles to try to end the legality of abortion."

The *Tribune* noted that Rosenblum had been chairman of the AUL board from 1989 to 1995, after Horan died, and was "part of the movement that is perhaps least noticed, but arguably most effective." Justice Antonin Scalia gave a tribute to Rosenblum at a memorial at Northwestern University Law School on September 29, 2006, saying Rosenblum's character justified calling him a "great man" and that through "his tireless devotion to the pro-life cause" his character "most vividly shone forth." Scalia said that when someone like Rosenblum:

> leaves our midst, I am struck first with a great sense of loss, and then with a great sense of wonder. How does such a man come to be? How have we deserved to have him among us? And will he be followed by others of equal worth? For the sake of our profession, and of our nation, I pray that he will.[4]

AUL's 2007 edition of *Defending Life* featured a tribute to Rosenblum written by Ed Grant, who described him as "a founder of AUL and a chief architect of the strategy to 'fence in' *Roe v. Wade* so as to bring about its ultimate demise."

The day after Rosenblum's March funeral, AUL attorneys began work on an *amicus* brief in *Gonzales v. Carhart*, in defense of the federal Partial-Birth Abortion Ban Act. AUL filed its brief in May 2006 in *Gonzales*, representing the American Association of Pro-Life Obstetricians & Gynecologists (AAPLOG), Sen. Tom Coburn, M.D., and other physician-members of Congress, and Drs. C. Everett Koop and Edmund Pellegrino. AUL cited medical data in support of the law, refuting the claim that partial-birth abortion was ever necessary for a woman's health.

Arguments were held at the Supreme Court on November 8, 2006. The debate over passage of the law had helped to positively shape public opinion, which almost certainly led to the Supreme Court's decision in *Gonzales v. Carhart* in April 2007, a significant victory implicitly overturning the Court's 2000 decision against Nebraska's partial-birth abortion ban in *Stenberg v. Carhart*. The additions of Roberts and Alito had been consequential, though their ultimate effects on the Court's abortion jurisprudence remained to be seen.

In the wake of the victory in *Gonzales*, AUL organized a legal conference in Washington, D.C., to examine the significance of the victory and to plan for the future. David McIntosh served as master of ceremonies, and speakers included Jim Bopp of the National Right to Life Committee and Kellyanne Conway, who spoke on abortion and public opinion.

Transitions in leadership continued with continuity in mission. At the beginning of 2007, Peter Samuelson retired as AUL president after a three-year tenure that boosted AUL's profile, and Forsythe returned as acting president, a role in which he served until the summer of 2008.

AUL suffered a tragic setback in June 2007 when Dan McConchie, vice president and executive director, suffered a serious motorcycle accident. Family and friends were shocked at the first sight of him in the hospital, laid out on a board with his arms spread and strapped down, unconscious, and behind a oxygen mask. By God's grace, he survived, and after months of healing and rehabilitation, he went on to become one of the most famous and effective pro-life lobbyists across the nation over the next eight years. In 2016, McConchie was elected to the state senate in Illinois, where he ultimately became Republican majority leader in 2021.

The Importance of Health and Safety Regulations

Though *Casey* enabled states to enact abortion regulations such as informed-consent measures, the Court virtually shut down clinic health and safety regulations in the states from 1973 to 2000 in a series of cases. AUL highlighted this troubling history in an article by Forsythe and Brad Kehr, "A Roadmap Through the Supreme Court's Back Alley," published by Villanova Law Review in 2012.[5]

However, after 2000, two federal appeals courts began to uphold clinic regulations for the first time. In an opinion by Judge Paul Niemeyer, the Fourth Circuit Court of Appeals upheld South Carolina's laws establishing standards for licensing abortion clinics.[6] The Fifth Circuit likewise upheld Texas's clinic regulations.[7]

That year, AUL counsel Denise Burke, later vice president of legal affairs, and Nik Nikas were both appointed deputy county attorneys, by the Maricopa County attorney's office, to defend Arizona's abortion-clinic regulations, passed in response to the death of Louanne Heron in a Phoenix abortion clinic. The case, *Tucson's Woman's Clinic v. Eden*, was tried in Tucson and then appealed to the U.S. Court of Appeals for the Ninth Circuit in San Francisco, where Burke argued the appeal on December 4, 2003. In June 2004, the Ninth Circuit upheld some of the regulations.[8] The case never reached the Supreme Court.

Tucson's Woman's Clinic was involved in subsequent litigation in 2009 when the abortionists challenged Arizona House Bill 2564, which amended Arizona's abortion laws in July 2009. After leaving AUL and founding the Bioethics Defense Fund (BDF), Nikas was involved in the Arizona litigation, as was AUL chief legal officer Steven Aden during his time at Alliance Defending Freedom prior to joining AUL.

Defending Life

Since AUL's founding, its policy strategy in the states has gone through four basic iterations. First, AUL focused on creating test cases against *Roe* in Illinois and supported abortion legislation from several other states. AUL went national after *Webster* in 1989, which brought greater attention to pro-life work in the states. After 2000, AUL published a growing number of model bills for the states. In 2005 AUL launched state report cards and in 2006 began publishing *Defending Life.*

McConchie and Burke developed the first-ever "AUL State Report Cards" in 2004, rating each state in terms of safety or danger for pregnant mothers and their unborn children. AUL's rankings established objective standards measuring state progress in protecting human life from beginning to end. Eventually, those standards encouraged states and legislators to compete for a higher ranking each year.

In 2006, AUL first published *Defending Life: A State-by-State Legal Guide to Abortion, Bioethics, and the End of Life*, edited by Denise Burke, AUL's vice president and legal director and co-written by Mailee Smith, who worked on the 50-state review and state report cards and wrote a chapter on end-of-life issues in state and federal law. For years, Burke and Smith were the creative minds and engines behind the annual production of *Defending Life*, a state-by-state legal guide to abortion and other bioethical issues.

As president and general counsel between 2004 and 2006, Peter Samuelson championed *Defending Life*, and wrote the introduction to the 2006 and 2007 issues. AUL board member Jeffrey Wright, who had a law degree from Georgetown University and an MBA from Columbia, underwrote the first issue of *Defending Life*, one of many contributions to AUL.

Defending Life 2006 focused on five legislative areas: abortion, protecting the unborn child from violence outside the context of abortion, biotechnology, end-of-life issues and assisted suicide, and rights of conscience for medical professionals. AUL included extensive reviews of the 2005 state-legislative sessions, recommendations for continued work in 2006, model legislation, and AUL's state rankings with analysis of each state. *Defending Life* covered the Court's abortion doctrine, the status of abortion limits, law and bioethics with a particular focus on stem-cell research, and a survey of state and federal laws.

The foreward to the first edition was written by then-Mississippi state senator Alan Nunnelee, who later became a congressman. The issue featured information on the Terri Schiavo case, especially in relation to assisted suicide and healthcare rights of conscience. McConchie and Erin Cox, AUL's creative and devoted communications coordinator, edited, distributed, and promoted the volume. From its first edition, *Defending Life* raised the standard for states and pro-life legislation.

The Roberts Court

The legacy of the Roberts Court continues to develop, shaped for better or worse by Presidential and Senate elections. The worst risks of the *Roe* Court—expanding a vague and ambiguous "right of privacy" to increase judicial power and diminish self-government—are behind us. But it remains possible that elections could reverse that trend over the next decade.

Roberts was first nominated to the U.S. Court of Appeals for the D.C. Circuit in 1992 by President George H.W. Bush, but his nomination was stalled by Democrat Senator Joe Biden, then-chairman of the Senate Judiciary Committee. During the Clinton presidency, Roberts became one of the most accomplished Supreme Court advocates of his generation. When George W. Bush was elected, Roberts was nominated again and confirmed to the D.C. Court of Appeals in 2003.

Roberts had worked in the George H.W. Bush Administration, and the senior Bush, like his son, supported overturning *Roe*. As assistant attorney general in September 1990, Roberts had filed a brief for the solicitor general in *Rust v. Sullivan*,[9] an important case involving limits on federal Title X family-planning funds and limits on pro-abortion counseling at Title X–funded clinics. Roberts argued:

> We continue to believe that *Roe* was wrongly decided and should be overruled. … The Court's conclusions in *Roe* that there is a fundamental right to abortion and that government has no compelling interest in protecting prenatal human life throughout pregnancy find no support in the text, structure, or history of the Constitution.

To support the Title X regulations, Roberts argued that "government need not finance the provision of information about abortion, whether the information is provided in the form of abortion counseling, referral, or advocacy." The Court, in an opinion by Chief Justice Rehnquist, adopted this position 5-4, though it did not heed the administration's request to overturn *Roe* in *Rust*.

Roberts also supported the administration's pro-life position in *Bray v. Alexandria Women's Health Clinic*,[10] that the Ku Klux Klan Act of 1871 did *not* apply to the actions of pro-life protesters. He represented the administration's position in interviews and argued before the Supreme Court. In a majority opinion by Justice Scalia, the Court held that the 1871 Act did not apply to protesters because the opposition to abortion was not "gender-based animus."

In an unprecedented decision in *Ayotte v. Planned Parenthood*,[11] reflecting the strategic savvy of Roberts and his desire for unanimity, the justices unanimously threw out the challenge to the New Hampshire law. The decision was a narrowly written one, penned by Justice O'Connor, the only unanimous decision in an abortion case and the last abortion opinion O'Connor wrote.

The Bush years ended with two new abortion-skeptical justices on the Court and greater movement on the issue at the state level. Replacing O'Connor with Alito shifted the Court's balance, leading to the *Gonzales v. Carhart* decision in 2007, which upheld the federal ban on partial-birth abortion. The growing pro-life momentum in the states would be even more evident during the presidency of Barack Obama. Federalism was vital to the movement's progress.

Chapter 11 Endnotes

1   Clarke D. Forsythe, *Litigation Strategies and Democratic Deliberation: Let the People Decide, in* Back to the Drawing Board: The Future of the Pro-Life Movement (Teresa R. Wagner ed., 2003).

2   546 U.S. 320 (2006). AUL's *amicus curiae* brief is available online. Brief of *Amici Curiae* New Hampshire Representative and HB 763 Sponsor Kathleen Souza, New Hampshire Senators John S. Barnes, Jr., Robert K. Boyce, Robert J. Letourneau, and Sheila Roberge, and New Hampshire Representatives Michael A. Balboni, Peter Batula, David J. Bettencourt, David L. Buhlman, Harriet E. Cady, Paul C. Ingbretson, Daniel C. Itse, Rogers J. Johnson, Phyllis M. Katsakiores, Thomas J. Langlais, Robert J. L'Heureux, Paul Mirski, Richard W. Morris, Sandra J. Reeves, and Robert H. Rowe in Support of Petitioner, *Ayotte*, 546 U.S. 320 (No. 04-1144), *available at* https://aul.org/wp-content/uploads/2018/10/Ayotte.pdf.

3   546 U.S. 243 (2006). AUL's *amicus curiae* brief is available online. Brief of *Amicus Curiae* Americans United for Life in Support of Petitioners, *Gonzales*, 546 U.S. 243 (No. 04-623), *available at* https://aul.org/wp-content/uploads/2018/10/Gonzales-vOregon04-623.pdf.

4   On file with author.

5   Forsythe, *A Road Map Through the Supreme Court's Back Alley, supra* ch. 4 note 1.

6   Greenville Women's Clinic v. Bryant, 222 F.3d 157 (4th Cir. 2000), *cert. denied*, 531 U.S. 1191 (2001); 317 F.3d 357 (4th Cir. 2002), *cert. denied*, 538 U.S. 1008 (2003).

7   Women's Med. Ctr. of N.W. Hous. v. Bell, 248 F.3d 411 (5th Cir. 2001).

8   371 F.3d 1173 (9th Cir. 2004).

9   500 U.S. 173.

10 506 U.S. 263 (1993).

11 546 U.S. 320.

CHAPTER 12

Returning to the Nation's Capital

D uring the 2008 presidential campaign, Charmaine Yoest, who earned a Ph.D. in Politics from the University of Virginia, became president of AUL, during a particularly difficult year.[1] Despite the election and national financial collapse that fall, AUL persevered and flourished under her leadership between 2008 and 2016.

After the 2008 election, Yoest moved AUL to Washington, D.C. The move resulted in the unfortunate loss of committed and talented team members, but it was a strategic move that made sense for AUL's mission over the long-term. Yoest was smart, tough, poised, politically connected, and knew the Washington press corps by name. She was well positioned to be a leading spokeswoman for life in Washington, the best place for AUL during the presidency of Barack Obama. The new headquarters allowed AUL to counter the administration's pro-abortion policies and judicial appointments, including Supreme Court nominations.

Fighting the Freedom of Choice Act (FOCA)

One of the first challenges from the new administration was the federal Freedom of Choice Act (FOCA). It would have been much better for President Obama, the cause of civil rights, and the country if, as the first African-American president, he had governed from the middle. He could have adopted Bill Clinton's rhetoric of wanting abortion to be "safe, legal, and rare," acknowledging that abortion wasn't a positive good but something to be avoided and limited. Instead, President Obama endorsed Planned Parenthood, the largest abortion provider in the U.S., and its agenda as a presidential candidate, and he promised in July 2007 and again in 2008 that, as one of his first acts, he would sign FOCA, then pending in the 110th Congress as S.1173.[2]

FOCA aimed to erase pro-life legislative gains made at the state level in the wake of *Roe*. By elevating abortion to the status of a "fundamental right" and prohibiting interference with or discrimination against abortion, FOCA would have nullified laws limiting abortion practice to physicians, informed-consent laws, waiting periods, parental consent and notification laws, health-and-safety regulations for abortion clinics, prohibitions on partial-birth abortion, limits on abortion after fetal viability, and conscience protections for medical professionals. And FOCA would have compelled public-funding of abortion.

Notably, pro-abortion groups did not deny that FOCA would have an immense effect on the country. Planned Parenthood declared that "FOCA will supersede anti-choice laws that restrict the right to choose, including laws that prohibit the public funding of abortions for poor women or counseling and referrals for abortions. Additionally, FOCA will prohibit onerous restrictions on a woman's right to choose, such as mandated delays and targeted and medically unnecessary regulations." "Medically unnecessary," in abortion law, means whatever regulations an abortionist deems "unnecessary."

During the transition, Planned Parenthood and other abortion-activism groups published marching orders for the incoming administration, a 55-page memorandum posted on the transition team's website, change.

gov, with goals and objectives for promoting abortion—the foremost of which was FOCA.

These were tragic developments for pro-life Americans, who looked to the civil-rights movement for inspiration and supported human rights for all Americans—including the 300,000 black unborn children killed every year by abortion—who were created equal and endowed by their Creator with unalienable rights.

With FOCA pending in Congress and the threat of candidate Barack Obama's promise to support it, Dan McConchie, AUL vice president of government affairs, launched AUL's online campaign to "Fight FOCA" in 2008.

Those radical gestures drove a wedge between President Obama and the pro-life movement and, more important, public opinion. At the start of 2009, the cause for life faced formidable challenges, including the inauguration of a president whose first priority was to sign FOCA and the most aggressive pro-abortion agenda the movement had ever encountered from a presidential administration. The country was suffering from a recession, and Americans faced an uncertain financial future. Approaching 36 years of legalized abortion on demand, pro-life Americans were discouraged.

Despite these challenges, Yoest supported an aggressive anti-FOCA campaign that significantly energized the cause for life. The "Fight FOCA" petition drive collected 700,000 signatures. Only when Republicans regained the majority in the U.S. House in the 2010 elections did the threat of FOCA temporarily recede. But since the 2020 elections, with Joe Biden in the White House and Democrats controlling Congress, the threat of FOCA has returned in the form of the so-called Women's Health Protection Act (H.R. 3755).

Public Education and Media

One of the hallmarks of Yoest's tenure at AUL was ramping up the group's media presence, and Yoest appeared on national news programs regularly. After the nomination of Elena Kagan to the Supreme Court, the *New York Times* published a piece analyzing AUL's influence in helping states pass abortion limits in 2010. The eleven states that passed abortion limits before the 2010 midterms were categorized as "an unusually high number of victories." In November 2011, Fred Barnes in the *Weekly Standard* chronicled the "unheralded gains of the pro-life movement," featuring Yoest and citing numerous examples of progress.

The Ed Show on MSNBC in July 2013 noted that "the rash of anti-abortion legislation sweeping the country isn't a coincidence. It can be traced back to one group—Americans United for Life, a legal team that has been involved in every abortion related case before the US Supreme Court since *Roe v. Wade*." In July 2015, *The Atlantic* profiled Yoest and AUL in an article by Olga Khazan entitled, "Planning the End of Abortions."

U.S. Supreme Court Nominations

When President Obama was inaugurated, he was determined to fulfill his promise to Planned Parenthood and appoint pro-abortion justices, which he did with Sotomayor and Kagan. When David Souter retired in the spring of 2009, Obama nominated Sotomayor, a federal-appeals court judge in Manhattan. After studying her record, including her board membership on a New York City legal organization showing support for abortion on demand, AUL mounted a full-scale campaign against the nomination, and Yoest testified against the nomination before the Senate Judiciary Committee on July 13, 2009. Nevertheless, she was confirmed on August 6, 2009. A year later, after pro-abortion Justice John Paul Stevens retired, Obama nominated U.S. Solicitor General Elena Kagan to replace him. AUL studied Kagan's record, including her authorship as a White House lawyer of an official policy statement in 1997 on partial-birth abortion for the American College of Obstetricians and Gynecologists (ACOG). AUL opposed Kagan's nomination and filed an extensive report in July 2010 against the nomination with the U.S. Senate. Yoest testified against the Kagan nomination before the Senate Judiciary Committee. Without the presidencies of Clinton and Obama, there would be no pro-*Roe* justices on the Court in 2022.

Abortion and Rationing in the Affordable Care Act

Healthcare was another early priority for Yoest and AUL. The best possible healthcare system helps protect human lives and promotes human flourishing and familial wellbeing, but when a presidential administration attempts to overhaul and control the entire healthcare system through one single law, the federal government amasses tremendous power over people's lives, the complexity is overwhelming, and the implications are vast and uncertain.

In 2009 and 2010, AUL opposed the Affordable Care Act (ACA) in Congress, *unless* it contained three pro-life protections: 1) it would have to expressly endorse the Hyde Amendment and apply "Hyde protections" throughout the ACA, because of the ACA's threat to directly and substantially increase federal support for abortion and the abortion industry, 2) it would have to protect the conscience rights of patients, doctors, and medical professionals, and 3) it would have to protect Americans against the rationing of healthcare as a budgetary consideration.

AUL was a leading voice in opposition to pro-abortion healthcare and launched a national grassroots campaign—Real Health Care Respects Life—to fight the abortion mandate in the ACA. In July and September of 2009, Yoest and AUL counsel Mary Harned, who would later work on Capitol Hill, met at the White House with the administration's policy advisers, urging them to amend the bill.[3]

The ACA's advocates claimed that the ACA would not fund abortion. Nevertheless, AUL's legal team, including senior vice president and senior counsel Bill Saunders, with staff counsels Anna Franzonello and Mary Harned, exposed this misinformation with analysis showing how the proposed "reform" would mandate abortion coverage—as well as violate providers' rights of conscience and threaten the ill, disabled, and elderly with denial of essential care.[4]

In March 2010, Yoest published a *Wall Street Journal* op-ed noting that the administration was willing to do anything to pass healthcare reform "except a ban on federal funding for abortion," despite the president's promise in September 2009 that "no federal dollars will be used to fund abortions, and federal conscience laws will remain in place."

AUL worked with Congressmen Bart Stupak (D-MI) and Joe Pitts (R-PA) on the Stupak-Pitts Amendment, which contained Hyde Amendment language and passed in the House. Unfortunately, President Obama disavowed the language in November of that year, and presidential advisers talked around the language, unwilling to act to ensure that abortion funding was excluded from the law.

When the ACA passed in March 2010, AUL launched a campaign to ensure that abortion would be excluded from the state exchanges created by the ACA. Section 1303 of the ACA stated that "[a] state may elect to prohibit abortion coverage in qualified health plans offered through an Exchange in such State if such State enacts a law to provide for such a prohibition."

As Sarah Kliff noted in *Newsweek* two weeks after the passage of the ACA, AUL "[led] the charge" by creating a "federal-abortion-mandate-opt-out-act" for states to pass, enabling states to opt-out of abortion funding. Missouri and Tennessee quickly introduced a version of AUL's "opt-out bill," and AUL was in touch with legislators and allies in 35 other states. At least 25 states eventually passed an opt-out amendment.

The ACA also threatened to use tax dollars for abortifacients, or abortion-inducing drugs, and overriding the conscientious objection of millions of Americans. The ACA required that non-grandfathered private health-insurance plans "provide coverage for and shall not impose any cost sharing requirements for … preventive care and screenings [for women]." The administration's regulatory mandate of August 1, 2011, implementing this provision, required these plans to fully cover, without a copay, all drugs and devices labeled by the Food and Drug Administration (FDA) as "contraception." But the FDA's definition of "emergency contraception" included drugs and devices with known post-fertilization mechanisms of action—in other words, drugs and devices that were really abortifacients and could end the life of an unborn child.[5] Forcing employers and employees to cooperate with the government in providing such drugs was an obvious violation of conscience.

When the Obama Administration's Department of Health and Human Services (HHS) issued the "contraception/abortion mandate" through a final rule in July 2013 and a so-called accommodation in August 2014, treating abortifacients as a "preventive service," AUL defended the conscience rights of those who objected to providing abortifacients through their healthcare program.

After the enactment of the ACA, the FDA approved the drug Ulipristal Acetate (*ella*) as an emergency contraceptive in 2010. The chemical makeup of *ella* is different from Plan B and similar to the abortion drug RU-486, or mifepristone, meaning that though it was marketed as a contraceptive, *ella* functions like mifepristone by blocking progesterone and ending a pregnancy after conception. The drug's effect as an abortifacient was acknowledged during the FDA advisory panel meeting.[6]

HHS therefore had mandated coverage for life-ending drugs and devices. This decision contradicted a colloquy between Sens. Barbara Mikulski (D-MD) and Bob Casey Jr. (D-PA) during Senate debate in December 2009, when Mikulski said that the ACA "does not cover abortion. Abortion has never been defined as a *preventive* service."[7] But, after the ACA passed, the federal agency defined it as such.[8]

In more than 20 briefs supporting numerous parties at the Supreme Court in 2013, 2014, and 2015, AUL represented eight national medical organizations to oppose the HHS mandate, including the Association of American Physicians and Surgeons (AAPS), American Association of Pro-Life Obstetricians & Gynecologists, Christian Medical Association, Catholic Medical Association, Physicians for Life, National Association of Pro Life Nurses, National Association of Catholics Nurses-USA, and the National Catholic Bioethics Center, and corporations such as Drury Inns.

AUL's briefs presented the medical evidence that the life of a human being begins at conception and thus that numerous Americans were justifiably concerned that these "contraceptive" mandates violated their conscience.[9] AUL counsel Mailee Smith led the effort to write and file these briefs, along with colleagues Denise Burke, Anna Paprocki, Mary Harned, and AUL general counsel Ovide Lamontagne. They summarized the scientific evidence "that a new, distinct human organism comes into existence during the process of fertilization—at the moment of sperm-egg fusion—and before implantation of the already-developing embryo into the uterine wall."[10]

Their work illustrated that the mandate required the AAPS and its members to arrange for coverage for *ella* contrary to religion and conscience, because *ella* and other drugs and devices had a "life-ending mechanism of action." They were "threatened with onerous fines if they follow their religious and conscientious beliefs," and while the mandate alleged accommodation, it "substantially burden[ed] religious beliefs" as the Supreme Court recognized in *Burwell v. Hobby Lobby* in 2014, in which AUL filed a brief.[11] That fight continued in 2020 with the appeal of the Little Sisters of the Poor before the U.S. Supreme Court.[12]

This campaign exemplified the skill with which Lamontagne managed AUL's work and expanded the group's reach. He joined AUL in May 2013 and served as general counsel until the end of 2015. Having run for public office in New Hampshire and been an accomplished litigator, Lamontagne brought an invaluable perspective to AUL's work and took to government relations with Congress with great skill. He worked to meld AUL's legal and legislative work, managing the talented legal team with skill, confidence, and understanding.

Twenty Week Limits on Abortion.

Meanwhile, AUL's strategy in the states emphasized legislative limits that would reduce abortions, increase legal protection for the unborn child from conception outside the context of abortion, decrease the supply and demand of abortion, and highlight abortion's negative impact on women.

The Court's 2007 decision in *Gonzales v. Carhart*, upholding the federal Partial-Birth Abortion Ban Act, suggested that a majority of the justices were concerned about late-term abortions. The 2010 midterms elections—which significantly increased the number of states with pro-life legislative majorities—were a great boost to AUL's work. *Gonzales* and the elections changed the landscape in the states, and AUL mounted a renewed effort to support a 20-week limit on abortion. In 2010, Nebraska led the nation by becoming the first state to enact a 20-week limit.

While the policy would protect prenatal human beings from late-term abortions, the limit was also needed to protect maternal health, since a widely-accepted medical study found a substantially higher maternal-mortality rate from abortions after 20 weeks of pregnancy.[13] Twenty-week limits were entirely consistent with the Court's opinion in *Roe* and its declarations that states had important interests in protecting fetal life and maternal health *before viability*.

However, these laws challenged a dogmatic adherence to the Supreme Court's arbitrary viability rule, which the Court said repeatedly in *Casey* was "essential" to *Roe*.[14] The 20-week limit highlighted errors and contradictions in *Roe* and the lack of reason in the viability rule.

In January 2012, Forsythe testified in support of a 20-week limit before an Arizona Senate Committee. Arizona passed the law in July 2012, and it was immediately challenged in federal court. The federal judge in Tucson, after carefully examining the facts and the law, upheld the 20-week limit as constitutional,[15] but the Ninth Circuit struck it down with a rigid application of the viability rule.[16] That same court struck down Idaho's 20-week limit.

AUL joined with the Alliance Defense Fund—including, at that time, attorneys Catherine Glenn Foster and Steven Aden—to support Arizona's appeal to the Supreme Court in *Horne v. Isaacson*. Unfortunately, the Court refused to hear Arizona's appeal on January 13, 2014.[17] By May 2020, 23 states had passed prohibitions on abortion between 18 and 20 weeks, and these laws have been enforced in most of those states because they were not challenged in court.

The Court's denial of review in *Horne* was a great disappointment, revealing the extreme scope of the abortion license in the U.S.: even a 20-week limit was not permissible under *Roe*.

Roe the Root, *Casey* the Branch

June 2012 marked the 20th anniversary of the Supreme Court's decision in *Casey*, which reaffirmed the result in *Roe*. AUL hosted a conference at the National Press Club in Washington D.C. in May 2012, "From *Planned Parenthood v. Casey* to the 'Day After *Roe*': *Casey*'s Impact on Abortion Jurisprudence." The conference featured Yoest, Saunders, Forsythe, Professor Michael Stokes Paulsen, and legal scholar Erika Bachiochi.

In opening remarks, Saunders outlined lessons from the "judicial disaster" of *Casey*. Saunders, a Harvard Law School graduate, bolstered AUL's scholarship and its international work in Central America while at AUL. In 2016, he left AUL to become director of the program in human rights at the Institute for Human Ecology at The Catholic University of America.

Bachiochi, later a visiting fellow at Harvard Law School, who had debunked equal-protection arguments for abortion rights in the Harvard

Journal of Law & Public Policy, addressed how abortion rights have harmed the cause of women's rights:

> Rather than make women more equal to men, constitutionaliz-
> ing the right to abortion, as the court did in *Roe*, has relieved
> men of the mutual responsibilities that accompany sex, and
> so has upended the duties of care for dependent children that
> fathers ought equally to share.[18]

Paulsen laid out why *Casey* was "the worst constitutional decision of all time," as he had done in a 2003 article in the Notre Dame Law Review.[19]

The *Casey* decision did not "reaffirm" *Roe* on the merits. In fact, the *Casey* court could not explain why any right to abortion was rooted in the Constitution or the nation's laws and traditions. Like *Roe*, *Casey* remains unsettled due to continuing political and legislative agitation. As now-Justice Amy Coney Barrett noted in a 2013 law review article, "*Casey* shows that the Court is quite incapable of transforming prece- dent into superprecedent by *ipse dixit*."[20]

Casey also opened the door to a number of life-saving laws since 1992, which has kept *Roe* unsettled, and reduced the number of abortions.[21] The AUL conference publication outlined the progress made since *Casey* in passing informed-consent laws, parental-involvement laws, ultrasound requirements, abortion-clinic regulations, and other limits.

Throughout 2012, Forsythe was finishing his book *Abuse of Discretion: The Inside Story of Roe v. Wade*, sponsored by AUL. Forsythe wrote the book in order to address the questions raised by *Roe*: Why did the Court issue such a sweeping and controversial decision that was subject to well-deserved legal and scholarly criticism? What did the Court know about abortion at the time? What kind of evidence did the Court have before it? The book focused on the two years of deliberations inside the Court in 1971 and 1972 leading up to the decision and highlighted the private papers of eight of the nine justices who had voted in *Roe*. These papers present a different history of the deliberations than the American public had been told, and they confirm the arbitrary nature of the Court's deliberations that lead to the *Roe* decision.

Kermit Gosnell and the Scandal of Abortion

One of the enduring problems of *Roe* is that the Court created a public-health vacuum by striking down the abortion laws of every state. The scandals in abortion clinics have been unceasing, as AUL has documented in numerous books, articles, and briefs. More than three years before Dr. Kermit Gosnell was convicted of several crimes—including manslaughter—AUL reported on the significance of the two raids of Gosnell's abortion clinic in Philadelphia in February 2010.

AUL's Denise Burke pointed out that the federal agents "found 'deplorable and unsanitary' conditions including blood on the floors ... and that the clinic's director, Dr. Kermit Gosnell ... sanctioned the performance of gynecological exams and the administration of controlled substances and prescription medication by non-licensed staff at the clinic." Burke noted that Gosnell's clinic was "not an aberration" and that the objective of clinic regulations was to "safeguard against unsanitary conditions, inferior equipment, and the employment of unsuitable and untrained personnel. They are also intended to put an end to substandard medical practices that injure and kill untold numbers of women each year."

Burke reported that "AUL has worked to remedy the epidemic of substandard conditions at the nation's abortion clinics, advocating for medically-appropriate and comprehensive health and safety regulations at abortion clinics and defending such laws when they are challenged in court by abortion providers more concerned with plying their trade without legitimate oversight and protecting their 'bottom-line' than with women's health and safety."

She also developed AUL's "Abortion Patients' Enhanced Safety Act," mandating that abortion clinics meet the same exacting standards as ambulatory surgical clinics, and AUL's "Women's Health Protection Act," prescribing minimum health-and-safety regulations.

Gosnell's trial in 2013 was a reminder of the back-alley conditions created by *Roe*.[22] The investigation and grand-jury report in his case confirmed several pro-life criticisms of *Roe* and of legalized abortion.

After the guilty verdict, Yoest appeared on Fox News' "Special Report" to discuss the significance of the case. Year by year, state by state, these types of problems continued, as AUL went on to document in *Unsafe* and other publications.

The Battle Against Planned Parenthood and the Abortion Industry

Under Yoest's leadership, AUL intensified its efforts to defund the abortion industry and highlight the role of Planned Parenthood as the nation's largest abortion provider. AUL had battled Planned Parenthood and other abortion providers in court since *Roe* and in the legislatures since the 1970s.

For years, Planned Parenthood has been an opponent of any abortion limits at the state level, and the group has instigated *hundreds* of lawsuits against state abortion laws in court. Those cases are often quite consequential: Planned Parenthood was the lead plaintiff in *Planned Parenthood v. Danforth* (1976) and *Planned Parenthood v. Casey* (1992), two landmark Supreme Court cases among many.

With an annual budget of more than $1 billion, Planned Parenthood has become the face of the abortion industry. Over time, the group has accumulated a greater "market share" of the annual number of abortions—somewhere between one-half and one-third of all abortions in the U.S. each year are done by Planned Parenthood—which was reflected in the group's support for Affordable Care Act and federally-funded abortion.

In July 2011, AUL published the first of three major reports exposing Planned Parenthood. The first, "The Case for Investigating Planned Parenthood: AUL Looks Behind the Closed Doors of the Nation's Largest Abortion Provider," was a 174-page report based on a review of 20 years of Planned Parenthood's reports and financial statements by AUL counsel Anna Franzonello and others. The report highlighted and documented eight major reasons that Congress should investigate Planned Parenthood and its use of hundreds of millions of federal dollars annually. Among other issues, AUL highlighted that the group's use of telemedicine to distribute mifepristone violated the FDA-approved protocol (at that time) for dispensing the drug: "a 'virtual visit' cannot accurately assess the gestational age or rule out ectopic pregnancy."[23]

In October 2012, AUL published its second major report, "The Planned Parenthood Exhibits: The Continuing Case for Investigating the Nation's Largest Abortion Provider." This documented the Obama Administration's loyalty to Planned Parenthood, which included withholding federal funds in order to coerce states into funding Planned Parenthood. It also discredited the claim that "abortion is only 3 percent of Planned Parenthood's services." That year's edition of *Defending Life 2012* also focused on Planned Parenthood and the abortion industry.

In June 2015, AUL published its third investigative report, a 41-page analysis, *"The New Leviathan: The Mega-Center Report, How Planned Parenthood Became Abortion, Inc."*[24]

A month later, pro-life activists launched a series of investigations into Planned Parenthood's practices of harvesting and selling fetal organs from aborted unborn children. The Center for Medical Progress (CMP) released the first of ten damaging videos involving Planned Parenthood's illegal profiting of aborted infants' organs.

Two months later, Yoest testified before the U.S. House Subcommittee on Health of the Committee on Energy and Commerce in favor of ending all taxpayer funding for Planned Parenthood in the wake of the videos.

AUL counsel Mary Harned moved to Capitol Hill in 2016 to join the *House Select Investigative Panel on Infant Lives of the House Energy & Commerce Committee*, which published a final report of more than 400 pages on December 30, 2016.[25] The report provided a thorough analysis of the ways in which Planned Parenthood affiliates had allegedly violated federal laws by its practice of fetal-tissue harvesting. The report provided the basis for the Senate Judiciary Committee to make eight criminal referrals to the Department of Justice and the FBI in December 2016.[26]

'Unsafe' and the Scandal of the Abortion Industry

In *Roe*, the Supreme Court created a "back alley" of sorts when it came to abortion, striking down every state law restricting abortion and creating a public-health vacuum that even Justice Harry Blackmun anticipated. The Court has perpetuated this state of affairs year after year in a series of cases that have invalidated state efforts to enforce health-and-safety regulations, including *Whole Woman's Health v. Hellerstedt*[27] in 2016 and *June Medical Services v. Russo* in 2020.[28]

To shine a spotlight on this continuing problem, and to show that the Court had ignored the problem entirely in *Whole Woman's Health*, AUL released the first edition of *Unsafe: How the Public Health Crisis in America's Abortion Clinics Endangers Women*, written by Denise Burke. Published in December 2016, the 204-page report and 235-page appendix told the stories of several women who were injured during an abortion procedure or died as a result of one. *Unsafe* found that 227 abortion providers in 32 states had been cited for more than 1,400 health-and-safety deficiencies between 2008 and 2016.

Unsafe exposed the tragic legacy of the Court's abortion doctrine and its inability to perform its self-appointed role as the national abortion control board, which it had just reaffirmed in *Whole Woman's Health*, striking down Texas' requirement that abortionists be credentialed and able to admit women to a local hospital if they suffered complications. *Unsafe* was intended to inspire state legislators to enact regulations and to serve as a rebuke to the Supreme Court's tragic decision to strike down the Texas admitting-privileges law.[29]

Unsafe was necessary because the Court had created an unregulated abortion industry. The federal government likely lacked the constitutional authority to step in, and the Court had prevented the states from doing it instead. No centralized federal agency regulates abortion clinics, and regulation in many states is inconsistent, haphazard, or non-existent.

During the summer of 2016, Regina (Luczyszyn) Maitlen served as an AUL legal fellow while a student at Temple University's Beasley School of Law. Maitlen reviewed abortion-facility reports and incidents state-by-state for *Unsafe*. The project was vast in scope, as she described the current difficulties of verifying abortion clinics' safety records:

> It was very important to the legitimacy of *Unsafe* to use verified sources such as public health reports and news stories. The public health data involved an official state inspection of the

facilities to determine what health code protections were violated. These official documents demonstrated how unsanitary clinics were and how supplies were often expired. There were some facilities that were repeat offenders with many violations. Reviewing the documents only bolstered our conviction that these clinics and the industry were not focused on the wellbeing of women.

I started with an interactive map online that listed each clinic in every state. I would then go to each state's public health website and try to obtain the documentation for clinic inspections. Some states required a public request (under the Freedom of Information Act (FOIA)) for the documentation in each case.

While a few states are very good at coordinating inspections, most rarely inspected the clinics. If there was no governmental record of violations, I would use other resources such as news stories or medical provider records to obtain information about specific clinics. It was very evident that neutral sources rarely address clinic conditions. In fact, clinics have worked to prevent the creation of a public record. They have strategically contracted with private first responders to ensure there is no public record. Members of the public often stand outside clinics and obtain video footage of the ambulances arriving at the facilities to transfer women to hospitals who are suffering distress from abortions. It is clear there are gaps in the inspections and the data reported to state entities.

It was quite evident that the reality of these clinic conditions is hidden in the depths of databases that hardly anyone looks at or frankly can even find. A woman can quickly find a restaurant inspection report with a quick search but would need to perform significant research to verify the safety record of an abortion clinic.

This is the public-health vacuum that the Court created in *Roe* and has perpetuated through its decisions, including *Whole Woman's Health* and *June Medical.*

A second edition of *Unsafe* was published in 2018. A third, expanded edition—with research and writing assistance from AUL legal fellow Amanda Stirone Mansfield—was published at the end of 2020. The latest edition came six months after the Court's decision in *June Medical Services,* in which five justices struck down Louisiana's laws. As Justice Alito illustrated in his dissent, Louisiana's policies were similar to those in Texas struck down in *Whole Woman's Health* but different in structure and scope.[30]

With major media regularly assisting the abortion industry in maintaining its secrecy, the lack of a federal law requiring abortion clinics to report complications or deaths, and the lack of a coherent national system of regulation, it remains necessary for AUL and others to investigate and report on the scandalous, dangerous practices of the abortion industry.

AUL's Mother-Child Vision

AUL's founding was animated in significant part by the negative effects that abortion has on women. There are two victims of abortion: the mother and child. Early feminist leaders such as Susan B. Anthony recognized that fact long before *Roe.*[31] From the beginning, AUL's leaders were concerned about the risks to women in addition to the violence against the unborn child.

AUL has a long history of consistent attention to this problem. Horan's 1971 brief in *Roe* and *Doe* presented the medical information existing at the time. After *Abortion and Social Justice* in 1973, AUL continued to cover the developing medical data on the risks to women. In 1978, AUL cosponsored a national conference on "The Psychological Aspects of Abortion," later published as a book in 1979 by University Publications of America and edited by former AUL executive director David Mall. In 1981, AUL published *New Perspectives on Human Abortion,* which included data on maternal mortality from abortion.

The focus on the negative effects of abortion has always been an essential part of the public argument against abortion and for protective legislation. The ethical principle of informed consent requires that women be fully informed of the risks of abortion. The evidence that abortion harms women became even more important when the Court in *Casey* allowed the states to enact informed-consent laws for abortion.

When the Court threw out the original rationale for the "abortion right" and adopted a new rationale—that women rely on abortion and need it for equal opportunity—the need for accurate and comprehensive data on the risks became more acute. In 2014, law professor Richard Myers observed that "this focus on equality" in contemporary Court decisions on abortion "suggests the importance of pro-life efforts to focus on and to prevent the harms to women from abortion."[32]

To memorialize the 30th anniversary of *Roe* in 2003, AUL cosponsored symposia on the ways abortion harms women, one in November 2002 in Washington, D.C., and another in January 2003 at Boston College Law School. Some of the papers from these symposia were published in 2004 in *The Cost of "Choice": Women Evaluate Abortion's Impact*, edited by Erika Bachiochi.[33]

During her time as AUL president, Yoest drew attention to the negative effects of abortion. Shortly after becoming president, she was diagnosed with breast cancer, and as a breast-cancer survivor, she discussed the need for reliable data, informed consent, and the dissemination of medical research to women.

At the time of *Roe*, there was no national system for collecting or reporting abortion data, and none exists today. Congress has never created one, and, under *NFIB v. Sebelius*,[34] Congress' authority to do so is doubtful unless attached to federal funding, which should be prevented for abortion.

Consequently, it has been necessary to look to public-health data from international sources. By 2014, there were nearly 33 international peer-reviewed studies finding an increased risk of breast cancer after abortion, 100 finding an increased risk of mental trauma after abortion, and more than 140 finding an increased risk of pre-term birth after abortion.[35]

Unfortunately, the U.S. today, still has no functional, reliable national system of abortion-data collection, a tremendous advantage to abortionists, who create their own statistics and produce their own reports proclaiming the safety of abortion, repeated by allies in the media. Analyzing accurate data about the risks of abortion is necessary to assess the risks to women, to present evidence for crafting public policy, to help courts properly apply the Court's abortion decisions, and enable scholars to accurately evaluate the legacy of the Court's abortion doctrine.

Because the U.S. has no functional system, international abortion data is critical for public education. Scandinavian countries, such as Finland and Denmark, have abortion registries because the countries pay for abortions and count them—abortions therefore become part of a woman's general medical history.

Abortion and Pregnancy Discrimination

The legalization of abortion nationwide spurred workplace discrimination against pregnant women. The "right" to abortion had unintended consequences the justices never imagined, due in large part to the lack of any evidentiary record in *Roe*.[36] The "liberty" put the burden squarely and directly on women alone to deal with an unintended pregnancy. Once the Court had created this right, employers expected women to use it, and some were not sympathetic when women chose not to.

Unfortunately, *Roe* and the right to abortion diminished the need for cultural support for changes in the workplace that might assist women in balancing work and family.[37] Some employers believed that pregnancy was inconvenient for the workplace and that women, with the right to abortion, had two choices—abort or lose their job. Members of Congress realized this problem within three years, and pro-life leaders and organizations supported the passage of the federal Pregnancy Discrimination Act (PDA), which was passed by pro-life Democrats and Republicans in October 1978.

In September 2014, AUL worked with a coalition of 23 pro-life organizations to file an *amicus* brief at the Supreme Court on behalf of Peggy Young in *Young v. United Parcel Service, Inc.*, to support a *broad interpretation* of the PDA, requiring employers to provide pregnant women with the same accommodations they afford to other employees with similar ability or inability to work.

The lower court erred by holding that the PDA allows employers to treat pregnant women as poorly as they treat their least-accommodated workers rather than requiring them to treat pregnant women as well as they treat their best-accommodated workers. In March 2015, the Supreme Court issued a narrow but favorable ruling for Young in a 6-3 decision, with Roberts and Alito joining the majority.[38] Alito's opinion— concurring in the judgment but offering a clearer rationale than Breyer's majority opinion—best captured the reasoning in the coalition's brief for a generous reading of the federal PDA in favor of pregnant employees. Young subsequently settled with UPS.

This is one of many examples in which AUL has worked with a network of allies with diverse expertise to achieve objectives in law and policy. The cause for life in the U.S. has flourished since the 1990s as a result of the proliferation and growth of conservative and pro-life organizations with complementary missions and special expertise that enhance the cause. Some key groups and partners in that project have been the American Association of Pro-Life Obstetricians and Gynecologists (AAPLOG), the Susan B. Anthony List, Students for Life, the American Center of Law and Justice, Alliance Defending Freedom, March for Life, Care Net, Heartbeat International, Live Action, National Right to Life, and the Heritage Foundation.

Momentum in the States

After every Supreme Court decision on abortion, states have worked to legislate to find the limits of those decisions. After *Casey* opened the door to informed-consent legislation and solidified the foundation for parental-consent laws, states were encouraged to promote such legislation throughout the 1990s.

Annual editions of *Defending Life* starting in 2006 gave legislators tools and data to continue productive state activity on the life issue. In 2009, AUL distributed 2,400 model legislative guides to more than 325 recipients—an increase over 2008—and actively consulted in 30 states on legislation and ballot initiatives, setting the stage for an explosion of pro-life legislation in future years.

In 2009, states enacted more than 60 pro-life measures, a marked increase from 2008. This prepared the foundation for the 2010 midterms, in which hundreds of pro-life legislators were elected at the state level. In *Defending Life 2010*, Denise Burke, then vice president of legal affairs, reported on state data and authored an analysis of the Freedom of Choice Act. Burke and Smith published surveys of state and federal abortion laws, of the 2009 state legislative sessions, the status of state parental-involvement and informed-consent laws, partial-birth abortion laws, and the status of regulations of abortion providers and facilities.

From 2011 to 2013, AUL received 3,400 requests for its model legislation. By 2010, AUL had published 32 model bills on a range of bioethical issues, and by 2017 that had increased to 50. In 2011 and 2012, AUL worked in 39 states to help pass nearly 50 new pro-life laws at the state level, about one-third of all the pro-life laws that were enacted during the two-year span. More abortion restrictions were enacted from 2011 to 2013 than in the entire previous decade, according to one of the foremost proponents of unrestricted abortion, the Alan Guttmacher Institute, which reported 189 such laws between 2001 and 2010 and 205 between 2011 and 2013.[39]

Have these state limits on abortion had any positive effect in reducing the number of abortions in the U.S.? In 2011, a statistical analysis by Dr. Michael New, published in *State Politics & Policy Quarterly*, found that legislative efforts to enact parental-involvement laws, informed-consent laws, and limits on taxpayer funding of abortion contributed to a 25-percent nationwide decline in the number of abortions performed since 1992.[40]

Media outlets were constantly monitoring AUL's impact. In November 2012, the *New York Times* reported that "around one-third of the [132] bills [passed in 2011 and 2012] were written by Americans United for Life." In fall 2012, AUL was featured in the left-wing tabloid *Mother Jones*'s survey of ultrasound–informed-consent legislation.[41] In January 2013, *Mother Jones* reported that AUL was "the anti-abortion group perhaps most responsible for the barrage of new state laws."

In 2013, AUL worked in 44 states and helped enact 16 new pro-life measures.[42] MSNBC reported that "this rash of anti-abortion legislation sweeping the country can all be traced back to one group: Americans United for Life."

The pro-life campaign in the courts, legislatures, and media had a measurable political effect. In 2018 and 2019, the last pro-abortion Republicans left the House of Representatives, as documented in the March 21, 2019, issue of the *Wall Street Journal*, which noted the retirements of "centrist Republican Reps. Charlie Dent of Pennsylvania and Rodney Frelinghuysen of New Jersey." This left only two Republican abortion-rights supporters in the Senate: Sen. Susan Collins of Maine and Sen. Lisa Murkowski of Alaska.[43]

Burke edited her final edition of *Defending Life* in 2017, with the help of staff counsel Deanna Wallace. The 2017 edition focused on AUL's Mother-Child Strategy, including AUL's Infant Protection Project and Women's Protection Project.

A Period of Transition

In 2016, AUL experienced another period of administrative transition. In a critical election year, Yoest left AUL to pursue national political commentary as the presidential campaign heated up. After President Trump was inaugurated in January 2017, Yoest moved into the Administration, directing public affairs for the Department of Health and Human Services (HHS), where she was able to establish pro-life goals for HHS's five-year plan.

After two and half years with AUL, General Counsel Ovide Lamontagne returned to private practice in Manchester, New Hampshire. Lamontagné had led AUL's legal department during the Obama administration's second term, from 2013 to 2015, with legal skill, poise, good humor, and a sophisticated understanding of politics and congressional relations.

Evangeline Bartz, who had been with AUL for seven years, helped guide AUL through 18 months of transition as chief operating officer and corporate counsel, overseeing human-relations work, company regulations, and compliance with a steady hand behind the scenes. Bartz broadened her role with legislative lobbying and state legislative testimony in the states from 2018 to 2019. Forsythe stepped in as acting president for 16 months.

AUL faced another shock when, on Saturday afternoon, February 13, 2016, the team learned that Justice Antonin Scalia had died. Within an hour or two, Senate majority leader Mitch McConnell (R-KY) announced that the Senate would hold no hearings for *any* Obama nominee to fill the seat. Instead, McConnell said the Senate would leave the matter to the American people, allowing them in the November election to determine who should nominate a successor. AUL supported McConnell's announcement, made more than a month before Obama nominated Judge Merrick Garland, who evidently had been vetted for his support for *Roe v. Wade* by Planned Parenthood and NARAL, who endorsed his nomination within minutes.

With his decision, McConnell ensured that the vacancy would continue as a 2016 campaign issue, highlighting the Court as an election issue perhaps for the first time since the 1968 elections. Along with Trump's Supreme Court shortlists released in May and September, many believe that McConnell's move—the future of the Court—was one of the most consequential factors in motivating a significant number of Americans to vote for President Trump.

From 2008 to 2016, with Yoest's leadership, AUL had prioritized key goals and gotten results, especially when opposing the pro-abortion policies of the Obama Administration. Those were difficult years in the courts, but states made immense progress, creating a solid foundation that prepared the way for greater momentum in courts and legislatures in 2017 and beyond.

Chapter 12 Endnotes

1   The AUL Board included Jay Cunningham, Bryan Clark, Thomas J. Donnelly (ex officio), Teri Goudie, Ed Grant, Dr. Donna Harrison, Ken Hansen, Terri Herring, Jeanneane Maxon, George Weigel. (Donnelly, a co-founder of Federated Investors in Pittsburgh and a wise and generous board member since the 1990s, died in April 2011.)

2   *See, e.g.*, Molly Moorhead, *Nothing to Sign; Bill Has Fizzled*, POLITIFACT (June 1, 2012), https://www.politifact.com/truth-o-meter/promises/obameter/promise/501/sign-the-freedom-of-choice-act/; Christine Cupaiuolo, *Obama: Freedom of Choice Act "Not Highest Legislative Priority,"* OUR BODIES OURSELVES (Apr. 30, 2009), https://www.ourbodiesourselves.org/2009/04/obama-freedom-of-choice-act-not-highest-legislative-priority/.

3   William L. Saunders & Anna R. Franzonello, *Health Care Reform and Respect for Human Life: How the Process Failed*, 25 NOTRE DAME J.L. ETHICS & PUB. POL'Y 593, 597 (2011).

4   *Id.*

5   *See, e.g.*, Christopher M. Gacek, *Conceiving Pregnancy: U.S. Medical Dictionaries and Their Definitions of Conception and Pregnancy*, 9 NAT'L CATHOLIC BIOETHICS Q. 543 (2009)

6   *Amicus Curiae* Brief of Association of American Physicians & Surgeons et al. at 16, Zubik v. Burwell, 136 S. Ct. 1557 (2016) (No. 14-1418), *available at* https://aul.org/wp-content/uploads/2019/03/Am.-Physicians-Su-Amicus-Brief.pdf.

7   *Id.* at 17 n.29, (citing 155 Cong. Rec. S12,274 (daily ed. December 3, 2009)).

8   *See* Helen M. Alvare, *No Compelling Interest: The "Birth Control" Mandate and Religious Freedom*, 58 VILL. L. REV. 379 (2013).

9   Maureen L. Condic, *When Does Human Life Begin? The Scientific Evidence and the Terminology Revisited*, 8 U. ST. THOMAS J.L. & PUB. POL'Y 44 (2013). *See also* SAMUEL B. CONDIC & MAUREEN L. CONDIC, HUMAN EMBRYOS, HUMAN BEINGS: A SCIENTIFIC & PHILOSOPHICAL APPROACH (2018).

10 *Id.*

11 Burwell v. Hobby Lobby Stores, Inc., 573 U.S. 682 (2014). AUL's *amicus curiae* brief is available online. *Amicus Curiae* Brief of Drury Development Corp. et al., *Burwell*, 573 U.S. 682 (2014) (No. 13-354), *available at* https://aul.org/wp-content/uploads/2018/10/13-354-13-356-bsac-Drury-Development-Corporation.pdf.

12 Little Sisters of the Poor Saints Peter & Paul Home v. Pennsylvania, 140 S. Ct. 2367, 2386 (2020) (upholding the authority of HHS and other federal departments to exempt from certain provisions of the Affordable Care Act (ACA) "the Little Sisters from the source of their complicity-based concerns—the administratively imposed

contraceptive mandate").

13   Bartlett, *Risk Factors for Legal Induced Abortion-Related Mortality in the United States, supra* ch. 4 note 28.

14   505 U.S. at 846, 869, 870, 871, 873, 880.

15   Isaacson v. Horne, 884 F.Supp.2d 961 (D. Ariz. 2012), *rev'd*, 716 F.3d 1213 (9th Cir. 2013), *cert. denied*, 571 U.S. 1127 (2014).

16   *Isaacson*, 716 F.3d 1213. AUL's *amicus brief* is available online. *Amicus Curiae* Brief of the Association of American Physicians & Surgeons and Other National Medical Organizations in Support of Defendants-Appellees and Affirmance of the District of Arizona, *Isaacson*, 716 F.3d 1213 (No. 12-16670), *available at* https://aul.org/wp-content/uploads/2018/10/Brief-12-16670-Isaacson-v-Horne-amicus-brief-of-AAPS-et-al.pdf.

17   Petition for Writ of Certiorari, *Horne*, 571 U.S. 1127 (No. 13-402), *available at* https://aul.org/wp-content/uploads/2018/10/Horne-v-Isaacson-cert-petition-Final.pdf.

18   Erika Bachiochi, *Amy Coney Barrett: A New Feminist Icon*, ETHICS & PUB. POL'Y CTR. (Oct. 15, 2020), https://eppc.org/publications/amy-coney-barrett-a-new-feminist-icon/. *See also* Bachiochi, THE RIGHTS OF WOMEN, *supra* ch. 10 note 4; Erika Bachiochi, *Embodied Equality: Debunking Equal Protection Arguments for Abortion Rights*, 34 HARV. J.L. & PUB. POL'Y 889 (2011).

19   Michael Stokes Paulsen, *The Worst Constitutional Decision of All Time*, 78 NOTRE DAME L. REV. 995 (2003).

20   Amy Coney Barrett, *Precedent and Jurisprudential Disagreement*, 91 TEX. L. REV. 1711, 1735 (2013)

21   New, *Analyzing the Effect of Anti-Abortion U.S. State Legislation in the Post-Casey Era, supra* ch. 9 note 20.

22   Forsythe, *A Road Map Through the Supreme Court's Back Alley, supra* ch. 4 note 1.

23   In 2020, a federal judge in Maryland issued a nationwide injunction against the FDA's in-person requirement for the administration of mifepristone and misoprostol. The FDA sought a stay of that injunction pending appeal, but the Supreme Court held the FDA's motion in abeyance in October 2020, with a dissent by Justice Alito, joined by Justice Thomas. *Food & Drug Admin.*, 141 S. Ct. 10.

24   The New Leviathan: *The Mega-Center Report, How Planned Parenthood Became Abortion, Inc.*, AMS. UNITED FOR LIFE (2015), https://aul.org/wp-content/uploads/2018/11/AUL-Mega-Center-Report-06-24-2015.pdf.

25   Oversight and Investigations, *The Select Investigative Panel Releases Final Report,* ENERGY & COM. REPUBLICANS (Jan. 4, 2017), https://republicans-energycommerce.house.gov/news/press-release/select-investigative-panel-releases-final-report/.

26   *See* Letter from Lindsey O. Graham, Chairman, Comm. on the Judiciary, & Charles E. Grassley, Chairman, Comm. on Fin., to William Barr, Att'y Gen., U.S. Dep't of Just., & Christopher Wray, Dir., Fed. Bureau of Investigations, (June 18, 2019), https://www.

judiciary.senate.gov/imo/media/doc/Graham%20Grassley%20Letter%20to%20DOJ%20 FBI%20on%20Human%20Fetal%20Tissue.pdf (citing the federal law that "bans the buying or selling of human fetal tissue," 42 U.S.C. § 289g-2)

27 136 S. Ct. 2292.

28 140 S. Ct. 2103.

29 Sabrina Tavernise & Sheryl Gay Stolberg, *Abortion Foes, Emboldened by Trump, Promise "Onslaught" of Tough Restrictions*, N.Y. Times (Dec. 11, 2016), https://www.nytimes.com/2016/12/11/us/abortion-foes-donald-trump-restrictions-politics.html.

30 *June Medical Servs.*, 140 S. Ct. at 2153 (2020) (Alito, J., dissenting, joined by Gorsuch, Thomas, and Kavanaugh, JJ., in significant parts).

31 *See* Dellapenna, *Dispelling the Myths*, *supra* ch. 1 note 3, at 376–398. *See also* Forsythe, *The Effective Enforcement of Abortion Law Before* Roe v. Wade, *supra* ch. 3 note 6.

32 Richard Myers, *Re-reading* Roe v. Wade, 71 Wash. & Lee L. Rev. 1025, 1044 & n.115 (2014).

33 With a preface by Jean Bethke Elshtain, the book included papers by Mary Ann Glendon, Paige Cunningham, Dr. Elizabeth Shadigian, Denise Burke, Dorinda Bordlee, Dr. Angela Lanfranchi, Dr. Joanne Angelo, Elizabeth Fox-Genovese, Professor Elizabeth Schiltz, Erika Bachiochi, Candace Crandall, and Serrin Foster

34 567 U.S. 519.

35 Forsythe, *The Medical Assumption at the Foundation of* Roe v. Wade *and Its Implications for Women's Health*, *supra* ch. 10 note 12 (including three appendices citing studies). *See also* Hush, *supra* ch. 4 note 101.

36 *See* Forsythe, Abuse of Discretion, *supra* ch. 2 note 46.

37 Bachiochi, *Embodied Equality: Debunking Equal Protection Arguments for Abortion Rights*, *supra* ch.12 note 18.

38 *Young v. United Parcel Serv., Inc.*, 575 U.S. 206 (2015). AUL's *amicus curiae* brief is available online. Brief of *Amici Curiae* 23 Pro-Life Organizations and the Judicial Education Project in Support of Petitioner Peggy Young, *Young*, 575 U.S. 206 (No. 12-1226), *available at* https://aul.org/wp-content/uploads/2018/11/Brief-for-23-Organizations-in-Young-v.-UPS.pdf.

39 *More State Abortion Restrictions Were Enacted in 2011-2013 Than in the Entire Previous Decade*, Guttmacher Inst. (Jan. 2, 2014), https://www.guttmacher.org/article/2014/01/more-state-abortion-restrictions-were-enacted-2011-2013-entire-previous-decade.

40 New, *Analyzing the Effect of Anti-Abortion U.S. State Legislation in the Post-Casey Era*, *supra* ch. 9 note 20

41 Kate Sheppard, *Wham, Bam, Sonogram! Meet the Ladies Setting the New Pro-Life Agenda*, Mother Jones, (Sept./Oct. 2012), https://www.motherjones.com/poli-

tics/2012/08/americans-united-for-life-anti-abortion-transvaginal-ultrasound/.

42   *AUL Action Releases 2013 State Legislative Session Report Detailing Successes in Protecting Women from a "Predatory Industry Indifferent to Abortion's Dangers"*, Ams. United for Life (Sept. 5, 2013), https://aul.org/2013/09/05/aul-action-releases-2013-state-legislative-session-report-detailing-successes-in-protecting-women-from-a-predatory-abortion-industry-indifferent-to-abortions-dangers/. AUL's influence was also highlighted in a 2013-2014 academic thesis by Kaitlin Reedy. The TRAP: Limiting Women's Access to Abortion through Strategic, State-level Legislation (2014) (Senior Thesis, Trinity College), https://digitalrepository.trincoll.edu/theses/387/.

43   *See* Ed Kilgore, *The Near-Extinction of Pro-Choice Republicans in Congress*, Intelligencer (June 28, 2018), https://nymag.com/intelligencer/2018/06/pro-choice-republicans-in-congress-are-nearly-extinct.html *and* Kristina Peterson, *House Republicans Now Unanimous in Opposing Abortion Rights*, Wall St. J. (Mar. 21, 2019), https://www.wsj.com/articles/house-republicans-now-unanimous-in-opposing-abortion-rights-11553172954.

CHAPTER 13

A Changing Culture and a Changing Supreme Court

For months, AUL had prepared for the dreadful prospect of a presidential administration led by Hillary Clinton, one of the most extreme proponents of unlimited abortion in the country. Clinton's unexpected defeat on November 8, 2016 removed a substantial threat and opened unexpected opportunities. AUL had witnessed growing state momentum after the 2010 midterms and another successful round of elections in 2014, but the 2016 election produced the best political conditions for AUL's work in Congress, the states, and the courts since *Roe v. Wade*.

If Clinton had won, she likely would have replaced Scalia and Kennedy with pro-abortion justices, creating a 6-3 pro-*Roe* majority, and she likely would have nominated hundreds of pro-abortion judges to lower federal courts. Such a Court majority might have overturned *Harris v. McRae*, the federal Hyde Amendment, and state limits on public funding of abortion by adopting Justice Ruth Bader Ginsburg's "equal protection" rationale for abortion rights, as articulated in her *Gonzales* dissent.[1] A Clinton Court would have threatened:

- the Reagan Administration's Adolescent Family Life Act (AFLA) under the Establishment Clause, overruling *Bowen v. Kendrick*;
- virtually all of the pro-life legislation passed by the states since 1973, including the 20-week limits on abortion that were in effect in some 20 states;
- *Gonzales v. Carhart*, which upheld the federal ban on partial birth abortion;
- the *Hobby Lobby* decision and given a narrow reading to the Religious Freedom Restoration Act of 1995 protecting rights of conscience;
- to allow the "contraception mandate" of the Affordable Care Act (ACA) to be applied to religious organizations, compelling them to fund abortions;
- *Vacco* and *Glucksberg*, the two assisted suicide decisions by the Supreme Court in 1997, which refused to create a national right to assisted suicide and allowed states to prohibit assisted suicide;
- free speech, by subordinating free speech to other "social values" like "privacy," "dignity," "equal citizenship," etc., that the majority would have identified;[2]
- *Citizens United v. FEC*,[3] the 2010 decision, which struck down federal limits on political speech by unions, organizations and corporations;
- to stifle the ability of non-profit organizations to educate the public about the voting records of pro-abortion politicians.

What a different America that would be.

Instead, Sen. McConnell's decision to hold open Scalia's seat proved to be a masterstroke, preserving the seat for a constitutionalist judge and likely influencing the outcome of the election by making the future of the Court a stark election issue. By the end of January 2017, President Trump had nominated Judge Neil Gorsuch to fill the Scalia seat.

Response to *Whole Woman's Health*

In the immediate wake of Scalia's death, AUL was deeply disappointed by the Court's 5-3 decision in *Whole Woman's Health v. Hellerstedt*,[4] invalidating Texas' health-and-safety regulations for abortion clinics. Once again, the Court made a stark exception for abortion: admitting privilege requirements that had applied for decades to ambulatory surgical centers generally could not be applied to abortion. The pro-abortion justices dismissed Kermit Gosnell's scandal in Philadelphia as an aberration and ignored the public-health crisis in Texas clinics. Once again the Court managed its self-appointed role as the national abortion control board by delegating health and safety standards to the abortionists. *Whole Woman's Health* threatened to undo progress in the states by empowering the federal courts to throw out state safety regulations. The decision proved to be a sword that abortion clinics would use in court against a broad range of state pro-life laws for four years, until the Court's decision in *June Medical* in June 2020.

But states were not intimidated, and they continued to pass abortion limits, though many were immediately enjoined under *Whole Woman's Health*, resulting in about 60 abortion cases pending in lower courts by 2020. To rebut *Whole Woman's Health*, AUL published the first edition of *Unsafe*, documenting the widespread existence of substandard providers and conditions in clinics across the country.[5]

Catherine Glenn Foster's Leadership

Catherine Glenn Foster succeeded Charmaine Yoest as AUL president in May 2017. A graduate of Georgetown University Law Center, one of the top law schools in the nation, Foster had been a litigator at Alliance Defending Freedom. She had devoted her career to exposing abortion, facing off against Planned Parenthood in the courts, and developing innovative approaches to pro-life legislation and courtroom advocacy. One of the best legal minds in the pro-life movement, Foster was the only female lawyer who led a national pro-life organization at that time.

Foster quickly became the leading public voice for AUL in the media and public square, speaking to a broad range of law and policy issues involving life, in both publications and interviews. She continued AUL's tradition of speaking regularly with media across the political spectrum, including the *Wall Street Journal*, the *New York Times*, the *Washington Post*, *Vox*, and *Mother Jones*. A lawyer with an energetic presence, Foster jumped into interviews, legislative testimony, writing and publishing, and executive responsibilities.

Just before the Mother's Day weekend in May 2020, AUL released myLIFEstory, enabling Catherine to tell her story and cast a spotlight on how many young women experience abortion. When Foster was 19 and a college student in Georgia, she became pregnant. Reluctant to tell her mother, she looked for solutions and found an abortion clinic. She began the abortion process and was led onto the operating table, when she decided it wasn't what she wanted. When she moved to get up, staff told her to stay down and restrained her until the abortion was complete, an incredibly painful experience.

Foster's witness aims to break the silence for women who suffered during or after an abortion, enabling women to share the pain of abortion and develop the ability to recover afterwards. There can be hope and healing after abortion.[6] "When we let shame and fear silence us, then we're taken out of community," Foster has testified. Those who have experienced the pain of abortion "have a voice, and that voice will be heard."

As an abortion survivor, Foster has a special credibility in explaining her experience, including the lack of information she received prior to choosing abortion. She's determined to show women the truth about abortion that she didn't have access to. That experience led her to serve Rockville Pregnancy Center, first as a board member and later as chair, strengthening her ability to inform and inspire an audience to understand and become engaged in the life issue. In 2020, Foster spoke in St. Louis to supporters of pro-life pregnancy center ThriVe on their crucial role providing alternatives to abortion for women who may feel they have no choice other than abortion:

> I wish every day that I had found a place like ThriVe when I was 19 years old. That someone had pointed the way to a place that hands out love and encouragement … I would have an 18-year-old now instead of an empty place in my heart. ThriVe builds a bridge with women and girls and partners and this community. And building real connections is one of the most critical things we can all do for each other, especially when people are hurting or struggling. For women and families in

> turmoil in the face of an unplanned pregnancy, an ear to listen, a sounding board, a helping hand, and maybe even a shoulder to cry on, that's imperative to helping them think through their options and ultimately making a choice for life. That's the thing I needed most. Being a mom, let's be honest, it's always a challenge, all the mamas in the audience know it! But when you feel like you have no support it can seem impossible. Encouragement can mean the difference between life and death. Being a positive force in the life of a friend can be the light in the darkness that they need to make the right choice.

More than perhaps any previous AUL president, Foster has made legislative testimony a priority, a focus to which she brought her abortion experience and legal expertise. In July 2018, Foster testified to the American Board of Medical Specialists, opposing the American Board of Obstetrics' petition for a subspecialty certification in "Complex Family Planning," or training in doing late-term abortions. In 2019, Foster submitted written testimony on abortion to the New Zealand Parliamentary Select Committee and testified on "Protecting Title X and Safeguarding Quality Family Planning Care" before a U.S. House subcommittee. In April 2019, Foster testified in support of S. 160, the Pain-Capable Unborn Child Protection Act, before the U.S. Senate Judiciary Committee.[7] In 2019 and 2020, Foster testified against abortion in at least nine states.

As president, Foster also made it a personal priority to hold the line against the legalization of assisted suicide, and in 2019 she submitted written testimony or testified in person in Colorado, Delaware, the District of Columbia, Maine, Massachusetts, Maryland, Minnesota, New Hampshire, New Jersey, and Rhode Island.

In 2019, AUL partnered with the National Constitution Center and its president Jeffrey Rosen to produce podcasts on *Roe v. Wade*. Forsythe[8] and Foster[9] were each featured in a 2019 podcast episode, and in March 2020 Foster participated in a third NCC podcast on *June Medical*.[10]

In fall 2019, Foster had a spirited debate with Kathryn Kolbert and Professor Mary Ziegler at the National Constitution Center in Philadelphia.[11] Kolbert has been a pro-abortion attorney with the ACLU for decades, and she argued *Planned Parenthood v. Casey* at the Supreme

Court against the overruling of *Roe* in 1992. Though Foster had a broken leg and was in pain at the event, she gave better than she got.

When the Supreme Court heard *June Medical*, Foster led AUL's media efforts. She spoke at a press conference organized by AUL at the National Press Club, featuring Louisiana state senator Katrina Jackson, U.S. Senator and physician Bill Cassidy (R-LA), and other members of the House and Senate. The following day, Foster addressed a rally on the steps of the Supreme Court while arguments were underway.[12]

Women Speak

Abortion activists and pro-abortion politicians, along with allies in the media, insist that women need abortion and that abortion is good for women. A majority on the Supreme Court held to some version of this notion from 1992 until *Dobbs* in 2022.

In *Casey*, the majority adopted a "reliance interest" rationale for preserving *Roe*, discarding the original rationale, based in history, for the abortion right created in *Roe*. Instead, the Court declared that it could not "go back" because women had come to rely on abortion for equal opportunity. But the evidence for women's reliance on abortion and the benefits to women had always been exceedingly weak.[13]

Since *Casey*, the reliance-interest rationale might be said to have morphed into the general notion that women need abortion or that abortion is good for women. Of course, this is a policy argument accessible to voters and legislation; it does not anchor abortion in the Constitution, nor does it justify a judicially-created right. In any case, the reliance-interest rationale for abortion requires constant rebuttal.

In addition to AUL's books, articles, and briefs rebutting this rationale, AUL hosted "Women Speak" in 2018, a conference focused on the negative effects of abortion on women, making the case that women can succeed without abortion. The conference in 2018 was co-hosted by and held at the Heritage Foundation in Washington, D.C. on June 13, 2018.

On May 1, 2019, AUL again held "Women Speak" at The Heritage Foundation. Charmaine Yoest, by then vice president of the Institute for Family, Community and Opportunity at The Heritage Foundation, opened the conference, introducing Foster.

A Reinvigorated Team

Upon becoming president in May 2017, Foster set about building AUL's team. She recruited Steven H. Aden, also a graduate of Georgetown University Law Center, to become AUL's chief legal officer and general counsel in August 2017. Prior to joining AUL, Aden had more than 25 years of legal experience in pro-life and religious-liberty law and litigation. In the decade before joining AUL, Aden was lead counsel or co-counsel in dozens of cases against Planned Parenthood and its affiliates. He was appointed special counsel by seven states to defend abortion limits and served as consulting counsel in dozens of other pro-life cases.

Since 2000, Aden has filed briefs in every Supreme Court case involving abortion. He has defended the conscience rights of physicians, nurses, pharmacists, and other healthcare professionals in numerous cases, including the defense of the Weldon Amendment from 2004 to 2006. He spearheaded legislation to defund Planned Parenthood and defended that legislation in several cases, and he argued cases in five federal circuit courts and in state courts. During his long career, Aden worked with state attorneys general in at least 15 states.

Shortly after becoming chief legal officer and general counsel, Aden filed a brief with AUL staff counsels Rachel Morrison and Deanna Wallace at the Supreme Court in *National Institute of Family & Life Advocates (NIFLA) v. Becerra*[14] on behalf of the American Association of Pro-Life Obstetricians and Gynecologists, the American College of Pediatricians, and the Christian Medical Association against the California statute compelling pregnancy-care centers in California to advertise the state's free abortion program. AUL's brief chronicled the ethical guidelines at pregnancy-care centers, arguing that coerced disclosure is not informed consent:

> There are certain narrow exceptions when the government can, in fact, compel speech, including in the commercial or professional context. But the disclosure required by the California Reproductive FACT Act is neither commercial speech

> nor professional speech … Information about State public pro-
> grams providing access to contraception and abortion is not a
> risk, consequence, or alternative to a pregnancy test, a limited
> ultrasound, or STI testing.

AUL's brief outlined the subtle but critical distinction between the legitimate regulation of informed consent within medicine and the unconstitutional, coerced disclosure compelled by California.

In June 2018, the Supreme Court held in a 5-4 decision that the California statute violated the First Amendment. The carefully reasoned
majority opinion by Justice Clarence Thomas tracked the reasoning of
AUL's brief.[15]

In 2020, Aden organized two moot courts for Louisiana Solicitor Gen-
eral Elizabeth Merrill in preparation for her argument in *June Medical*.
Foster, Aden, AUL counsel Katie Glenn, and AUL counsel Natalie Hejran
filed a brief on behalf of 207 members of Congress in the Supreme
Court, the most members, at the time, on an abortion-related brief since
Harris v. McRae.

A week after the *June Medical* argument, the COVID-19 pandemic shut-
down the nation, but AUL maintained its productivity working remotely. During the pandemic, Aden wrote and filed a brief at the Supreme
Court in *Baker v. Planned Parenthood South Atlantic*—which involved
a defense of South Carolina's exclusion of Planned Parenthood from the
state's Medicaid program—urging the Court to hear the case. He also
spearheaded a new edition of *Unsafe*. The team was disappointed when
the Court refused to hear *Baker* in October 2020.[16] In May 2022, however, South Carolina again asked the Supreme Court to hear the case,
and Americans United for Life filed a brief in support of the petition.[17]

In fall 2020, Aden wrote a brief for a federal court of appeals in *Food
and Drug Administration (FDA) v. American College of Obstetricians
and Gynecologists (ACOG)*, in defense of the FDA's 20-year-old limits on
chemical-abortion drugs mifepristone and misoprostol, which required
that they be prescribed only during an in-person meeting with a physician, rather than by mail or over the counter. When the Supreme Court

refused to stay the district court's injunction against the FDA requirements, Justice Alito dissented, joined by Justice Thomas.[18]

Katie Glenn joined AUL as government affairs counsel in June 2019.
A graduate of the University of Florida Law School, Glenn worked on
Capitol Hill in the office of Louisiana Congressman Steve Scalise. Before
joining AUL, Glenn spent five years planning and drafting state legislation. In her first nine months with AUL, Glenn testified in several states
and filed written testimony in several more. Working on Capitol Hill
with allies, Glenn recruited 39 Senators and 168 Representatives to join
AUL's brief in *June Medical*, which Justice Alito cited in his dissent.[19]
Glenn also recruited 102 members of Congress to join Aden's brief in
the FDA appeal. Glenn worked on 100 bills in her first year with AUL,
about two dozen of which dealt with issues of especially high intensity,
including fetal-remains legislation, 20-week limits, post-*Roe* legislation,
conditional laws, ultrasound-notification requirements, admitting privileges, emergency-transfer laws, and heartbeat laws.

Tom Shakely, AUL chief engagement officer, and Noah Brandt, AUL
communications director, launched AUL's "Life, Liberty, and Law" podcast in July 2019. "Life, Liberty, and Law" would run for more than three
years, releasing 168 episodes featuring conversations on the human
right to life meant to inspire, encourage, and uplift listeners.[20] Shakely
and Brandt spoke with a multitude of guests on topics across the spectrum of life issues.

"Life, Liberty, and Law" guests included Sen. Steve Daines (R-MT) on
his leadership in founding the U.S. Senate Pro-Life Caucus, Sen. James
Lankford (R-OK) on the battle to preserve the Hyde Amendment, Dr.
Hadley Arkes on natural rights, natural law, and moral reasoning as
essential for law and policy, David French on originalism, the U.S. Constitution, and the achievements of the pro-life movement, Dr. Catherine
Ruth Pakaluk on American birth rates and pro-family policies, Mayra
Rodriguez, a former Planned Parenthood director turned whistleblow-
er, Jeanne Mancini on the March for Life's advocacy in Washington and
across the states, and Professor Joseph W. Dellapenna on his book
Dispelling the Myths of Abortion History.

Shakely and Brandt connected the American pro-life movement with
international pro-life advocacy and threats to human rights in conver-

sations with guests like Ambassador Sam Brownback on international religious freedom and the right to life, Jean-Paul Van De Walle on abortion activism at the European Parliament and the human right to life in Europe, Obianuju Ekeocha on the culture of life across Africa and the threat of ideological neocolonialism and philanthropic racism, and Wesley J. Smith on the rise of China and its human rights record.

"Life, Liberty, and Law" also occasionally aired audio from the archives of AUL, featuring advocates like Dr. Bernard Nathanson, M.D., on the realities of abortion and what physicians owe to their patients, Congressman Henry Hyde on standing up for the powerless and opposing partial birth abortion, and Dr. Leon Kass on the hubris of human reproductive cloning and the threat of radical forms of child abuse.

Throughout the decades, there have been countless talented and committed individuals selflessly devoting their skills to AUL. Like Gideon's 300, it has always been a small but devoted team, implementing the essential legal strategy that Horan, Rosenblum, Gorby, Trueman, and Marzen launched in the 1970s.

Defending Life 2018, 2019, 2020, and 2021

Aden picked up the editorship of *Defending Life* in 2018, 2019, and 2020, working with AUL staff counsel Natalie Hejran. A graduate of Notre Dame Law School, where she was a student of Amy Coney Barrett, Hejran began working with AUL as a legal fellow in the fall of 2017 and came to AUL full time in July 2018 as staff counsel. She assumed the enormous task of researching and writing *Defending Life* 2020 and 2021, and has written and edited briefs and legislative testimony.

With endorsements from Vice President Mike Pence, Oklahoma governor Mary Fallin, and Arkansas governor Asa Hutchinson, the 467-page *Defending Life 2018* focused on the AUL report *Unsafe* and the public-health crisis in America's abortion clinics. It also gave a detailed review of the best and worst states for life issues and ranked the states, with recommendations for pro-life priorities for every state. It concluded with a list of AUL's 50 model bills, published and updated since the 1970s.

With the same endorsements the following year, the 492-page *Defending Life 2019* began with a focus on the strategy for reversing *Roe* in light of the confirmations of Justices Gorsuch and Kavanaugh, as well as the possible implications of overturning *Roe*. The volume included state rankings and state report cards. AUL outlined the bills comprising the Infants Protection Project, the Women's Protection Project, and the Patient Protection Project. *Defending Life 2019* added, for the first time, a note on the status of abortion law in each state when *Roe* is overturned.

In 2020, *Defending Life* was endorsed by Vice President Pence, Tennessee Sen. Marsha Blackburn, and Meghan McCain. The edition contained a recap of successes in 2019, written by Glenn. *Defending Life 2020* focused on 20 model bills on abortion and euthanasia and contained a feature article by Forsythe on "Eight Reasons Why *Roe v. Wade* is Unworkable." Though not an aspect of *Roe* that Americans often think about, the workability of Court decisions is a standard paradigm that justices examine when reconsidering a precedent, an important perspective that spotlights the problems with *Roe* and *Casey*.[21]

In 2019, *USA Today* produced an analysis finding that "Americans United for Life was behind the bulk of the more than 400 [pro-life] bills introduced in 41 states." The *Washington Post* concluded that "Americans United for Life … frames proposals that will be palatable to state legislatures, can be discussed in ways that will generate less political backlash and will appeal to the courts that will eventually have to review legislative intent and discussion."

On the surface, the proliferation of model bills for abortion may seem like hair-splitting minutiae, but they are necessary for advancing the cause for life for several reasons. They apply important ethical arguments to the practical consequences and present traditional arguments in new ways. They employ a wide variety of arguments, complementing the essential argument that the unborn child is a human being from conception. They specify a number of types of harms, including the many ways abortion harms the prenatal child and the way it harms women. They spotlight the problems and contradictions in the Court's control of the abortion issue. They utilize the most recent data and encourage the collection and analysis of demographic data to facilitate public argument over abortion. They provide affirmative protection of the prenatal child that didn't exist before and show that such protection is reasonable, enforceable, and effective. Criticizing abortion has always

been and always will be multifaceted, exposing the ways in which the
Court's doctrine has failed. This same reasoning can be applied effectively to other areas of bioethics that threaten human life and dignity.

Roe Unsettled

Before the 2016 election, most legal and political commentators would
have thought it fanciful that the Supreme Court would ever overturn
Roe. After the election, countless commentators on both sides of the
issue began to think that the Court might sooner or later overturn *Roe*
and said so publicly. This was a significant development because the
Court considers "settled expectations" when determining whether to
overturn a previous decision.

State legislation, test cases, judicial and scholarly criticism, political opposition, and the work of the pro-life movement kept *Roe* unsettled for
decades, and the moment finally looked ripe to urge the Court majority
to expressly reconsider and overturn *Roe*.

In many ways, *Roe* contained the seeds of its own destruction. Even
pro-abortion scholars admitted that the Court's opinion had been an
embarrassment. The broad edict legalizing abortion went far beyond
public support, and the Court had ignored proper procedural and
evidentiary requirements. There was no trial or evidentiary proceeding
in the lower courts in *Roe* or *Doe*; all the factual assertions in Justice
Blackmun's majority opinion were assumptions, derived from inter-
est-group briefs or Blackmun's research at the Mayo Clinic during the
summer of 1972.

The justices in the majority made a political miscalculation, believing
they could settle the issue and refusing to grapple with the possible unintended consequences of their move. When members of Congress and
voters failed to fall in line, the justices dug in their heels and doubled
down, sparking grassroots opposition that led to the election of several
presidents who openly opposed the decision.

When the Court subsequently attempted to defend *Roe*, its defenses
were weak. It never identified a rationale based in the text or history
of the Constitution. The *Akron* decision in 1983 relied on *stare decisis*,
and it was written by Justice Louis Powell, who later privately acknowledged the flaws of *Roe* and *Doe*. *Thornburgh* did the same, insisting on

sticking to *Roe* as precedent (*stare decisis*) but without articulating a coherent, constitutional rationale. *Casey* overturned *Akron* and *Thornburgh* with its own weak rationale, which was strongly criticized by justices and scholars.[22]

Dr. Bernard Nathanson, an abortionist in the 1960s and founder of what was then called the National Association for Repeal of Abortion Laws—today called NARAL Pro-Choice America—pointed out in the *New England Journal of Medicine* shortly after *Roe* that medical developments had begun to reveal the reality of abortion:

> There is no longer serious doubt in my mind that human life exists within the womb from the very onset of pregnancy, despite the fact that the nature of the *interviewer* in life has been the subject of considerable dispute in the past. Electrocardiographic evidence of heart function has been established in embryos as early as six weeks.
>
> Electroencephalographic recordings of human brain activity have been noted in embryos at eight weeks. Our capacity to measure signs of life is daily becoming more sophisticated, and as time goes by, we will doubtless be able to isolate life signs at earlier and earlier stages in the fetal development … Life is an inter-dependent phenomenon for us all. It is a continuous spectrum that begins in utero and ends at death—the bands of the spectrum are designated by words such as fetus, infant, child, adolescent, and adult … we must courageously face the fact—finally—that human life of a special order is being taken. And since the vast majority of pregnancies are carried successfully to term, abortion must be seen as the interruption of a process that would otherwise have produced a citizen of the world. Denial of this reality is the crassest kind of moral evasiveness.[23]

Roe remained unsettled not only because of continued scientific advancements but because of ongoing scholarly criticism and political opposition and because the Court continued to alter its standard of review for state pro-life laws. Between *Stenberg, Gonzales, Whole Woman's*

Health, and *June Medical*, spanning two decades, the Court switched its standard for state abortion restrictions each time.

To demonstrate why *Roe* was susceptible to being overturned by the doctrine of precedent (*stare decisis et quieta non movere*), Forsythe published "A Draft Opinion Overruling *Roe v. Wade*" in 2018.[24] Since *Roe*, a network of political activists, lobbyists, lawyers, scholars, and researchers had continued making the case against the decision.

In 2019, the state legislative sessions featured blue states such as Illinois and New York enacting extreme abortion-legalization laws and red states such as Alabama passing strong prohibitions on abortion. Both trends indicated that states expected the Court might overturn *Roe* in the near-term, and they were preparing the ground for the day after *Roe*. Meanwhile, abortion jurisprudence had been at the center of confirmation battles for decades, ever since Judge Robert Bork's nomination, which Senate Democrats blocked in large part over fear that he'd vote to overturn *Roe*. During the hearings for Justices Gorsuch, Kavanaugh, and Barrett, opponents of the nominations made clear that they wanted to block the nominees for fear that they would oppose *Roe*.[25]

At the end of 2020, AUL released its "State Legislative Session Report," which reflected that, though the pandemic closed the legislative sessions of 2020, opposition to *Roe* remained steady, and perhaps even grew.[26]

June Medical and the New Court Majority

Four years after *Whole Woman's Health v. Hellerstedt*, the Court heard Louisiana's appeal in *June Medical Services v. Russo*, with Justice Kavanaugh as successor to Justice Kennedy. On the surface, both cases involved an admitting-privileges requirement, mandating that surgeons, including abortionists, have the ability to admit a patient who suffers complications to a local hospital. That's where the similarities ended.

June Medical was not simply a retread of *Whole Woman's Health*. Louisiana had a different history of substandard conditions in abortion clinics, and its law, Act 620, was structured differently from the law in Texas. It would have had a different impact on clinics, and Louisiana had assembled a stronger set of facts to defend the law in court.[27]

Before joining AUL, Aden was co-counsel for Louisiana at trial in June

2016 and through the first appeal. Several weeks before the trial began, he got a call from the trial attorney for Louisiana, asking him to come aboard the trial team and help prepare for trial in Baton Rouge. The attorneys for June Medical Services, the abortion provider challenging the law, were well-staffed and had immense resources.

Aden joined the trial team, which included Dorinda Bordlee of the Bioethics Defense Fund, and spent the next several weeks preparing. He helped try the two-week case in Baton Rouge, including five days of testimony, and interviewed medical witnesses. It was a non-stop race to obtain information on witnesses and prepare examination and cross-examination. The team compiled one of the best factual records in any abortion case since *Roe*, and Aden knew that the case was likely to hinge on the fight to assemble the facts and present them persuasively.

Later, Louisiana solicitor general Liz Merrill told the Supreme Court about the extensive legislative record her staff had relied on in trial, highlighting the fact that an abortionist used his admitting privileges to follow up with a woman in a hospital and fix his surgical mistake to stop her bleeding. Merrill also informed the Court that Louisiana's abortion industry had no information on complication rates because their clinics and doctors didn't keep records, one reason why the legislature had to step in with the admitting-privileges law.

When Louisiana prepared to file its appeal, state officials asked AUL to write an *amicus* brief on the dangers of the abortion industry, in support of the state's petition asking the Supreme Court to hear the case. After the Court agreed to hear the case, several AUL lawyers spent December 2019 briefing the case at the Court. Thanks to Glenn's work recruiting members, AUL submitted a brief on behalf 39 Republican senators and 168 representatives. The brief recounted the detailed history of unsafe abortion practices that Act 620 addressed and called on the Court to reconsider *Roe*.

AUL filed a second Supreme Court brief in *June Medical*, co-authored by Aden and Forsythe, based on the latter's groundbreaking article "A Draft Opinion Overturning *Roe v. Wade*," and focused on the *stare decisis* reasons for overruling *Roe*.

AUL worked closely with Louisiana's legal team preparing for oral argument, participating in moot courts in New Orleans and Washington.

AUL coordinated a coalition of more than 20 pro-life partner organizations to cooperate on messaging for the case, establish a website, and plan the "Protect Women, Protect Life Rally" in front of the Court on March 4, 2020, the morning of the oral argument. AUL also led a coalition of lawmakers, doctors, and pro-life advocates for a press event at the National Press Club the day before the argument, including Act 620's sponsors, Louisiana state senators Katrina Jackson and Regina Barrow. The event also featured the Republican Attorneys General Association's female leaders, the American Association of Pro-Life Obstetricians and Gynecologists, Congressman Mike Johnson (R-LA), additional congressmen, and several pro-life organizations.

Throughout the process, AUL served as a recognized authority on the case, with senior legal team members providing commentary and offering interviews to national media and organizations, including *National Law Journal*, the *Wall Street Journal*, *SCOTUSBlog*, the ABA Journal, the *Washington Post*, the *New York Times*, USA Today, and the Federalist Society.

The Supreme Court released its decision on Monday, June 29, 2020, the 28th anniversary of the Court's decision in *Casey*, and AUL immediately issued a white paper with legal and legislative analysis on the implications of the ruling.[28] Early media reports focused on the 5-4 ruling striking down Louisiana's law, but they overlooked the implications of Chief Justice Roberts's concurring opinion,[29] as well as the four dissents from Justices Thomas, Alito, Gorsuch, and Kavanaugh.

Together, those five opinions illustrated a new Court majority—Roberts, Thomas, Alito, Gorsuch, and Kavanaugh—that would apply the more lenient standards of *Casey* to state abortion limits in future cases.

In his dissent, Alito wrote, "[T]here is ample evidence in the record showing that admitting privileges help to protect the health of women by ensuring that physicians who perform abortions meet a higher standard of competence than is shown by the mere possession of a license to practice."[30] Justice Alito added, "The record shows that the vetting conducted by hospitals goes far beyond what is done at Louisiana abortion clinics."[31] Alito noted that, contrary to Roberts's conclusion, *Whole Woman's Health* and *June Medical* were not identical: "Both opinions [the plurality and that of Roberts] try to create the impression that this case is the same as *Whole Woman's Health* and that *stare decisis* therefore commands the same result. In truth, however, the two cases are very different. While it is certainly true that the Texas and Louisiana *statutes* are largely the same, the two cases are not." Alito's dissent was his most critical opinion to date of the Court's abortion doctrine.

Still 'Unsafe'

During the COVID-19 pandemic, AUL produced a new edition of *Unsafe*, an expanded edition that was the product of months of research by legal fellow Amanda Stirone Mansfield. The new edition was based on a national survey of health-inspection reports available from all reporting states, which AUL obtained through Freedom of Information Act (FOIA) requests. The widespread reality of substandard providers and dangerous conditions in abortion clinics still exists, which is not surprising considering the Court's dismissive decisions in *Whole Woman's Health* and *June Medical*. In remarks offered in the fall of 2020, Foster shared some of the findings:

> One of the reports that I can't stop thinking about comes from Planned Parenthood in Birmingham, Alabama, from 2014. A state health violation report tells us the story of a 14-year-old girl ... When this little girl in Birmingham went into Planned Parenthood, she already had two living children. Planned Parenthood aborted her third child. Did they at least report suspected sexual abuse to the authorities? No. They sent her right back into what we can only assume was an abusive situation. Tragically, if not surprisingly, just four months later, this same girl came in again, and Planned Parenthood performed another abortion, no questions asked. Once again, no suspected abuse was reported, and this young girl got no help—just Planned Parenthood repeatedly performing an abortion, taking her money, and sending her on her way, twice in four months. During this child's second abortion, seven of the 16 mandated health and legal records were missing or incomplete.

This problem wouldn't end until the Court decided either to permit states to require abortion clinics to meet the same standards as other ambulatory surgical centers, or overturn *Roe*.

COVID-19 and the 2020 Presidential Election

A week after *June Medical* arguments, the COVID-19 pandemic shut down the nation.

The pandemic highlighted the fact that abortion is not healthcare. Ninety-five percent of abortions are chosen for social reasons, not for reasons of health, and that holds true even for abortions after fetal viability. But immediately after the pandemic began, media outlets began to insist that the disease might cause prenatal defects and that pregnant women should rush to get an abortion, despite the BBC's report on March 17 that "the government says limited evidence suggests there are no coronavirus-related complications in pregnancy."

Abortion activists insisted that abortion clinics had to stay open, even as most other businesses were forced to shut down and elective health-care procedures were canceled. The pandemic made it all the more urgent for women with an unplanned pregnancy to obtain real counseling away from the ideological bias of an abortion clinic.[32] As abortion proponents began to push for expanded chemical abortions obtained via telemedicine and the mail, Glenn wrote in the *Washington Examiner* to highlight the risks to women from the abortion pill.[33] In the first quarter of 2020, AUL renewed its quarterly conference calls with researchers and allies on medical risks to women from abortion, featuring Drs. Paul Sullins, Byron Calhoun, Donna Harrison, and James Studnicki, Ph.D, who discussed newly published data.

In June 2020, Foster spoke to the Center for Bioethics and Human Dignity on the bioethical aspects of the pandemic and in October she traveled to St. Louis to speak at a fundraiser in support of ThriVe. The entire team remained productive, even though the D.C. government closed offices from March 2020 through the end of the year. After arguments in *June Medical*, the team worked online and held weekly meetings to complete *Unsafe* and *Defending Life* and kept up a hectic pace with media interviews, especially during the Barrett nomination battle.

Lincoln Proposal

As the 2020 presidential contest between President Trump and former

Vice President Biden raged, Foster joined leading pro-life advocates Josh Craddock, affiliated scholar with the James Wilson Institute, and Dr. Chad Pecknold, professor at The Catholic University of America, as authors of AUL's "Lincoln Proposal" policy paper.

The "Lincoln Proposal: A Constitutional Vision for an Executive Order to Restore Constitutional Rights to All Human Beings,"[34] was released in late 2020 with the intention of shaping the priorities of future pro-life presidents. The essential insight of the Lincoln Proposal was that, whatever might happen with *Roe v. Wade*, pro-life presidents need not accept the notion of total judicial supremacy on the issue of abortion.

AUL's "Lincoln Proposal" underlined that the executive, legislative, and judicial branches each share constitutional interpretive authority, and consequently that pro-life presidents possess the power to issue executive orders to interpret the constitution as being fundamentally incompatible with abortion. AUL's "Lincoln Proposal" was modeled on President Abraham Lincoln's response to the Supreme Court's landmark 1857 decision in *Dred Scott v. Sandford*. The "Lincoln Proposal" explains:

> As a Senate candidate, Lincoln acknowledged the Court's decision as binding upon the parties, but denied the opinion possessed precedential effect. Once elected President, Lincoln reaffirmed his commitment to resisting Dred Scott in his First Inaugural Address, warning that "if the policy of the government, upon vital questions affecting the whole people, is to be irrevocably fixed by decisions of the Supreme Court … the people will have ceased to be their own rulers, having to that extent practically resigned their government into the hands of that eminent tribunal."

> Lincoln's attorney general quickly drafted a lengthy legal opinion arguing that "the president and the judiciary are co-ordinate departments of government, and the one not subordinate to the other."

> Thus, the Executive must be able "to act out its own granted powers, without any ordained or legal superior possessing the

power to revise and reverse its action." The Lincoln administration then put its theory into practice, disregarding Dred Scott's central argument against black citizenship and issuing passports and patents to black Americans, acts within his purview as the Chief Executive. Lincoln also exercised his authority over the federal territories and the District of Columbia by signing bills that abolished slavery in those jurisdictions despite Dred Scott's assertion that the territories were constitutionally required to permit slavery. Most famously, Lincoln's Emancipation Proclamation, issued on January 1, 1863 in the midst of the Civil War, declared "that all persons held as slaves" within the warring Southern states "are, and hence-forward shall be free." That act, based upon the president's authority as Commander in Chief of the Union forces, permitted freed African-Americans to enter the army; and by the end of the war, nearly 200,000 had fought for their freedom.

These great American presidents provide an example for the President to follow. The President may exercise his independent constitutional authority to interpret the Fourteenth Amendment's safeguards of due process and equal protection to extend to all human beings, born and not yet born, irrespective of the Supreme Court's position in *Roe*.

AUL's "Lincoln Proposal" also articulated more recent historical precedent for such an executive order, as well as the practical consequences of such a prudential use of presidential power:

In 1988, President Reagan issued a proclamation recognizing that "[t]he unalienable right to life is found not only in the Declaration of Independence but also in the Constitution that every President is sworn to preserve, protect, and defend. Both the Fifth and Fourteenth Amendments guarantee that no person shall be deprived of life without due process of law." Reagan therefore undertook to "proclaim and declare the unalienable personhood of every American, from the moment of conception until natural death." Invoking his solemn constitutional duty, President Reagan promised to "take care that the Constitution and laws of the United States are faithfully executed for the protection of America's unborn children."

An Executive Order from the President could give legal effect to the proclamation first announced by President Reagan over three decades ago. Such an order would constitute a binding and authoritative interpretation of the Constitution within the executive branch, including its constitutive departments and agencies. The President could direct the departments and agencies to examine their regulations and programs to ensure they align with the President's Executive Order, and to initiate rulemaking or issue guidance bringing those regulations and programs into compliance with the President's interpretation as necessary.

The "Lincoln Proposal" outlines a variety of specific orders for such an executive order to include, illustrating the impressive scope of executive branch power for effecting positive pro-life policies. The authors of AUL's "Lincoln Proposal" conclude:

The exercise of prudence in public life calls political leaders to bring about the greatest good possible in a given situation. Americans need not accept an interminable status quo of indifference toward the rights of the child, due either to the timidity of our political elite or to the presumption of our judiciary class. It is a political imperative to lead with both prudence and principle. An Executive Order would be the culmination of earlier presidential actions to guarantee constitutional protections to all human beings, following in the footsteps of President Lincoln in the aftermath of Dred Scott. Adopting the logic of Lincoln's approach would likewise be a step away from a false federalism wherein the most basic and fundamental of all rights could continue to be unjustly withheld in hostile jurisdictions. No doubt such an order would be the greatest pro-life accomplishment in decades, introducing the logic of abolition to America's body politic. And indeed, such an order would vindicate that most precious unalienable right named in the Declaration of Independence: the right to life. ...

> The Lincoln Proposal focuses presidential energy not merely on abortion's regulation, but rather on the ultimate goal of abortion's abolition.

The debut of AUL's "Lincoln Proposal" led to significant conversation with the pro-life movement for its concrete and precedential proposal for the prudential exercise of executive power, as well as interest from the states for a version of the "Lincoln Proposal" for pro-life governors.

The Barrett Nomination

The long-term prospects for *Roe* suffered several hammer blows in the years following *Whole Woman's Health*: the 2016 elections, the confirmations of Justices Gorsuch and Kavanaugh, the new majority in *June Medical* that abandoned *Whole Woman's Health*, and the confirmation of Justice Barrett.

On September 18, 2020, Justice Ruth Bader Ginsburg died after a long fight with cancer. AUL issued a statement recognizing her pioneering work as a legal advocate for equal opportunity for women. The Trump Administration moved immediately to fill the empty seat.

President Trump nominated Seventh Circuit Court of Appeals Judge Amy Coney Barrett. Confirmation hearings in the Senate Judiciary Committee began on Monday, October 12, 2020, and lasted for four days.

Barrett sailed through the hearings, exhibiting more confidence and poise than any nominee in living memory. But she offered an insight that no nominee had since 1973. When asked if *Roe* was "super-precedent," a well-worn label used to describe the rulings like *Brown v. Board of Education*, Barrett replied, "I'm answering a lot of questions about *Roe*, which I think indicates that *Roe* doesn't fall into that category." Barrett's confirmation on October 26, 2020 heightened the risk to *Roe*. As the first pro-life female justice on the Court in its history, Barrett's role would soon prove to be pivotal

Training the Next Generation of Lawyers

But who will be on the Supreme Court in 2030 or 2040?

From its earliest days—beginning with the efforts of Victor Rosenblum,

Dennis Horan, and John Gorby—AUL has recruited law students to help with research, legislation, litigation, and publications.

Law students who assisted in the preparation of AUL's brief in *Danforth* in 1975 and 1976 included Patrick Trueman, Valerie Bruech, Mary Schmuttenmaer, and Douglas Scovil of John Marshall Law School, where Gorby taught, and Thomas J. Marzen, who was a law student at Illinois Institute of Technology, Chicago-Kent College of Law. Trueman later became executive director of AUL, and Marzen served as general counsel of AUL until 1984.

In 1978, after the tragic death of David Louisell, AUL launched the Louisell Summer Internship for law students in his honor. In 1975, Louisell had become a member of the National Commission for the Protection of Human Subjects of Biomedical and Behavioral Research and issued a dissenting opinion to the commission's recommendations for fetal experimentation, advocating that "[n]o research should be permitted on a fetus to be aborted that could not be permitted on one to go to term."[35] When Louisell died unexpectedly in August 1977, colleagues wrote a tribute still available online:

> David's devotion to the problems of church and state, of abortion and other humanistic causes, exposed him to constant demand as a public speaker, legal advocate, and counselor. These calls on his time and energy he rarely felt able to turn down, despite exigent commitments to teaching and research. He was an outstanding and inspiring classroom teacher of the grand style, peppering his lessons of legal analysis with memorable aphorism and towering voice. Amidst many outside engagements, he accepted several important and distinguished visiting professorial appointments in recent years (Minnesota, 1971-72; Virginia, 1975-76). He was a splendid colleague, ever ready to dispense counsel and friendship. Perhaps most admirable of all was his devotion to his wife, which sorely taxed his resources in the last year of his life during her terminal illness and must have contributed to his own untimely death.

For two decades thereafter, AUL's summer legal fellowship was named after Louisell.

Foster and Forsythe began their work at AUL after learning of the organization through the Louisell internship at law school. Forsythe contacted Marzen by letter in November 1983 after graduating from law school and offered to volunteer. After a year of volunteering, Forsythe interviewed for a staff counsel position and accepted it in February 1985. Former AUL legal fellow Brian Hagedorn was elected to the Wisconsin Supreme Court in 2018.

AUL's summer Legal Fellows Program hit its stride in 2020 with six law students: MaryJayne Caum (Mercer), Noelle Daniel (Kansas), Molly Hogan (Georgetown), Carolyn McDonnell (U. St. Thomas), Hugh Phillips (Liberty), and Shane Rider (Oklahoma). Though held remotely as a result of the COVID-19 pandemic, AUL and the students benefited tremendously. Students received 15 hours of classroom instruction online, a significant learning experience during which they heard from legal experts and received instruction on the law of bioethics, abortion, and end-of-life issues. The group produced legal memos on legislation and litigation, covering approximately 20 legal projects, including brief drafting, a white paper on the *June Medical* decision, and updated model legislation for *Defending Life*. Several students explored questions on chemical abortion, assisted-reproductive technologies, and end-of-life issues. Each added a passion for protecting human life through the law, and the group contributed significantly to AUL's work.

As 2020 demonstrated, from federal and state policy issues related to the pandemic to the Supreme Court's decision in *June Medical,* the American legal profession will always need lawyers to protect human life in American law amidst the never-ending complexity of bioethics and technology.

The Biden Presidency

The 2020 election posed a stark choice between President Trump's policy record and the positions taken by Democratic nominee, Joe Biden. Though he had described himself throughout his decades-long political career as "personally pro-life," Biden had a long history of support for *Roe* and the right to abortion. One pro-life position he had held, however, was support for the Hyde Amendment, saying that pro-life

Americans should not be required to fund a procedure with which they fundamentally disagreed.

But in June 2019, Biden rejected that position, adopting instead the stance of his party: full opposition to Hyde and support for federally-funded abortion on demand. September 30, 2020 marked the 44th anniversary of the Hyde Amendment. As Dr. Michael New put it:

> The Hyde Amendment has … saved over 2.4 million lives since 1976. It enjoys broad public support—and even garners significant support from Democrats and people who identify as "pro-choice." It has also stood as evidence both political parties can find common ground. The original Hyde Amendment passed with the support of 103 House Democrats. Presidents Bill Clinton and Barack Obama routinely signed funding bills with Hyde Amendment protections. However, despite this outstanding track record, the Hyde Amendment is now in greater danger than ever. After years of supporting the Hyde Amendment, last summer Joe Biden reversed his position and now opposes the Hyde Amendment. Additionally, over 180 House Democrats have publicly stated their opposition to the Hyde Amendment. Additionally the Democratic Party platform now explicitly calls for eliminating the Hyde Amendment, thus forcing taxpayers to pay for the destruction of innocent human life.[36]

Since becoming president, Biden has not swerved from his opposition to Hyde. He swiftly ended the Mexico City policy, which had forbidden federal foreign-aid money from underwriting groups that perform or promote abortions, and he signed a COVID-19 stimulus bill that allowed funding for abortion and funded Planned Parenthood.

Nevertheless, the Trump Administration had been a success for the pro-life movement, the most effective presidential administration since *Roe* at implementing pro-life policy. The administration reshaped the Court with three new justices, and officials throughout the administration worked to end federal support for abortion and strengthened federal protection of conscience rights.

During the Trump Administration, there was increased momentum in the states, and the results of the 2020 election did not set back pro-life legislators at the state level. Pro-life strength increased in the House and in a number of states. With Justice Barrett's confirmation, the cause for life had more hope that the Court might remove itself from the "abortion-umpiring business" and permit leaders at all levels of government to uphold natural rights and human dignity and protect human persons in law and policy.

Chapter 13 Endnotes

1   550 U.S. at 172 (2007) (Ginsburg, J., dissenting) ("legal challenges to undue restrictions on abortion procedures do not seek to vindicate some generalized notion of privacy; rather, they center on a woman's autonomy to determine her life's course, and thus to enjoy equal citizenship stature").

2   *See* The Constitution in 2020 (Jack M. Balkin & Reva B. Siegel eds., 2009), especially Dawn E. Johnsen, *A Progressive Reproductive Rights Agenda for 2020, in* The Constitution in 2020 255–266.

3   558 U.S. 310.

4   136 S. Ct. 2292.

5   *See The Public Health Crisis in America's Abortion Clinics is Unsafe Conditions*, Ams. United for Life, https://unsafereport.org/ (last visited June 7, 2022)..

6   *See* Hush, *supra* ch. 4 note 101. *See also* Priscilla K. Coleman, *Post-Abortion Mental Health Research: Distilling Quality Evidence from a Politicized Professional Literature*, 22 J. Am. Physicians & Surgeons 38 (2017); David M. Fergusson et al., *Does Abortion Reduce the Mental Health Risks of Unwanted or Unintended Pregnancy? A Re-appraisal of the Evidence*, 47 Australian & N.Z. J. Psychiatry 819 (2013); Priscilla K. Coleman, *Abortion and Mental Health: A Quantitative Synthesis and Analysis of Research Published* 1995-2009, 199 British J. Psychiatry 180 (2011); Peace Psychology Perspectives on Abortion (*Rachel M. MacNair ed., 2016); David C. Reardon, Abortion Decisions and the Duty to Screen: Clinical, Ethical and Legal Implications of Predictive Risk Factors of Post-abortion Maladjustment*, 20 J. Contemp. Health L. & Pol'y 33 (2003).

7   Catherine Glenn Foster, *Testimony Before the U.S. Senate Judiciary Committee on S. 160, the Pain-Capable Unborn Child Protection Act*, Ams. United for Life (Apr. 9, 2019), https://aul.org/2019/04/09/testimony-before-the-u-s-senate-judiciary-committee-on-s-160-the-pain-capable-unborn-child-protection-act/.

8   We the People, *Will* Roe *Be Overturned?: Abortion and the Constitution Part 1,* Nat'l Const. Ctr. (May 23, 2019), https://podcasts.apple.com/us/podcast/will-roe-be-overturned-abortion-and-the-constitution-part-1/id83213431?i=1000439178679.

9   We the People, *The Future of Abortion Laws at the Supreme Court*, Nat'l Const. Ctr. (Feb. 28, 2019), https://podcasts.apple.com/us/podcast/the-future-of-abortion-laws-at-the-supreme-court/id83213431?i=1000430842591.

10 We the People, *Louisiana Abortion Law at the Supreme Court*, Nat'l Const. Ctr. (Mar. 12, 2020), https://podcasts.apple.com/us/podcast/louisiana-abortion-law-at-the-supreme-court/id83213431?i=1000468271908.

11 America's Town Hall, *Should* Roe *v.* Wade *Be Overturned?*, Nat'l Const. Ctr. (Sept. 24,

2019), https://www.youtube.com/watch?v=ddSsLg7Zj78.

12   Protect Women, Protect Life Rally at the United States Supreme Court (Mar. 4 2020), *available at* https://www.facebook.com/AmericansUnitedforLife/videos/protect-women-protect-life-rally/483436305868435.

13   *See* Helen M. Alvare, *Nearly 50 Years Post-*Roe v. Wade *and Nearing its End: What is the Evidence that Abortion Advances Women's Health and Equality?*, 34 Regent U. L. Rev. 165 (2022).

14   138 S. Ct. 2361 (2018). AUL's *amicus curiae* brief is available online. Brief *Amici Curiae* of the American Association of Pro-life Obstetricians and Gynecologists, American College of Pediatricians, and Christian Medical Association in Support of Petitioners, *NIFLA*, 138 S. Ct. 2361 (No. 16-1140), *available at* https://aul.org/wp-content/uploads/2018/10/AUL-Amicus-Brief-NIFLA-Becerra.pdf.

15   *Id.* at 2373–74.

16   Planned Parenthood S. Atl. v. Baker, 941 F.3d 687 (4th Cir. 2019), *cert. denied*, 140 S. Ct. 550 (2020). AUL's *amicus curiae* brief is available online. Brief *Amicus Curiae* of Americans United for Life in Support of Petitioners, *Baker*, 140 S. Ct. 550 (No. 19-1186), *available at* https://aul.org/wp-content/uploads/2020/11/19-1186-Amicus-Brief-of-American-United-for-Life.pdf.

17   Kerr v. Planned Parenthood S. Atl., No. 21-1431 (petition for cert. filed May 6, 2022). AUL's *amicus curiae* brief is available online. Brief *Amicus Curiae* of Americans United for Life in Support of Petitioner, *Kerr*, No. 21-1431, *available at* https://aul.org/wp-content/uploads/2022/05/AUL-amicus-brief-in-Kerr-v.-Planned-Parenthood-South-Atlantic.pdf.

18   *Food & Drug Admin.*, 141 S. Ct. 10. AUL's *amicus curiae* brief filed in the Fourth Circuit is available online. Brief *Amici Curiae* of 102 Members of Congress, *supra* ch. 10 note 34.

19   *June Med. Servs.*, 140 S. Ct. at 2156 n.3 (Alito, J., dissenting).

20   *Life, Liberty, and Law Archives*, Ams. United for Life, https://aul.org/topics/life-liberty-and-law/ (last visited June 1, 2023).

21   *See* Forsythe, *Stare Decisis, Workability, and* Roe v. Wade, *supra* ch. 10 note 6.

22   *See* Forsythe, *A Survey of Judicial and Scholarly Criticism of* Roe v. Wade *Since 1973*, *supra* ch. 3 note 1 (compiling judicial and scholarly criticism of *Roe v. Wade, Doe v. Bolton*, and *Planned Parenthood v. Casey*).

23   Bernard N. Nathanson, *Deeper into Abortion*, 291 New Eng. J. Med. 1189 (1974). Dr. Nathanson spoke at an AUL conference in Chicago in October 1986. Life, Liberty, & Law, *Dr. Bernard Nathanson, M.D. on Abortion as Between "A Woman and her Doctor" and What Physicians Owe to their Patients*, Ams. United for Life (Jan. 31, 2022), https://podcasts.apple.com/us/podcast/dr-bernard-nathanson-m-d-on-abortion-as-between-a/id1472791329?i=1000550636268.

24   Clarke D. Forsythe, *A Draft Opinion Overruling* Roe v. Wade, 16 Geo. J.L. & Pub. Pol'y

445 (2018).

25 *See* Mollie Hemingway & Carrie Severino, Justice on Trial: The Kavanaugh Confirmation and the Future of the Supreme Court (2019).

26 Katie Glenn, *AUL's 2020 State Legislative Sessions Report*, Ams. United for Life (Oct. 13, 2020), https://aul.org/2020/10/13/2020-state-legislative-sessions-report/.

27 *June Med. Servs.,* 140 S. Ct. at 2155 (Alito, J., dissenting). AUL's *amicus curiae* briefs are available online. Brief *Amicus Curiae* of Americans United for Life in Support of Respondent and Cross-Petitioner, *June Med. Servs.*, 140 S. Ct. 2103 (No. 18-1323), *available at* https://aul.org/wp-content/uploads/2020/01/18-1323-Amicus-Brief-of-Americans-United-For-Life.pdf; Brief Amici Curiae of 207 Members of Congress in Support of Respondent and Cross-Petitioner, *June Med. Servs.*, 140 S. Ct. 2103 (No. 18-1323), *available at* https://aul.org/wp-content/uploads/2020/01/18-1323-Amicus-Brief-of-207-Members-of-Congress.pdf.

28 *Disappointment and Opportunity: Americans United for Life Assesses the Supreme Court's Decision in* June Medical Services *and Surveys the Road Ahead*, Legal Memorandum from Ams. United for Life to State Legal Officers, Lawmakers, and Policy Advocates (July 31, 2020), https://aul.org/wp-content/uploads/2020/08/2020-07-31-AUL-on-JMS-Disapointment-and-Opportunity.pdf.

29 *June Med. Servs.*, 140 S. Ct. at 2133 (Roberts, C.J., concurring in the judgment).

30 *Id.* at 2155 (Alito, J., dissenting).

31 *Id.* at 2156.

32 In November 2020, the ACLJ filed a brief in the Supreme Court in support of a state appeal pointing out that the abortion advocates' claim that abortion is safer than childbirth cannot be verified and is contradicted by reliable medical evidence. *Amicus Brief* of the American Center for Law and Justice in Support of Petitioners, Slatery v. Adams & Boyle, P.C., (No. 20-482) (Jan. 25, 2021), *available at* http://media.aclj.org/pdf/Slatery-v.-Adams-&-Boyle-ACLJ-Cert.-Stage-Amicus-Brief-Filed-11.12.20_Redacted.pdf.

33 Katie Glenn, Opinion, *At-home Abortion is no Magic Pill*, Washington Examiner (Apr. 8, 2020), https://www.washingtonexaminer.com/opinion/at-home-abortion-is-no-magic-pill.

34 *Lincoln Proposal: A Constitutional Vision for an Executive Order to Restore Constitutional Rights to All Human Beings,* Ams. United for Life, https://aul.org/law-and-policy/lincoln-proposal/ (last visited June 1, 2023).

35 Louisell, *National Commission for the Protection of Human Subjects of Biomedical and Behavioral Research, supra* ch. 6 note 25, at 317.

36 New, *Hyde @ 40, supra* ch. 4 note 47.

CHAPTER 14

Dobbs and the
Seismic Reversal of *Roe*

Before the 2016 election, most legal commentators dismissed the overruling of *Roe* as impossible. But after the 2016 election, a growing chorus of commentators began warning of a possible reversal. Whether the warnings were genuine, designed to garner political contributions, or foster grassroots mobilization, they nevertheless proved that *Roe* was unsettled and undermined any reasonable expectation that *Roe* would remain the law.

Since Richard Nixon and the 1968 presidential election, no presidential candidate successfully made the Supreme Court an issue until 2016. Within hours of Justice Antonin Scalia's death on Saturday, February 13, 2016, Senate Majority Leader Mitch McConnell announced that the Senate would not approve any nominee to fill the vacancy until after the presidential election.[1] That served to put the Court at the center of the presidential election throughout 2016, and numerous analysts have since concluded that the vacancy influenced a significant number of votes.

A series of additional signs that *Roe* might be vulnerable began to appear to careful observers, especially the confirmation of Justice Gorsuch and the replacement of Justice Kennedy by Justice Kavanaugh. At her confirmation hearing, Judge Amy Coney Barrett, responding to a question by Sen. Amy Klobuchar (D-MN) as to whether *Roe* was a "super-precedent" immune from reconsideration, forthrightly and artfully responded, "I'm answering a lot of questions about *Roe*, which I think indicates that *Roe* doesn't fall in that category."[2] In other words, if *Roe* was settled, Senators wouldn't be asking all the questions about *Roe*.

How and Why *Roe* Fell

In May 2021, the Court agreed to hear *Dobbs v. Jackson Women's Health Organization*, involving Mississippi's 15-week limit on abortion, which would not have happened while Justices Kennedy and Ginsburg were on the Court. The State (joined by 25 other states) directly argued that *Roe* should be reconsidered. At oral argument on December 1, 2021, Chief Justice Roberts and Justices Thomas, Alito, Gorsuch, Kavanaugh, and Barrett asked numerous questions about the validity of *Roe* and *Casey*,[3] dramatically distinguishing *Dobbs* from the oral arguments in *Planned Parenthood of Southeastern Pennsylvania v. Casey* in 1992, during which few questions directly explored the validity of *Roe*. Instead, several justices spent considerable time exploring the nuances of the specific sections of the Pennsylvania abortion law, suggesting an emphasis on how those laws might be upheld *without* reexamining *Roe*.[4]

Then, of course, all the signs climaxed on May 2, 2022, when Justice Alito's entire draft opinion, showing that a majority supported the overruling of *Roe* and *Casey*, was leaked to, then released by, *Politico*.[5] Despite enormous pressure day by day over the next seven weeks, Justices Alito, Thomas, Gorsuch, Kavanaugh, and Barrett kept to their vote to overturn *Roe* and *Casey*.

On Friday, June 24, 2022, the Supreme Court, by a 5-4 vote, expressly overruled *Roe v. Wade* and *Planned Parenthood of Southeastern Pennsylvania v. Casey*.[6]

The majority opinion by Justice Samuel Alito, joined by Justices Thomas, Gorsuch, Kavanaugh, and Barrett, addressed the overruling of *Roe* head-on, and forthrightly and thoroughly explained why *Roe* and *Casey* were wrongly-decided and constitutionally illegitimate. The final opinion was stronger than the February draft, amplified to address the Chief Justice's position that overruling *Roe* should be postponed, to address the dissent, and to include two appendices totaling 29 pages with detailed citations of the state abortion laws that protected the pre-natal human being at "all stages of development" when the Fourteenth Amendment was ratified in 1868.

Roe's declaration of a right to abortion—and the Court's exercise of power over state abortion laws—could not be justified by the federal Constitution. Consequently, the abortion issue had to be returned to the people and their elected representatives.

While Chief Justice John Roberts joined the decision to uphold the Mississippi 15-week limit, he expressly refused to join the overruling of *Roe*, writing that an early right to abortion might be justifiable and that the overruling of *Roe* should be considered in a *future* case.[7] No other justice joined his opinion. The majority directly and thoroughly responded, turning the Chief Justice's prior opinions about *stare decisis* against him. His refusal to join the overruling of *Roe* is mystifying, given his personal knowledge of the 40-year campaign for originalism and his personal experience with the growing attack on the Court because *Roe* was unsettled. His role and his influence would have strengthened the overruling with a 6-3 vote.

Many factors contributed to *Roe v. Wade*'s demise. *Roe* was inherently defective. The Court rushed to judgment in 1971–72 because a tem-porary minority of four justices wanted to declare a right to abortion before President Nixon could confirm two justices to fill the vacancies left by the retirements of Justices Black and Harlan in September 1971. To accomplish this, the Court used two cases—out of the more than 20 abortion cases in the courts at that time—that had no trial or evidentia-ry record on the abortion issue. In deciding *Roe* and issuing a sweeping judgment, the Court violated many procedural, evidentiary, and pruden-tial rules in its rush to judgment. Thereafter, there was a concerted ef-fort over decades, galvanized by states and state public officials, to keep *Roe* unsettled. There was widespread criticism of the decision. There was a focused goal of overturning *Roe*, not just fixing it. Indeed, some scholars have identified *Roe* as the beginning of the modern concern with judicial activism and constitutional interpretation, spearheaded by the conservative legal movement.

Moreover, following the tack taken by every anti-*Roe* justice since 1973, these advocates formulated and consistently emphasized the most realistic manner in which *Roe* might be overruled by a majority of justices—a federalist manner that modestly returned the issue to the states, which had prohibited the procedure since the 1600s, rather than a Supreme Court declaration of constitutional personhood by which the unborn child would be protected as a "person" under the Fourteenth Amendment, which would have the effect of continuing to centralize the abortion issue in the Supreme Court.

The Supreme Court's opinion in *Dobbs* reiterated the main criticisms of *Roe* which have been articulated by numerous scholars, historians, and judges over decades, which fit the traditional standards of *stare decisis: Roe* was unsettled, wrongly decided, relied on a false history, not rooted in precedent, unworkable in practice, with no legitimate reliance interests. These fit, too, the factors articulated by Abraham Lincoln in his famous criticism of *Dred Scott* in 1857.[8] Even Justice O'Connor at one time referred to the Court's application of *Roe* to state regulations as an abortion "distortion" and decried the reality that "no legal rule or doctrine is safe from ad hoc nullification by this Court" when the Court applied its abortion doctrine to state abortion laws.[9]

The fatal defects of *Roe* were baked into the original opinion that was issued in January 1973. As federal appeals judge Amul Thapar forthrightly acknowledged in an abortion case in 2021, "[t]here are rules for most cases, and then there are rules for abortion cases."[10] The result-oriented willfulness that motivated four pro-abortion justices in 1971 to sweep away the abortion laws using the two cases of *Roe* (from Texas) and *Doe* (from Georgia) is reminiscent of the May 2023 Durham Report on the blunders by the FBI and its leadership during the Trump-Russia collusion investigation.[11] The Court in *Dobbs* decried "*Roe*'s abuse of judicial authority."

Repeated claims that a majority of Americans supported *Roe* never dealt with the reality that few Americans understood what *Roe* said or did. As the 1990 Gallup Poll "Abortion and Moral Beliefs" documented, and

James Davison Hunter explained in his 1994 book, *Before the Shooting Begins: Searching for Democracy in America's Culture Wars*, public opinion did not understand what *Roe* or the Court's 1989 decision in *Webster* did. When asked, public opinion did not accept specific elements of *Roe*. In fact, Gallup polling showed that a supermajority of Americans support a legal prohibition on abortion after 12 weeks.[12]

The Failure of the *Dobbs* Dissenters

The dissent by three justices in *Dobbs* was shocking.[13] After nearly 50 years of criticism of the *Roe* decision by judges, legal scholars, Congress, and state legislators, the *Dobbs* dissenters could not articulate any reason to anchor abortion as a constitutional right or justify *Roe* as rightly decided. After nearly five decades, the dissent could not articulate a stronger rationale for *Roe* other than the original rationale given by the Court in 1973. They relied, as *Roe* did, on an *ipse dixit*: women need abortion because we say so. The dissenters relied on policy reasons for legal abortion that are not found in the Constitution and are more accessible to legislators than to judges, as demonstrated by the Court's confused handling of facts and data about abortion in numerous cases over decades.

The Court's majority opinion in *Dobbs* leveled a direct and strong critique against the dissent.[14] The most striking thing about the *Dobbs* dissent by Justices Breyer, Sotomayor and Kagan is that it rewrites history and rewrites *Roe*. They could not be frank with the nation about the scope of *Roe*. They could not admit that the right to abortion in *Roe* and *Casey* extended up to birth. They could not admit that the "health" exception after fetal viability, adopted by *Roe* and *Doe* and reiterated in *Casey*, was limitless, allowing abortion for any "emotional" reason up to birth. And they refused to confront the problems with *Roe* addressed by lawyers, scholars, and judges since 1973. They would have reaffirmed *Roe* as originally written—something virtually no legal scholar in the country has been willing to do since 1973. They pretended that *Roe* was a shining example of the Supreme Court's success.

They ignored the entire 50-year controversy over *Roe* in Congress, the states, the courts, and among legal scholars and lawyers, and they simply pronounce that *Roe* was "settled" law. Of course, the *Dobbs* case would never have been heard by the Court—they would have dismissed it, refused to hear it—if *Roe* were a great success and indeed settled law. The dissenters simply could not deal with reality and admit that they have no adequate response.

They raised fears that the states would prosecute women, but ignored decades of state policy going back before *Roe* which treated women as the "second victim" of abortion, and ignored language in numerous modern federal and state abortion laws that *expressly* state that women cannot be prosecuted for abortion.

Like the plurality in *Casey* which devised new precedential rules (*stare decisis*) to save *Roe* in 1992, the *Dobbs* dissenters set up a new *stare decisis* standard: the Court should never overrule precedent unless it can "point[] to major legal or factual changes undermining a decision's original basis."[15] They basically picked two of the several *stare decisis* factors traditionally applied by the Court which they thought were the strongest in defending Roe. The "major" condition, of course, allows unlimited equivocation.

The *Casey* decision in 1992 was simply incoherent.[16] The plurality emphasized *stare decisis* but expressly overruled *Akron* and *Thorn-burgh*. It refused to overrule *Roe* due to political pressure but failed to acknowledge the political pressure on both sides. It suggested that abortion was "*sui generis*," even though there is a long Anglo-American tradition protecting prenatal life, and extensive state protection in pre-natal injury, wrongful death, and fetal homicide law. It talked about a "covenant," but not the Anglo-American legal protection for the prenatal human that historically parallels that covenant. It called "the contending sides ... to end their national division by accepting a common mandate rooted in the Constitution" but failed to explain how an abortion "right" was "rooted in the Constitution." It only justified the "right" by repeating the *ipse dixit* of *Eisenstadt* ("If the right of privacy means anything, it is the right ..."). And the "mystery" passage necessarily ignores the reality that state legal protection specifically protects the prenatal human *as a human being*. *Casey* did not "reaffirm" *Roe* on the merits but only on *stare decisis* (because it was decided). *Casey* did not provide a consti-tutional foundation for *Roe* in text, history, or structure. *Casey* did not demonstrate that an abortion right is "deeply rooted in this Nation's history and tradition." *Casey* failed its own test: "a decision without principled justification would be no judicial act at all." The closest the plurality in *Casey* came to addressing the merits of the constitutional "right" was an *ipse dixit*: they simply asserted that the abortion right is in the "Due Process Clause of the Fourteenth Amendment." The *Dobbs* dissent praised *Casey* but *Casey* admitted that *Roe* was unsettled, that parts of it were unworkable, and that the Court had erred. But in the *Dobbs* dissent, there was no admission of any error and no expression of any humility.

The *Dobbs* dissenters can't admit that *Roe* and *Casey* didn't strike a "balance" and instead imposed a national right to abortion for any reason, at any time of pregnancy, in all 50 states—a position held by 7% of Americans, and a policy that made the U.S. one of only five nations (of 195) that allows abortion for any reason after 20 weeks gestation. A position not supported by majority opinion and extreme by international standards.

They continue to tell the American people—as Justices Blackmun, O'Connor and Breyer did in previous writings—that *Roe*'s right to abortion only extended to "the first stages of pregnancy."[17] It's a confirmation of *Roe*'s extreme scope and unpopularity that the dissenters can't be frank with Americans—after almost 50 years—as to what *Roe* precisely did and meant. They rewrite *Roe* in a way they think would be reasonable to a majority of Americans, the *Roe* of their imagination, not the *Roe* actually imposed by the federal courts for 50 years.

They suggest that the Court in *Roe* "understood the difficulty and divisiveness of the abortion issue."[18] In fact, the Court decided *Roe* without any trial or evidentiary record of any kind. The *Roe* justices understood very little of anything about abortion. The *Roe* Court was clueless. They were then surprised by the negative reaction and criticism in Congress, by the constitutional amendments introduced in the next few months, by the numerous abortion bills introduced in the states in 1973–74, by the scholars who proceeded to criticize *Roe*, and by technological developments like obstetric ultrasound and in vitro fertilization that demonstrated that the embryonic life of a human person begins with the union of sperm and egg.

The dissent discourages extensive use of the Fourteenth Amendment's history because it was ratified by men, and thus "not perfectly attuned to the importance of reproductive rights for women's liberty, or for their capacity to participate as equal members of our Nation."[19] But if the Fourteenth Amendment can be so easily dismissed—if it can't be a source of authority about the constitutionality of abortion—then it cannot have been the source of an abortion right for 50 years.

The dissent applied the doctrine of *stare decisis* in the narrowest way possible to make a case for sticking to *Roe*. But the dissent refused to acknowledge that *Roe* and *Casey* were unsettled, the heart of *stare decisis et quieta non movere*. Precedent is only entitled to *stare decisis* respect if it is settled. They refused to acknowledge what numerous scholars and judges have acknowledged since 1973—that *Roe* was poorly reasoned and based on a false history. They refused to acknowledge the legal changes since *Roe* in substantive due process doctrine (involving unenumerated rights) that the Court had adopted in a series of decisions since *Roe*, such as *Washington v. Glucksberg* (1997),[20] *McDonald v. City of Chicago* (2010),[21] and *Timbs v. Indiana* (2019)[22] (written by Justice Ginsburg). Those decisions engaged in a careful historical analysis of the claimed right and required that unenumerated rights be "fundamental to our scheme of ordered liberty" and "deeply rooted in this Nation's history and tradition."

The *Dobbs* dissent repeatedly hit upon a very shallow criticism: that *Dobbs* happened because the Court's personnel changed. This says too much; what the dissent said of *Dobbs* was true of *Brown v. Board of Education*: *Brown* happened because of a change in Court personnel. Warren, Frankfurter, Black, Douglas, Jackson, Murphy, etc. *saw segregation differently* from their predecessors on the Court. The Court has overruled itself 235 times;[23] very few cases were overturned by the same group of justices. The great majority were overturned by different justices. This serves to show that it's difficult for justices to admit their errors, and correction must come from outsiders with a more objective perspective.

It is clear the dissenters have learned virtually nothing from nearly 50 years of *Roe* and more than 33 abortion cases decided by the Court. They simply refuse to acknowledge the constitutional crisis and the controversy. By refusing to acknowledge any of these errors, mistakes, and criticisms, the dissenters showed just how far they would go to distort areas of constitutional law and doctrine—even the doctrine of precedent itself—in order to "save *Roe*."

What *Dobbs* Accomplished

Because neither "privacy" nor "abortion" is mentioned in the U.S. Constitution, the *Roe* Court put considerable emphasis on history to justify an implied or unenumerated right to abortion. The Court in *Dobbs* therefore thoroughly re-examined the Anglo-American history of legal treatment of prenatal human beings because the *Casey* Court in 1992 failed to examine that history. *Roe* failed to justify abortion as a constitutional right under the constitutional standards that the Court had applied up to 1973. Instead, *Roe* was based on an *ipse dixit*: the Court simply declared "we believe that the right of privacy is broad enough to include a right to abortion."

The *Dobbs* Court concluded that no abortion right is deeply rooted in Anglo-American history and corrected the serious mistakes of history made by the *Roe* Court. In fact, the *Dobbs* Court referred at least 19 times to the fact that the states protected the prenatal human at "all stages" of development. In two appendices, Justice Alito sets out in great detail the legal protection of prenatal human beings ("criminalizing abortion at all stages of pregnancy") that the states had enacted as of 1868, when the Fourteenth Amendment was ratified. He emphasized that by the end of 1868, twenty-eight of the thirty-seven states in the Union prohibited abortion throughout pregnancy, not just after quickening.

Abortion was prohibited by the English common law and the Americans colonies adopted the English common law of abortion decades before the states adopted and ratified the Federal Constitution in 1788. Abortion is rightfully an issue for state governance under our federalist system unless the U.S. Constitution or a subsequent amendment takes that authority away from the states. While some states may get the abortion issue grievously wrong and legalize abortion on demand—as many have—this doesn't in itself justify judicial control of abortion.

Few have recognized how much the Court in *Dobbs* did. It erased the false history of abortion conjured in *Roe v. Wade* and gave the nation a detailed, accurate account of our history. It gave America back its long legal and cultural heritage of protection for the prenatal human being from its earliest stages. The Court *expressly* overruled both *Roe* and *Casey* in several passages. The Court gave a strong justification based in precedent (*stare decisis*) for doing so. The Court declared that *no implied or unenumerated* right to abortion was lurking elsewhere in the Constitution. And the Court affirmed that the 50 states have a *rational basis* to preserve "prenatal life at all stages of development."

Besides its correction of the historical record that showed no right to abortion existed in Anglo-American history, the *Dobbs* decision was solidly based in precedent (*stare decisis*). In 1992, *Casey* distorted *stare decisis* to preserve *Roe* (abortion distortion). The *Dobbs* Court noted that the *stare decisis* rationale in *Casey* was flawed, unconvincing, and an orphan: after *Casey*, the Court never applied *Casey*'s version of *stare decisis* in any subsequent decision, demonstrating that it was concocted to preserve *Roe*, influenced no future decision, and was not persuasive to any future Court.

The *Casey* Court admitted that *Roe* was unsettled but never addressed how that affected its analysis of the doctrine of precedent, despite the fact that settled caselaw is at the heart of *stare decisis*. In contrast, the *Dobbs* dissenters could never admit that *Roe* was radically unsettled and refused to consider that or explain how sticking with *Roe* in 2022 would settle *Roe* after 50 years.

In fact, numerous factual changes eroded *Roe*, especially advances in medical technology such as ever-more powerful ultrasound technologies. Numerous laws changed that eroded *Roe*, including fetal homicide and other prenatal injury laws. The most important change was the Court's own foundational doctrine of substantive due process, which was the foundation for *Roe*. The historical foundation for *Roe*—which the *Roe* Court acknowledged was required by substantive due process— was false and fabricated, as the *Dobbs* showed in great detail. In contrast, the *Dobbs* dissenters said that the history surrounding the Fourteenth Amendment was irrelevant, thus detaching the Court's exercise of power from the Amendment.

It's important to recognize that the *Dobbs* Court relinquished power, rather than aggrandized power. The *Dobbs* Court decentralized the issue of abortion by sending it to the people and their elected representatives in Congress and the states.

Few have noticed that *Dobbs* also decentralized *the debate over the risks to women* from abortion. The *Roe* Court in 1973 pronounced abortion "safer than childbirth." That was the key sociological fact on which the *Roe* Court relied to formulate the superstructure of *Roe* and the rules that would govern abortion, even though there was no trial or evidence in *Roe* or *Doe* which supported that assumption. And the *Roe* Court assumed the self-appointed role as the national abortion control board. In that role, the Court continued to dismiss data on the risks (proffered by abortion activists) over the decades. By striking down state limits on abortion after *Roe*, the Court said or implied that the risks of abortion did not justify the state laws. With *Dobbs*, the Court will no longer act as the national abortion control board. By decentralizing the debate over the physical and psychological risks of abortion, the Court is no longer the "national abortion control board" that issues pronouncements on the safety of abortion. The decentralization will open up the debate—as the medical debate over the COVID-19 vaccines and the best way to combat COVID-19 was decentralized—recognizing that state governors exercise their police power to care for the public health at the state level. So too, the debate over the risks will not be foreclosed by the Supreme Court; instead, studies and the data can be openly examined by state public officials and state health departments.

However, the risks of abortion are real. Coerced abortion is real. No medical and sociological data demonstrate that abortion is necessary for women's health or for women's equality. Instead, abortion is justified as an act of autonomy. The challenge will be to effectively disseminate medical studies on the risks and maintain a robust debate and ensure that women get fully informed consent before any abortion.

The Immediate Impact of *Dobbs*

A week after the *Dobbs* decision, a Rasmussen Reports poll found that "50% of likely U.S. voters approve of the Supreme Court abortion ruling, including 38% who Strongly Approve of the decision, which means that each state can now determine its own laws regarding abortion.

Forty-five percent (45%) disapprove of the Supreme Court's new ruling, including 38% who Strongly Disapprove."[24]

The most important practical question when *Dobbs* was issued was whether state officials would stand up and enforce their pro-life laws, including their abortion limits. *Dobbs* repeatedly stated that *Roe* and *Casey* were expressly overturned, and state officials acted immediately to enforce the abortion laws on their books, and state and federal courts immediately implemented *Dobbs* by allowing state abortion laws to go into effect. Within weeks of the *Dobbs* decision, more than 30 federal court cases were dismissed because *Dobbs*, by overturning *Roe*, erased the legal foundation for those federal challenges to state abortion laws. The laws could be enforced, and state governors or attorneys general acted to do so. This demonstrated federal and state judicial obedience to *Dobbs*, as well as widespread admission that *Roe* was overturned.

Within days, thirteen states announced plans to enforce their laws. That included Missouri, South Dakota, Arkansas, Kentucky, Louisiana, Ohio, Utah, Oklahoma, Alabama, Mississippi, South Carolina, Texas and Tennessee. Later West Virginia, Idaho, and Georgia made similar announcements as well.

In July, Arizona Governor Ducey signed a 15-week limit (SB 1164), as did Florida Governor DeSantis (HB 5). By September, Indiana Governor Holcomb had signed an early gestational prohibition (with exceptions for rape and incest), which was enjoined by a state court, but eventually went into effect.

Enforcement of state abortion limits was the most important thing to happen after *Dobbs*. It demonstrated that *Roe* and *Casey* were overruled and that public officials were acting based on that reality.

With federal and state officials now directly responsible, and with the media spotlight shining hotly on them, we especially need states and state officials to stand up and enforce state laws. It is particularly important that purple states enforce whatever is on the books. Even in purple states, majorities tend to support prohibition after 12 weeks.

Substantive progress starts with an enforceable line, a sustainable beachhead from which further progress can be made.

Implications for Future Supreme Court Decisions

While the majority emphasized that *Dobbs* applied only to *Roe* and not to other past decisions, there are some clear implications for *future* decisions and questions of implied or unenumerated rights. *Dobbs* reinforced federalism and representative government and downgraded judicial supremacy. The *Dobbs* Court frankly admitted that the *Roe* Court was seriously wrong. *Dobbs* has significant implications for substantive due process, the doctrine that has undergirded unenumerated rights for decades. *Dobbs* strongly indicates that states will have authority under their police power for the regulation of medicine and biotechnology. This is reinforced as well by the Supreme Court's decisions since 2020 on the COVID-19 pandemic.

To preserve *Roe*, the Court distorted numerous legal doctrines. That eventually included the doctrine of precedent itself. As *Roe* was challenged after 1973, Justice Blackmun got his back up and dug in his heels, refusing any "compromise" and expanded *Roe* to eliminate more and more regulations of abortion. Justices adopted a "strong" version of precedent that was unrealistic and, frankly, unprecedented. It refused to acknowledge that settled law was at the heart of *stare decisis* and that unsettled decisions might be defective. It suggested that Justices could do no wrong. It was rooted in judicial supremacy rather than constitutional supremacy. It was rooted in the "living constitution" rather than the document ratified by the people. It was repeated by the dissent in *Dobbs*.

Hopefully, *Dobbs* may rectify the confusion of *stare decisis* that developed to save *Roe*. Now that *Roe* is gone, the Court has an opportunity to return to an understanding of precedent that is more humble and more willing to admit that justices make mistakes and that the ratified text is supreme over the decisions that justices may reach from time to time. *Dobbs* also employed an originalist judicial philosophy anchored in the constitutional text as ratified by the people, thereby preserving self-government.

What's Happened in the Year Since *Dobbs*

Was the cause for life ready for *Dobbs?* The question is ironic given that expectations until the November 2016 election were that overturning *Roe* would never happen.

The cause for life indicated that it was ready first by the abortion laws that were quickly enforced by public officials who had been support- ed by pro-life voters and organizations like Susan B. Anthony Pro-Life America, the National Right to Life Committee, and state pro-life politi- cal action committees (PACs), second by the court cases against pro-life laws getting dismissed, third by the thousands of pregnancy resource centers (PRCs) across the country who continued decades of good work by reaching out to pregnant women in need, and, finally, by the political mobilization before the November 2022 elections which re- elected dozens of pro-life state officials and helped the Republicans win the House of Representatives.

In September 2022, Sen. Lindsey Graham (R-SC) introduced a bill in Congress to protect pain-capable unborn children by establishing a federal limit on abortion at 15-weeks.[25] AUL leadership stood alongside Sen. Graham and other pro-life partners and called on Congress for action after *Dobbs.*

If some feared a wholesale Republican election debacle after *Dobbs,* it didn't happen. In November 2022, a dozen pro-life governors who supported or enforced early gestational limits were elected or re-elect- ed. The $500 million poured into pro-abortion ads in the 2022 election cycle most likely blunted any "red wave" and led to a narrow Republi- can majority in the U.S. House and a narrow Democratic majority in the U.S. Senate. In one sense, the pro-abortion money fought Republicans to a draw at the *federal* level.

The one thing that enabled state pro-life public officials to be as ready as they were for *Dobbs* was their decades of work on state abortion bills. Those years of work—combined with election campaigns involv- ing those bills and the fundraising and organizing that equipped these officials to win elections—enabled them to be ready to work for the strongest possible abortion limits after *Dobbs*. Pre-*Dobbs* and post-*Dobbs* was a matter of degree in state legislatures. The decades of work by pregnancy resource centers enabled them to be strong after *Dobbs* and available to help women.

There is evidence that *Dobbs* is becoming settled, and such actions need to continue year by year. States have enforced abortion laws. States have assumed control. States have voted. People are deciding.

The loss of the Kansas ballot initiative in August 2022 (which would have overturned a state version of *Roe v. Wade* and made the state constitution abortion neutral) was deeply disappointing, as was the Kentucky ballot initiative and the Michigan ballot initiative in November 2022.

In the 2023 state legislative sessions, states moved ahead with additional legislative limits. In March, Wyoming debated a limit on abortion[26] and on chemical abortion.[27] Strong majorities supported the abortion limit in the House (49-10) and the Senate (25-5). Wyoming Governor Mark Gordon allowed the abortion limit, Life is a Human Right Act (HB 152), to become law without his signature. But he signed a different bill prohibiting abortion pills (SF 109), which AUL supported with written testimony in January.

In May 2023, North Carolina's House and Senate voted to override Governor Cooper's veto of an abortion limit after 12 weeks of pregnancy.[28] The same month, South Carolina heard an extensive debate over a heartbeat limit in their Senate and House. It eventually passed both houses and was sent to Governor McMaster for his signature.[29] Likewise in May, Nebraska's unicameral legislature passed a prohibition on abortion after 12 weeks and it was signed by Governor Jim Pillen.[30]

At the federal level, efforts by the Biden Administration and Garland Department of Justice to erase state prolife initiatives failed. Federal policy is pro-life policy; federal laws that were enacted in the decades before *Dobbs* are pro-life.[31] For example, the federal Emergency Medical Treatment and Active Labor Act (EMTALA) law protects the unborn child explicitly.

States that have enacted and enforced gestational limits on abortion will need to track how women do in states with abortion limits. Each state needs to publish a "Women's Wellness Index" because we need public health and socio-economic data in order to show how women do in states with abortion limits and prohibitions.

AUL's Leadership in a Post-*Roe* America

On May 2, 2022, the same day that *Politico* would publish a leaked version of the *Dobbs* majority opinion, AUL released a short film entitled "What Does a Post-*Roe* America Look Like?"[32] Due in part to the providential timing of its debut only hours prior to the *Dobbs* leak, AUL's vision and message went on to be widely seen and discussed within the pro-life movement.

"We've never wanted *Roe*'s reversal simply to mean that America moves from a constitutionally pro-abortion attitude to a constitutionally indifferent attitude," the AUL narrator states in the short video, alluding to the organization's ultimate strategic aim of achieving constitutional protection for every member of the human family. "Abortion is fundamentally unjust," the AUL narrator continues, "because it deprives our brothers and sisters of the equal protection of the laws. It turns equals into unequals. It empowers the strong at the expense of the vulnerable. And it makes us all less human and less humane along the way."

"What Does a Post-*Roe* America Look Like?" set the stage for AUL's continuing work after the by-that-point anticipated decision in *Dobbs* to reverse *Roe*, and made clear that the grand strategy of both AUL and the pro-life movement remained the same as it ever was: arriving at the day where all are welcomed throughout life and protected in law. "Americans United for Life advances the human right to life in culture, law, and policy," the short video continues, "because we recognize that our role is this: to make the most justice-focused, most powerful, and most constitutional arguments possible on behalf of our plaintiffs—the preborn child, the mother and father vulnerable to abortionists, and the families and communities diminished by the deadly indifference of the law across the spectrum of life issues."

Later that month, the Democrat-controlled House Committee on the Judiciary called a hearing on abortion in response to the *Dobbs* draft opinion leak. At the hearing, Rep. Hank Johnson (D-GA 4) read excerpts[33] from "What Does a Post-*Roe* America Look Like?" into the Congressional record, feigning surprise at AUL's declaration that, "We never really wanted *Roe*'s reversal to make abortion a state issue where some states protect life and other states continue to kill and dismember. After *Roe*, we don't want more victims, we want abortion abolition."

While closely tracking national and state level abortion conversations in the weeks and months after *Dobbs* was finally handed down and *Roe* was overturned, AUL developed and in November 2022 launched its American Life Initiative.[34] The American Life Initiative (ALI) represented AUL's vision for the pro-life movement post-*Roe* and for leaders and elected representatives in every branch and across every level of government to strive for a constitutional order that equally protects all members of the human family. Steven H. Aden, AUL chief legal officer & general counsel, articulated "The Post-*Roe* Road Ahead and Our Final Destination,"[35] namely the achievement of constitutional personhood for the preborn child. As the surest approach, AUL proposed an Abortion Abolition Amendment[36] to the U.S. Constitution, offering language modeled on the 13th Amendment abolishing slavery. AUL offered the following as draft language for such a constitutional amendment, for the pro-life movement to consider:

Abortion Abolition Amendment

Section 1. Neither abortion nor any form of intentional termination of a human life in utero shall exist within the United States, or any place subject to their jurisdiction; provided, however, that the term "abortion" shall not include medical procedures to resolve a miscarriage or ectopic pregnancy, or necessary to preserve the life of a pregnant woman or to address a serious risk of substantial and irreversible impairment of a major bodily function.

Section 2. Congress and the several States, as well as the territories of the United States, shall have power to enforce this article by appropriate legislation.

Section 3. Any citizen of a State or territory of the United States shall have the right to bring an action in federal district court of the district wherein that citizen resides for equitable relief to enforce the provisions of this article, and upon prevailing, shall recover reasonable costs and attorney's fees., but the suit otherwise shall be brought in accordance with the articles of the Constitution.

Carolyn McDonnell, AUL litigation counsel, wrote alongside Regina Maitlen, AUL research fellow, on "The States in Congress: Federal Strategies for Defending Life After *Roe*,"[37] stressing the role that federal action will play after *Roe* to "protect unborn children, mothers, and families in even the most anti-life states." The ALI also offered new pro-life model legislation for elected representatives in the states, including the Ready for Life Act, Empowering Families to Thrive Act, Pregnancy Options Tax Credit Act, and Free Speech for Life Act.

In January 2023, in advance of the March for Life's 50th Anniversary, AUL released the policy paper "Make Birth Free: A Vision for Congress to Empower American Mothers, Families, and Communities."[38] After *Roe*, with abortion remaining a scourge from coast to coast, AUL's "Make Birth Free" vision was authored with the simple conviction that pregnancy and childbirth should be cheaper than the cost of abortion. AUL's policy paper proposed eliminating the direct costs of pregnancy and childbirth to American families, either by adapting successful policy precedents through Medicare and Medicaid or by adopting the approach of the Affordable Care Act by mandating that private medical insurers eliminate co-pays and deductibles relating to prenatal care, birth, and related services.

AUL's "Make Birth Free" policy proposal sparked healthy and widespread conversation, leading to an endorsement by newly elected Sen. J.D. Vance (R-OH)[39] as well as Sen. Chris Murphy (D-CT) who affirmed that "our nation should have far more policies that promote childbirth, and universal free childbirth is a really worthwhile idea."[40]

"Make Birth Free" was applauded by the Institute for Family Studies as a proposal "conservatives must strongly consider,"[41] was described as "compelling" and "a proposal that deserves bipartisan support" by pro-life social scientist Dr. Michael New,[42] and was hailed by bioethicist Wesley J. Smith for having "opened an important conversation."[43] Bradley Devlin at The American Conservative applauded "Make Birth Free" in his article "Babies Are Good,"[44] and Carmel Richardson unpacked how the proposal would "address our deference to medical management [of birth] that is driving up charges in the first place."[45] Christianity Today spotlighted many voices praising "Make Birth Free," including Prof. Daniel Bennett who stated, "I am encouraged to see an unapologetically pro-life group recognize the complexity of living in a post-*Roe* world."[46] Kelly Rosati, formerly of Focus on the Family, praised "Make Birth Free" as a proposal that "recognizes the unique, sacred, and practical imperatives to structure a society whose fiscal priorities include welcoming new life and fostering the next generation."[47] Lyman Stone, demographer and economist, described "Make Birth Free" as "laudable" and observed that "[i]f the proposal on offer became law tomorrow, we would have fewer abortions, more healthy babies, and a stronger culture of life in our society."[48]

Terry Moran, senior national correspondent at ABC News, spotlighted "Make Birth Free" to his nearly one million Twitter followers, calling it "an idea progressives, moderates, [and] conservatives might agree on."[49] People's Policy Project endorsed "Make Birth Free" and contributed to the dialogue by outlining one approach to implementation.[50] The *Pittsburgh Post-Gazette* editorial board endorsed "Make Birth Free" and called it a "refreshingly bi-partisan" proposal that creates "common ground" for those with the "courage and wisdom to see it."[51]

Dr. Allan C. Carlson, author of *The American Way: Family and Community in the Shaping of the American Identity* and *Fractured Generations: Crafting a Family Policy for Twenty-first Century America*, praised "Make Birth Free" for having "resurrected a sharp, if now largely forgotten, policy debate over the very same issues conducted a century ago: the triumph and eventual failure of The Sheppard-Towner Maternity and Infancy Act." After passing overwhelmingly in Congress and being signed into law by President Harding, thus enshrining into law America's first universal maternal and infant healthcare program, "Sheppard-Towner nurses, commonly in distinctive uniforms with dramatic, flowing capes, spread out across the land" throughout the 1920s and across 45 states. "The nurses accomplished much," wrote Carlson. "By 1929, they had held 183,252 prenatal and child-health conferences, helped to established nearly 3,000 permanent maternity clinics, visited 3,131,996 homes, and distributed 22,030,489 pieces of literature, including the popular booklets Prenatal Care and Infant Care. Home visits provided direct support for mothers breastfeeding their babies.

The overall infant mortality rate fell by about 10 percent. Deaths from gastrointestinal disease—those most preventable through education—fell by 45 percent." Carlson, who served on the National Commission on Children (1988-1993) by appointment of President Ronald Reagan, connected Congress's sunsetting of the Sheppard-Towner Act in 1929—despite its enormous popularity and, tragically, on the eve of the Great Depression—to continuing opposition of the American Medical Association. "An important lesson from the Sheppard-Towner experience," reflected Carlson, "is that big ideas enacted democratically, rather than as public charity, have powerful and positive effects. 'Make Birth Free' would be a wonderful affirmation of all young families. It would enhance the life prospects of children. It should reduce the turn to abortion. And it could allow for more humane and less medicalized birthing alternatives to flourish."[52]

In March 2023, months after AUL and the pro-life movement had secured the long-sought reversal of *Roe* and with AUL's vision for the next generation launched, Catherine Glenn Foster departed AUL to pursue new opportunities for shaping public sentiment. Kevin Tordoff, AUL chief strategy officer and a past AUL board member, stepped into the role of interim president as the organization began its search for its next generational leader.

In April 2023, The Catholic University of America's Institute for Human Ecology hosted a public debate on "Make Birth Free" between Tom Shakely, AUL chief engagement officer, and the *Washington Post*'s Megan McArdle.[53] EWTN Pro-Life Weekly endorsed "Make Birth Free," with anchor Prudence Robertson stating, "Making birth free relies on reprioritizing what's important in our culture" and that "healthcare must be focused on the future of humanity."[54] In May 2023, Marvin Olasky, coauthor with Leah Savas of *The Story of Abortion in America* and former editor of WORLD Magazine, endorsed "Make Birth Free," calling it "an easy-to-understand and helpful proposal for the pro-life movement to get behind."[55]

Although abortion remains the pre-eminent pro-life concern, AUL has continued to emphasize that issues pertaining to the human right to life span a broad spectrum.

In early May 2023, Carolyn McDonnell published the AUL policy paper,

"A Time to Choose: Suicide Assistance or Suicide Prevention?"[56] Mc-Donnell outlined the legal status of physician-assisted suicide across the nation and underscored why so-called safeguards put in place by states that have made assisted suicide lawful cannot protect vulnerable persons as well as how increasing suicide access undercuts successful suicide prevention policies.

"Assisted suicide threatens vulnerable patients, poses grave informed consent issues, and blatantly discriminates against the elderly and persons with illnesses and disabilities," writes McDonnell.[57] "The practice undermines suicide prevention policies and increases the rates of non-assisted suicide."[58] McDonnell concludes that "physician-assisted suicide exploits vulnerable patients and degrades the integrity of the medical profession."[59] AUL's policy paper stresses roles for both Congress and the states in protecting patients vulnerable to suicide and in safeguarding human dignity for those truly facing end-of-life realities.

In mid-May 2023, Hannah Ward, AUL project specialist, published "The Surrogate Mother and the Child She Bears," raising awareness about the true costs and consequences of commercial surrogacy.[60] "Children have a natural right to be brought into the world in an act of selfless love," wrote Ward. "'Womb renting,' as surrogacy is commonly called, completely distorts this gift."

"Commercial surrogacy is, in fact, incompatible with a free society and the human right to life understood in its fullness," concludes Ward. The startling reality is that "surrogacy perpetuates women's health issues, distorts parental roles, and may depend on abortion clauses embedded in the contracts." Ultimately, Ward reflects, the "realities of motherhood and the rights of children are not so easily reducible to the vocabulary of consent, free markets, or financial compensation. Mother and child, and the relationship between the two, are irreducible."

Over the course of the year since the *Dobbs* majority opinion draft first leaked, AUL's vision and voice have continued to guide leading thought and conversation within the pro-life movement and the cultural, legal, and policy priorities for the cause for life.

Shaping Public Sentiment

If the current Supreme Court majority holds, *Dobbs* indicates that the abortion issue will be left to the democratic and legislative process for the foreseeable future. The key challenge for the cause for life after *Dobbs* is shaping public sentiment in favor of respecting and protecting human beings. This is a contest of ideas.

In this, the cause for life should look to Abraham Lincoln. During the Lincoln-Douglas Senate debates of 1858, Lincoln told the crowd at Ottawa IL: "In this and like communities, public sentiment is everything. With public sentiment, nothing can fail; without it nothing can succeed. Consequently, he who moulds public sentiment, goes deeper than he who enacts statutes or pronounces decisions. He makes statutes and decisions possible or impossible to be executed."[61] By this statement, which Lincoln repeated over the years to different audiences, Lincoln did not mean that public opinion establishes the moral standard, but that public opinion is powerful in a republic, based on representative government.

Abraham Lincoln exhibited a democratic disposition. Lincoln was committed to studying and understanding public sentiment. As the Lincoln Douglas Senate debates of 1858 show, Lincoln made public *arguments* but did so in a homespun way that relied on shared understandings of life, shared faith.

Lincoln respected people but he was not a slave of public opinion. As Allen Guelzo has written, Lincoln sought to understand public opinion "not so much for the purpose of molding his policies after public opinion, as in determining how to navigate through public opinion toward political goals that he never offered up for compromise."[62] As his Cooper Union address in 1860 and his Second Inaugural showed, Lincoln refused to directly condemn southern slaveowners, even if he forthrightly said that slavery was an evil.

In the aftermath of *Dobbs*, strong public support of abortion law enforcement is essential. If it is absent—in major metro areas for example—the laws won't be enforced.

The cause for life needs a democratic disposition, a genuine willingness to see their neighbors as fellow Americans, a disposition to persuade rather than dismiss the public as immoral, an optimistic expectation that America can improve. We must respect Americans and view them as our fellow citizens.

This approach to political persuasion will require leaders of a certain character who are optimistic about the future, who like and respect their fellow citizens. It will require effective means to changing public understanding of abortion and its negative impact on women and children.

It will require the broadest possible argument against elective abortion. Abortion is not just about "the babies." It is about human flourishing, caring for women in need, and hope for the future. The best primer for this after *Dobbs* is Ryan Anderson and Alexandra DeSanctis's June 2022 book, *Tearing Us Apart: How Abortion Harms Everything and Solves Nothing*. We need to ask pointed questions about abortion that bring out abortion's downside and risks, e.g., what percentage of abortions are coerced?

Because the electoral system limits our choices, we don't get to vote for great leaders all the time. Sometimes we have to vote against the worst. Pro-life citizens will also have to be wise and discerning voters.

It will require a generational strategy because *Dobbs* was limited in its effect. *Dobbs* could not do away with the social and political forces promoting unlimited abortion. The obstacles to a culture of life in American politics and culture are still imposing. And yet we should be confident and inspired by the reality that the cause for life in America—which defends the Declaration of Independence and its doctrine of natural rights and protects human beings as human beings—is essential to preserving the American Republic.

Chapter 14 Endnotes

1 Burgess Everett & Glenn Thrush, *McConnell Throws Down the Gauntlet: No Sca-lia Replacement Under Obama*, Pᴏʟɪᴛɪᴄᴏ (updated Feb. 13, 2016), https://www.politico.com/story/2016/02/mitch-mcconnell-antonin-scalia-supreme-court-nomina-tion-219248.

2 Brian Naylor, *Barrett Says She Does Not Consider Roe v. Wade 'Super-Precedent'*, NPR (Oct. 13, 2020), https://www.npr.org/sections/live-amy-coney-barrett-su-preme-court-confirmation/2020/10/13/923355142/barrett-says-abortion-rights-deci-sion-not-a-super-precedent.

3 Transcript of Oral Argument, Dobbs v. Jackson Women's Health Org., 142 S. Ct. 2228 (2022) (No. 19-1392).

4 Transcript of Oral Argument, *Casey*, 505 U.S. 833 (No. 91-744).

5 Josh Gerstein & Alexander Ward, *Supreme Court Has Voted to Overturn Abortion Rights, Draft Opinion Shows*, (updated May 3, 2022), https://www.politico.com/news/2022/05/02/supreme-court-abortion-draft-opinion-00029473.

6 *Dobbs*, 142 S. Ct. 2228.

7 *Id.* at 2310–2317 (Roberts, C.J., concurring in the judgment).

8 Lincoln, *Speech on the Dred Scott Decision, supra* ch. 2 note 32, at 390–403.

9 Thornburgh v. Am. Coll. of Obstetricians & Gynecologists, 476 U.S. 747, 814 (1986) (O'Connor, J., dissenting).

10 Memphis Ctr. for Reprod. Health v. Slatery, 14 F.4th 409, 437 (6th Cir. 2021) (Thapar, J., concurring in judgment in part and dissenting in part).

11 *See* Jᴏʜɴ H. Dᴜʀʜᴀᴍ, U.S. Dᴇᴘ'ᴛ ᴏғ Jᴜsᴛ., Rᴇᴘᴏʀᴛ ᴏɴ Mᴀᴛᴛᴇʀs Rᴇʟᴀᴛᴇᴅ ᴛᴏ Iɴᴛᴇʟʟɪɢᴇɴᴄᴇ Aᴄᴛɪᴠɪ-ᴛɪᴇs ᴀɴᴅ Iɴᴠᴇsᴛɪɢᴀᴛɪᴏɴs Aʀɪsɪɴɢ Oᴜᴛ ᴏғ ᴛʜᴇ 2016 Pʀᴇsɪᴅᴇɴᴛɪᴀʟ Cᴀᴍᴘᴀɪɢɴs (2023).

12 Randy Beck, *State Interests and the Duration of Abortion Rights*, 44 McGᴇᴏʀɢᴇ L. Rᴇᴠ. 31, 41 (2013).

13 *See Dobbs*, 142 S. Ct. 2317–2350 (Breyer, Sotomayor, & Kagan, JJ., dissenting).

14 *Id.* at 2259–2261 (majority).

15 *Id.* at 2337 (Breyer, Sotomayor, & Kagan, JJ., dissenting).

16 *See Casey*, 505 U.S. 833.

17 *Dobbs*, 142 S. Ct. at 2317.

18 *Id.*

19 *Id.* at 2324.

20 521 U.S. 702.

21 561 U.S. 742.

22 139 S. Ct. 682.

23 Constitution Annotated, *Table of Supreme Court Decisions Overruled by Subsequent Decisions*, Libr. of Cong., https://constitution.congress.gov/resources/decisions-over-ruled/ (last visited June 1, 2023).

24 *Abortion: Half of Voters Approve Supreme Court Ruling*, Rasmussen Reps. (June 28, 2022), https://www.rasmussenreports.com/public_content/politics/general_politics/june_2022/abortion_half_of_voters_approve_supreme_court_ruling.

25 Protecting Pain-Capable Unborn Children from Late-Term Abortions Act, S. 4840, 117th Cong. (2022).

26 H.B. 152, 67th Leg., Gen. Sess. (Wyo. 2023) (enacted).

27 S.F. 109, 67th Leg., Gen. Sess. (Wyo. 2023) (enacted).

28 S.B. 20, Gen. Assemb., 2023 Sess. (N.C. 2023) (enacted).

29 S. 474, Gen. Assemb., 125th Sess. (S.C. 2023) (enacted).

30 L.B. 574, 108th Leg., 1st Sess. (Neb. 2023) (enacted).

31 Carolyn McDonnell, *Federal Policymakers' Guide to a Post-Roe America*, Ams. United for Life 1, 3–4 (Nov. 14, 2022), https://aul.org/wp-content/uploads/2022/11/Feder-al-Policymakers-Guide-to-a-Post-Roe-America.pdf.

32 Americans United for Life, *What Does a Post-Roe America Look Like?*, YouTube (Apr. 28, 2022), https://www.youtube.com/watch?v=dEwCNvGZfi8.

33 *Revoking Your Rights: The Ongoing Crisis in Abortion Care Access Before the H. Comm. on the Judiciary*, 117th Cong. 58 (2022).

34 *American Life Initiative: Our Vision for the Pro-Life Movement Post-Roe*, Ams. United for Life, https://aul.org/ali/ (last visited June 1, 2023).

35 Steven H. Aden, *The Post-Roe Road Ahead and Our Final Destination*, Ams. United for Life (Nov. 9, 2022), https://aul.org/2022/11/09/the-post-roe-road-ahead-and-our-final-destination/.

36 Steven H. Aden, *Introducing the Abortion Abolition Amendment*, Ams. United for Life (Nov. 9, 2022), https://aul.org/2022/11/09/introducing-the-abortion-abolition-amend-ment/.

37 Carolyn McDonnell & Regina Maitlen, *The States in Congress: Federal Strate-gies for Defending Life After Roe*, Ams. United for Life (Nov. 9, 2022), https://aul.org/2022/11/09/the-states-in-congress-federal-strategies-for-defending-life-after-roe/.

38 Catherine Glenn Foster & Kristen Day, *Make Birth Free: A Vision for Congress to Empower American Mothers, Families, and Communities,* Ams. United for Life (Jan. 2023), https://aul.org/law-and-policy/make-birth-free/.

39 *American Moment, Make Birth Free | Sen. JD Vance*, YouTube (Apr. 7, 2023), https://www.youtube.com/watch?v=wsBi3v2nntM.

40 Chris Murphy (@ChrisMurphyCT), Twitter (Mar. 5, 2023, 11:51 AM), https://twitter.com/ChrisMurphyCT/status/1632438660770430979.

41   Institute for Family Studies (@FamStudies), Twitter (Jan. 18, 2023, 7:57 AM), https://twitter.com/FamStudies/status/1615709909081026562.

42   Michael New (@Michael_J_New), Twitter (Jan. 18, 2023, 10:31 AM), https://twitter.com/Michael_J_New/status/1615748746754789377.

43   Wesley J. Smith (@theWesleyJSmith), Twitter (Jan. 18, 2023, 12:44 PM), https://twitter.com/theWesleyJSmith/status/1615782234161561615.

44   Bradley Devlin, *Babies Are Good*, Am. Conservative (Jan. 20, 2023), https://www.theamericanconservative.com/babies-are-good/.

45   Carmel Richardson, *Why Birth Costs So Much*, Am. Conservative (Jan. 27, 2023), https://www.theamericanconservative.com/why-birth-costs-so-much/.

46   Stefani McDade, *Should Christians Support Making Birth Free?*, Christianity Today (Jan. 25, 2023), https://www.christianitytoday.com/ct/2023/january-web-only/make-birth-free-pro-life-proposal-roe-anniversary-christian.html.

47   *Id.*

48   *Id.*

49   Terry Moran (@TerryMoran), Twitter (Jan. 18, 2023, 12:29 PM), https://twitter.com/TerryMoran/status/1615778374860816396.

50   Matt Breunig, *It Would Be Easy to Provide Universal Pregnancy Coverage*, People's Pol'y Project (Jan. 19, 2023), https://www.peoplespolicyproject.org/2023/01/19/it-would-be-easy-to-provide-universal-pregnancy-coverage/.

51   Editorial Board, *Making Birth Free: A Bipartisan Way to Reduce Abortions*, Pittsburgh Post-Gazette (Jan. 22, 2023), https://www.post-gazette.com/opinion/editorials/2023/01/23/maternal-neonatal-healthcare-abortion/stories/202301230010.

52   Allan C. Carlson, *The Forgotten History of America 'Making Birth Free'*, Institute for Family Studies (Feb. 7, 2023), https://ifstudies.org/blog/the-forgotten-history-of-america-making-birth-free

53   Institute for Human Ecology, *Should Birth Be Free?*, YouTube (Apr. 26, 2023), https://www.youtube.com/watch?v=MgaoCaMpXpI&t=854s.

54   EWTN, *Speak Out: What the Government & Church Can Do to Promote Life | EWTN Pro-Life Weekly*, YouTube (May 6, 2023), https://www.youtube.com/watch?v=nyvo1lYKpJw.

55   Marvin Olasky (@MarvinOlasky), Twitter (May 11, 2023, 7:52 AM), https://twitter.com/MarvinOlasky/status/1656643420503326722.

56   Carolyn McDonnell, *A Time to Choose: Suicide Assistance or Suicide Prevention?*, Ams. United for Life 1 (May 1, 2023), https://aul.org/wp-content/uploads/2023/04/2023-05-A-Time-to-Choose-Suicide-Assistance-or-Suicide-Prevention-Web.pdf.

57   *Id.* at 3.

58   *Id.*

59   *Id.* at 23.

60 Hannah Ward, *The Surrogate Mother and the Child She Bears*, Ams. United for Life (May 16, 2023), https://aul.org/2023/05/16/the-surrogate-mother-and-the-child-she-bears/.

61 Stephen A. Douglas & Abraham Lincoln, *First Lincoln-Douglas Debate, Ottawa, Illinois, in* Abraham Lincoln, Speeches and Writings, *supra* ch. 2 note 32, at 495, 524–525.

62 Allen C. Guelzo, *"Public Sentiment Is Everything": Abraham Lincoln and the Power of Public Opinion, in* Lincoln and Liberty: Wisdom for the Ages 171, 181 (Lucas E. Morel ed., 2014).

CHAPTER 15

The Bioethical Challenges
of the 21st Century

Five major bioethical issues most directly affecting the protection of human life will continue to challenge American society for the foreseeable future: abortion, euthanasia and suicide, healthcare policy and care for the chronically and terminally ill, informed consent, and protecting conscience rights of medical professionals in American medicine.

In addition, genetic engineering, gene editing, and the constant evolution of new technology will force us to continue asking: What harms human beings?[1] A culture of life, secured by the law, requires protecting human life in each of these areas, which should be priorities for the cause for life. If implemented, the United States will serve as a model for countries throughout the world.

The Challenge to Human Rights from Moral Skepticism

The fundamental challenge to human rights is not technological but rather philosophical and cultural. Our country's natural-rights heritage and tradition of human rights are threatened by the moral skepticism that has plagued American universities and culture for decades.

The Declaration of Independence, influential to advocates for freedom and human dignity around the globe, proclaims objective, self-evident moral truths, including the equal dignity of human beings. It is the Declaration, based on the common law, which reminded us "[t]hat to secure these rights [including "Life, Liberty and the pursuit of Happiness"] Governments are instituted ..., deriving their just powers from the consent of the governed..." And that protection for equality must go deeper than race, sex, or ethnicity to capture the intrinsic equality of human beings "endowed by their Creator."

Moral skepticism has influenced American law for much of the last century.[2] In 2022, our elites and institutions are profoundly skeptical of moral truth, including the inherent dignity of human beings. Human rights are under assault from a number of prominent ideologies—as they were for much of the 20th century—including the renewal of Marxism among intellectuals and elites in the American academy and American politics.

Moral skepticism isn't a new phenomenon, but it is more pervasive today throughout elite legal institutions than it was a century ago, having a significant effect on legislation and the judiciary. Consider, for instance, the philosophy and legal positions of the American Constitution Society, which supports a constitutional right to unlimited abortion even though there is no originalist or textualist defense of *Roe*.[3]

Because of this legal and political culture, it remains necessary to defend natural rights and natural law in a way that can appeal to the American people. That educational campaign requires a corresponding commitment to defend human dignity in the public square and protect it in law. Such an effort is morally and politically legitimate and has thus far been legally and politically effective.[4]

Post-*Roe* Abortion Policy

While the Supreme Court has left many bioethical issues to the democratic process, the Court made a grave error—a self-inflicted wound—by taking the abortion issue out of the hands of the American people.[5]

Overturning *Roe* means that abortion is now an issue for the American people and their elected representatives.

Imposing an absolute ban on abortion may risk a serious political backlash in many states, and it will likely be most prudent to enact limits on abortion in stages. The best time to debate whether to permit abortion in cases of rape and incest is after a state already has laws restricting most other abortions, rather than jumping straight from abortion on demand to banning all abortion, including in the so-called hard cases. As pre-*Roe* history shows, unless there is public support for a law, enactment does not necessarily mean that enforcement will be strong, effective, or consistent. District attorneys may not be willing to enforce laws, especially in cities, and state leaders need to understand public opinion in their state before they act.

Ramesh Ponnuru articulated a prudent strategy in his book, *The Party of Death*. The legislative goals "should be first to provide the maximum feasible legislative protection that can be sustained over time, and second to expand the limits of what is feasible."[6] In a sense, first establish a sustainable beachhead and make progress from there.

Even in states enacting strong limits on abortion, pro-life lawmakers should not expect that their efforts will be "one and done." Effective enforcement will require time, especially considering the legal vacuum that has lasted several decades, as well as the public's lack of experience with enforcement. The prudent goal is to pass the strongest possible legal limits on abortion that public opinion allows while working to increase support for complete protection of prenatal human life from conception.

For effective enforcement, it will be enough for the law to target abortion providers. Since Planned Parenthood's campaign to legalize abortion, activists for legal abortion have promoted the falsehood that pro-life laws target women and criminalize them for seeking abortion. One abortion activist, Robin Marty, promoted this myth in her 2019 book, *Handbook for a Post-Roe America*. In reality, nearly every major abortion law, such as the federal Partial-Birth Abortion Ban Act, expressly excludes women from prosecution.

Planned Parenthood, NARAL, and NOW have claimed—without evidence and contrary to the well-documented practice of all 50 states—

that women were prosecuted and jailed before *Roe* and will be punished similarly now that *Roe* is overturned. This claim, which is so frequently repeated that it has risen to the level of an urban legend, rests on two falsehoods.

First, before *Roe*, states with abortion prohibitions almost uniformly targeted abortionists, not women. Abortion laws targeted those who artificially induced elective abortion, and in fact, some states expressly referred to women as the second victim.[7] Abortionists were the exclusive target of the criminal law, and abortion was considered a crime for the same reason that homicide is a crime: It kills a human being. Men and women who sought abortions sometimes were prosecuted under anti-solicitation laws, broadly prohibiting the solicitation of any crime, but such instances were rare.

Prior to *Roe*, there are only two cases in which a woman was charged with participating in her own abortion: in Pennsylvania in 1911 and Texas in 1922. *There is no documented case in the U.S. since 1922 in which a woman has been charged for seeking or obtaining an abortion.*[8]

There were three main policy judgments undergirding the choice not to prosecute women for obtaining an abortion: Abortion law exists primarily to punish abortionists, prosecuting women often is counterproductive to that purpose, and women actually are the victims of an abortion procedure.

In fact, rather than states prosecuting women, something close to the opposite was true. To protect themselves, it was abortionists who, when prosecuted, brought women into court and asked the court to treat them as accomplices involved in abortion—exemplified in the 1968 case of Ruth Barnett in Oregon. As a matter of criminal law, if the court treated the woman as an accomplice, she could not testify against the abortionist, and the case against the abortionist would collapse.

Second, the notion that women will now be jailed for abortion in a post-*Roe* world rests on the myth that overturning *Roe* has resulted in the immediate re-criminalization of abortion in every state.

Legislatures in states without abortion laws would have to enact new laws, and these would almost certainly continue the uniform state policy before *Roe* of targeting abortionists and treating women as the second victim of abortion. In many states, there won't even be prosecutions of abortionists unless lawmakers pass new laws restricting abortion earlier in pregnancy.

The merits of abortion activists' argument on this point are not up for speculation. The lengthy historical record of states treating women as the second victim of abortion is easily accessible. States prosecuted the "principal," the abortionist, and did not prosecute someone who might be considered an "accomplice," the woman, in order to enforce the law against the principal more effectively.

States should also consider effective tax, economic, and employment policies to influence the work-family balance of citizens and indirectly assist in reducing abortions. Such policies might include prohibitions on pregnancy discrimination in employment. Such federal law exists, but not every state has one.

Most of all, pro-life Americans should be realistic about new possibilities in the wake of the overturning of *Roe*; it will require patience and perseverance, not to mention a commitment to progress over the longterm.

A careful study of the rise and fall of Reconstruction after the Civil War offers a useful comparison. The Thirteenth Amendment abolished slavery in 1865, and Congress adopted some legal protections like the Civil Rights Act of 1866. But by 1876, public support for protecting freedmen was waning, and African Americans went on to suffer the Black Codes, Jim Crow, segregation, and discrimination for another century, at least. The U.S. adopted civil rights laws in the 1960s, but they didn't solve every problem, and the racial tensions that emerged in 2020 came as a surprise to some, revealing that all was still not well.

That sad history should erase any notion that abortion will be easily abolished or that the time will soon come when pro-life Americans can pack up and go home. Such a strategy and attitude would resemble something like the Compromise of 1876.

Preventing Assisted Suicide

In part because of public resistance to *Roe* in the 1970s and 1980s, the

Supreme Court in 1997 refused to create a national right to assisted suicide, leaving the issue to the states, a significant victory for human life.

A decision finding a constitutional right to assisted suicide would be disastrous, resembling the right to abortion and all that followed from it. Such a decision would put the Court's blessing on the "right" and immunize it from congressional or state oversight. Under the guise of "privacy," it would insulate assisted suicide from public oversight or scrutiny, as has happened with abortion in the U.S. and assisted suicide in several U.S. states and in foreign countries.

Proponents of assisted suicide are conducting a persistent campaign to legalize the practice state by state, a reality that requires strong opposition and vigilance. Legalization would be a detriment to caring for the terminally and chronically ill. It has been well documented that legalizing assisted suicide and euthanasia eventually expands to ever broader categories of persons than just the "terminally ill." John Keown's book *Euthanasia, Ethics and Public Policy: An Argument Against Legalisation* describes how futile it is to attempt a regime of assisted suicide with a limiting principle. States and countries that have tried to do so have failed.

What's more, as we said above, legalization would undermine medical standards for all of us. If a life can be ended with a relatively inexpensive pill or injection, why invest in cancer treatment, palliative care, or new medical innovations? Insurance companies, among others, would almost certainly encourage, enable, or promote the cheaper option. Preventing legalization prevents that cheapest option from becoming the norm when care for the chronically ill or elderly becomes burdensome or expensive.

Healthcare Policy: Caring for the Chronically and Terminally Ill

Preventing direct killing through abortion or assisted suicide is not enough for a comprehensive culture of life. A broader social context of effective healthcare is necessary to protect human dignity and prevent legal, social, and financial pressures that encourage taking human life.

However, for reasons of technology, demography and government, healthcare and healthcare policy have become overwhelmingly complex over the past 50 years, and the dynamics of healthcare for 330,000,000 people entails constant challenges. Caring for human beings in a pro-life society requires a healthcare system that offers efficient and equitable healthcare to as many citizens as possible, promotes healthy living, seeks to avert disease, and cares for the chronically and terminally ill. Though it has fallen short, the U.S. today aims for such a system, and trillions of tax dollars have been spent in an effort to construct it.

Both political parties bear responsibility for that enormous price tag. Democrats seek total governmental control through costly and inefficient single-payer healthcare, while Republicans have failed by downplaying the issue and failing to remedy the problems inherent in the Affordable Care Act.

Technological and demographic challenges require constant innovation in medical biotechnology, some of which will contribute to well-being and others of which might be harmful. For example, telemedicine involves "the use of technology and electronic communications to provide healthcare to patients" and became popular during the pandemic of 2020-2021 because it is believed that it "can address barriers to healthcare access such as physician shortages in rural areas." While it has "the potential to change how medicine is delivered, expanding access and addressing provider shortages," *it can also be used to facilitate abortion or assisted suicide.*[9]

States need flexibility to create and monitor effective health insurance markets so that people have more choices for affordable coverage, with protection for the vulnerable and people with pre-existing conditions. Likewise, we must avoid government rationing of healthcare, which will be unavoidable if the federal government controls our healthcare system as a central part of the budget.

That problem can be avoided by means of federalism and decentralization. During the COVID-19 pandemic, many were concerned that early cases would overwhelm the hospital system, especially in high-population areas, and that healthcare providers would have to ration ventilators. Production and advanced planning mitigated that threat, an important lesson for broader healthcare rationing.

Centralization of power in the federal government is unlikely to advance the protection of human life and would undermine the progress that the culture of life has made through the states since the 1960s.

Greater government control would enable leaders to introduce further pro-abortion and pro-assisted suicide policies, and one national election could result in a complete turnover. Decentralized government better resists such policies, as witnessed by state resistance since *Roe*. Decentralization distributes power and better allows innovation.

Except for issues involving the direct killing of human beings such as abortion, euthanasia, and suicide, the cause for life largely has been on the sidelines of the healthcare debate. But alternative plans are available, and it is necessary to improve the ACA. It's time to get involved.

Fully Informed Consent

It has been a fundamental principle of American medicine that patients have a right to refuse any medical treatment by a doctor. In recent decades, that principle has been bolstered by the concept of informed consent, which entails providing patients with adequate information about their healthcare.

This is essential as medical technology advances and experimental treatments expand. Informed consent is particularly crucial for elective procedures, which are not medically indicated and where there is no medical abnormality or problem requiring intervention.

Abortion is the most obvious case of such a procedure. In nearly all cases, abortion is elective. Cosmetic surgery is another example. With medically-indicated procedures—when there is a condition that requires a medical intervention—the risks of the intervention can be weighed against the risks of doing nothing, or the risks of one type of intervention can be compared with the risks of another.

With an elective procedure, there is no direct or immediate medical risk involved in doing nothing, because no medical abnormality exists. With abortion, health-related conditions that require medical intervention are rare. Another contemporary example is so-called gender-reassignment surgery, which aims to surgically alter sex characteristics when a patient suffers from gender dysphoria, or a feeling of misalignment with his or her biological sex. Are patients—or parents, in the case of minors—fully informed about the risks of such a course of action?

As medical technology expands, these bioethical questions about elective procedures will continue to grow. Consider germ-line genetic editing or brain enhancement procedures. Can we accurately assess the risks of such procedure? Can doctors clearly communicate the uncertainty of these types of experimental procedures?

In a consumer culture such as ours, patients must be given adequate information to mitigate against risks and uncertainty. If certain procedures aren't prohibited outright, patients at least need fully informed consent, which respects human dignity.

Protecting Conscience in Medicine

Since the Founding, freedom of conscience has been one of our most cherished liberties.[10] The importance of this right has been magnified not only by contemporary debates over health care but by long-term technological changes in the healthcare industry.

Over the past 300 years, diverse groups of Americans have defended freedom of conscience, including Quaker pacifists in the colonial era, religious dissenters in the Founding era, abolitionists in the 1840s and 1850s, draft dissenters in the 1920s and 1960s, civil-rights activists in the 1950s and 1960s, and healthcare workers over the past four decades.

When Dr. Martin Luther King Jr. spoke against the Vietnam War in April 1967 at Riverside Church in Manhattan, he began by saying that he spoke "because my conscience leaves me no other choice."

Conscience is a timeless principle of individual liberty that can be threatened by government power or public opposition. We protect conscience because of the protection of liberty in our common law and our constitutional traditions, and because human beings are rational creatures with free will who are responsible to a Creator who has endowed them with unalienable rights.

Freedom of conscience is essential to preserve a zone of individual liberty from governmental coercion. Protection of conscience was the first freedom that animated the American colonists and led to the structural protections of our Constitution and the Bill of Rights.[11]

The protection of conscience means the right to dissent from majority opinion in a democratic society. We recognize that minority rights must be protected within majority rule. We protect conscience because of the

witness of the great souls in history who have awakened prior generations in America and around the world to tyranny and oppression.

Protection of conscience is necessary to safeguard our moral integrity
as individuals. If you drill down to the core of any notion of privacy,
you find freedom of conscience. If society won't protect conscience,
what's left of privacy?

Consider the history of medical science specifically. History is rife with
examples of common practices that were later shown to be harmful—
lack of hand washing, bleeding and purging, surgery without sterilizing
instruments, and so on. Doctors risked their careers and reputations in
objecting to these practices.

Alan Pell Crawford has written that, in the history of the world, "the
only societies in which true science has ever thrived are those established on the principles of classical liberalism. Where government is
limited, science can flourish because it is only under such conditions
that free inquiry—on which science depends—is protected."[12]

It should be no surprise that the American people by and large tend
to support freedom of conscience. A poll in 2011 found that 87 percent of respondents said it is important to "make sure that healthcare
professionals in America are not forced to participate in procedures and
practices to which they have moral objections."

Opposition to conscience in medicine is often based on misunderstand-
ings of the nature of conscience and its limits. Opponents often misun-
derstand the doctor-patient relationship, ignoring the critical difference
between the profession of medicine and the function of a technician
who provides a service.

Those who oppose conscience rights tend to assume that doctors are
simply contractors. In effect, they say, "Conscience is fine, but I'm a
consumer, and I want this now." Other times, they exaggerate the role
of individual healthcare professionals as so-called "gatekeepers." They
fail to distinguish between *elective* and *medically-indicated* treatments,
or they fail to distinguish between providing information and being
required to perform an act. These are not legitimate objections to pro-

tecting freedom of conscience, and those distinctions should guide our analysis.

A physician is not an employee of the patient but a professional in the healing arts. Every physician makes professional judgments about treatment, just as lawyers make professional judgments about which cases they are willing to be responsible for. Some lawyers want to tell doctors how they must provide care but would not mandate that lawyers file any given suit simply because a client insists. If government coerces physicians into complying with patient demands, it eliminates the physician's professional judgment.

Medical professionals are not mere contractors; their profession is defined and governed by an ethical code, derived from the Hippocratic Oath. At the heart of medicine is a conscientious physician or nurse, meaning that there are some things—guided by long-standing ethical principles—that doctors cannot and will not do. Conscience is subjective in the sense that it is personal, but it is objective in the sense that it is guided by a set of ethical standards.

During the Supreme Court oral arguments in *Roe* and *Doe*, Justice Blackmun referred to the Hippocratic oath as "the only definitive statement of ethics of the medical profession," and called the oath "the definitive statement of medical ethics for centuries."[13] This does not mean that the Hippocratic oath is the only source of medical ethics but rather that it is the dominant enduring alternative to viewing doctors as if they were contractors.

Viewing doctors as if they were contractors is not in the patient's best interest. Take the tragic death of Michael Jackson, who demanded stronger and stronger doses of certain drugs and died of an overdose in large part because his doctor, Conrad Murray, complied.

Those who espouse the "doctor as contractor" view seem to except abortion, arguing that abortionists should remain completely unregulated and left to self-police. Despite the fact that 90 percent of abortion patients never meet the abortionist until they are gowned and in stirrups, many believe that he should be permitted to act as the gatekeeper for information about risks and alternatives in that vulnerable moment.

The doctor-patient relationship is unique, and both patients and doctors have rights and responsibilities. Conscientious physicians provide medical care that, in their best judgment, promotes patient health and avoids harm. One of the realities of medicine, perhaps more apparent today than it was a century ago, is the disparity in technical knowledge between doctor and patient. Since the knowledge of a physician dwarfs that of the patient, the ethical principles guiding a doctor's conscience tend to benefit patients. Exalting patient "autonomy" skews the balance between doctors' and patients' rights and responsibilities, usually to the detriment of patients.

Of course, conscience is not unlimited. While patients are protected by law and ethical standards, they have a responsibility to be informed and to know what the doctor does or does not provide. Conscience is not a defense of malpractice, negligence, or poor communication. But, according to the American tradition, conscience is highly protected and subject only to the harm principle. Thomas Jefferson wrote in his *Notes on Virginia* in 1782, "The rights of conscience we never submitted, we could not submit. We are answerable for them to our God. The legitimate powers of government extend to such acts only as are injurious to others."

It's interesting that such a view accords with Hippocratic ethics, which reinforce the first principle of ethics for doctors: First, "do not harm." Do doctors really harm patients by refusing to provide an elective procedure? Do they harm patients by refusing to prescribe a drug with risks the patient might not know about? Might a doctor harm a patient by doing whatever the patient demands?

Apply this "vending machine" approach to the case of infertility treatment. Should a doctor implant eight embryos in a woman's womb just because she demands it?

Patients are protected by an open marketplace and by the proliferation and diversity of healthcare options. When patients have a pharmacy on every street corner, and Google to offer them information, this is not a question of "access" or of too little information about options.

In such a marketplace, patients should find a doctor who shares their values rather than force a physician with a different ethical framework to leave the profession. Some years ago on CBS Radio, a pediatrician urged families with pets to choose their veterinarian with care. Among the questions one should ask is, "Do you offer the range of services that meet my needs?" If that's a simple question one should ask a veterinarian, isn't it even more important to pose such a question to a physician? If you forget to ask until you want an elective procedure six months down the road, is the logical reaction that the physician must leave the profession instead?

There's an essential distinction between elective and medically indicated treatments. Ethical objections legitimately extend only to the procedure, not to an individual, meaning that conscience rights could never justify a medical professional categorically refusing to treat an AIDS patient, for example.

This is obvious in many cases, including that of pharmacists. Since free enterprise has led to pharmacies on practically every street corner, with the exception of some rural areas, it makes little sense to coerce individual pharmacists into either filling prescriptions or leaving the profession, especially when they have an ethical and medical obligation to exercise their independent judgment.

A few years ago, a woman brought her prescription to the pharmacist who examined it and said, "I don't think you should use this." It was not a prescription for contraception; it was medicine for her child's ear problem. The pharmacist explained, "That's a very powerful drug for a young child and I think you should get a second opinion." The mother did, and the second doctor determined that the child didn't even need that particular medicine. The pharmacist should have an even greater freedom of conscience in the case of elective drugs or procedures than in the case of ear medicines that might actually treat illness.

Freedom of conscience protects human life and dignity. Physicians who follow the Hippocratic Oath morally object to procedures that cause harm to patients, and no physician is obligated to perform a procedure, which, in his or her medical judgment, will harm the patient. When it comes to end-of-life care, the famous 20th century sociologist Margaret Mead recognized the power of Hippocratic ethics to protect vulnerable patients, writing:

> Throughout the primitive world the doctor and the sorcerer tended to be the same person. He with the power to kill had the power to cure. With the Greeks [referring to the Hippocratic

> Oath], the distinction was made clear. One profession was to be
> dedicated completely to life under all circumstances regardless
> of rank, age or intellect. This is a priceless possession which
> we cannot afford to tarnish. But society is always attempting
> to make the physician into a killer. To kill the defective child
> at birth, to leave the sleeping pills beside the bed of the cancer
> patient. It is the duty of society to protect the physician from
> such requests.[14]

Given our legal and constitutional respect for conscience, given the
great good that freedom of conscience has served, an imagined example of misplaced conscience cannot be used to rescind or reduce freedom of conscience. Patients gain, generally speaking, when healthcare
professionals exercise freedom of conscience. Freedom of conscience
protections keep the proper balance of rights and responsibilities between doctor and patient, guide doctors by objective standards, protect
human life and dignity, improve healthcare and informed consent, positively build the patient/physician relationship, and make it possible to
retain better medical professionals. Freedom of conscience in medicine
is constantly under assault. It must be strengthened in law and policy in
the 21st century.

What Harms Human Beings?

Human lives have been immeasurably blessed by science and technology over the past century. And yet, many have written with wisdom and
insight into the challenges to human life and dignity from biotechnology.[15]

The bioethical challenges of the future are likely to be even more difficult than the issues of abortion and assisted suicide, because abortion
and assisted suicide involve direct killing. The bioethical issues of the
future, provoked by culture, technology, and ideology, may involve sub-
tler violations of human life and human dignity.

Protecting human life is necessary to preserve the vision of the Declaration of Independence and to preserve humane relationships in our
society. We should respect people not because they belong to a par-

ticular identity group or tribe but because they are, first and foremost, human beings.

In addition to the culture of moral skepticism in law, medical technology will continue to create challenges to the protection of human life and dignity. During the 2020 pandemic, doctors promoted telemedicine as a means of distributing medical care economically and efficiently. Abortion activists took advantage of this trend to push chemical abortion via telemedicine, and their campaign included litigation attacking the Food and Drug Administration's "in-person requirement" for the administration of RU486 (mifepristone) abortion pills. Suicide activists also saw an opening, promoting "teledeath."[16]

As they have throughout the 20th century, culture, technology, politics, and the crisis of ethics in American law and medicine will continue to challenge the legal protection of human life. Use of technology has been guided throughout our history by democratically-adopted law, and the case for the legitimacy of public control of technology through law needs to be made in the public square.

One bioethical question that has risen to the top of social consciousness is that of personal identity. There is a story of Jesus Christ sometime around 34 A.D., when he was with his disciples on the Sea of Galilee in Palestine. As one historian records it:

> Jesus said to his disciples, "Let's go over to the other side of the lake." So they got into a boat and set out. As they sailed, he fell asleep. A squall came down on the lake, so that the boat was being swamped, and they were in great danger. The disciples went and woke him, saying, "Master, Master, we're going to drown!" He got up and rebuked the wind and the raging waters; the storm subsided, and all was calm. "Where is your faith?" he asked his disciples. In fear and amazement they asked one another, "Who is this?"

Human beings have grappled with the question of personal identity throughout history. In one way or another, many humans have asked, "Who am I?" We see it in 2022 in the issues of transgenderism and gender dysphoria. In this particular context, the law should insist on fully informed consent, especially for the young and vulnerable and especially with regard to procedures that are elective and not medically indicated.

Many questions in bioethics come down to the question of harm to human beings. How can we identify harm? How does the law define it? These questions have yet to be answered fully.

Chapter 15 Endnotes

1   *See, e.g.*, EBEN KIRKSEY, THE MUTANT PROJECT: INSIDE THE GLOBAL RACE TO GENETICALLY MODIFY HUMANS (2020).

2   *See e.g.*, ALBERT W. ALSCHULER, LAW WITHOUT VALUES: THE LIFE, WORK, AND LEGACY OF JUSTICE HOLMES (2000).

3   This is made clear by THE CONSTITUTION IN 2020, *supra* ch. 13 note 2, a 2009 book edited by Yale Law Professors Jack Balkin and Reva Siegel, containing numerous essays by members of the American Constitution Society (ACS).

4   That view is defended as a prudential judgment in Princeton Professor Robert P. George's MAKING MEN MORAL: CIVIL LIBERTIES AND PUBLIC MORALITY (1993).

5   John Keown, *Back to the Future of Abortion Law:* Roe*'s Rejection of America's History and Traditions*, 22 ISSUES L. & MED. 3, 37 (2006) ("*Roe*'s invention of a constitutional right to abortion represented a radical rejection of America's long-standing history and traditions.").

6   RAMESH PONNURU, THE PARTY OF DEATH: THE DEMOCRATS, THE MEDIA, THE COURTS, AND THE DISREGARD FOR HUMAN LIFE 248 (2006).

7   Forsythe, *The Effective Enforcement of Abortion Law Before* Roe v. Wade, *supra* ch. 3 note 6.

8   Paul Benjamin Linton, *Overruling* Roe v. Wade*: The Implications for the Law*, 32 ISSUES L. & MED. 341 (2017).

9   *See, e.g.*, Pien Huang & Mara Gordon, *Telehealth Abortion Demand is Soaring. But Access May Come Down to Where You Live*, NAT'L PUB. RADIO (May 20, 2022), https://www.npr.org/sections/health-shots/2022/05/20/1099179361/.

10   *See* Michael W. McConnell, *The Origins and Historical Understanding of Free Exercise of Religion*, 103 *Harv. L. Rev.* 1409 (1989).

11   *See* Paulsen & Paulsen, *The Constitution, supra* ch. 10 note 16, at 98–105.

12   Alan Pell Crawford, *Freedom of Inquiry,* WALL ST. J. (Feb. 11, 2010) https://www.wsj.com/articles/SB10001424052748704140104575057631549120478.

13   FORSYTHE, ABUSE OF DISCRETION, *supra* ch. 2 note 46, at 225 (citations omitted).

14   Margaret Mead, Address to the Rudolph Virchow Medical Society (1962); Margaret Mead, *Introduction* to MAURICE LEVINE, PSYCHIATRY AND ETHICS 17 (1972).

15   *See, e.g.*, Snead, *supra* ch. 2 note 34; Kilner, *supra* ch. 2 note 38; Sandel, *supra* ch. 2 note 38; Smith, *supra* ch. 2 note 38; THE PRESIDENT'S COUNCIL ON BIOETHICS, *supra* ch. 2 note 38; IN DEFENSE OF HUMAN DIGNITY, *supra* ch. 2 note 27; Fukuyama, *supra* ch. 2 note 38; Kass, *supra* ch. 2 note 38; Ramsey, *supra* ch. 1 note 8.

16   *See, e.g.*, *Telemedicine*, PATIENTS RTS. COUNCIL, https://www.patientsrightscouncil.org/site/telemedicine/ (last visited June 10, 2022).

Conclusion

Abraham Lincoln recognized that America was flawed but that Americans had inherited ethical and political ideals which they must strive to more fully realize.

Lincoln saw these in the Declaration of Independence, referring to it as "my ancient faith." It was, in his words in June 1857 in Springfield, "a standard maxim for free society, which should be familiar to all, and revered by all; constantly looked to, constantly labored for, and even though never perfectly attained, constantly approximated, and thereby constantly spreading and deepening its influence, and augmenting the happiness and value of life of all people of all colors everywhere."

He repeatedly drew his audiences back to the Declaration, urging Americans in the 1850s, and as President in the 1860s, to live up to the ideals of the Declaration. Frederick Douglass and Martin Luther King, Jr. also lauded the Declaration, even while they challenged Americans and elected officials to live up to its ideals. Our best presidents and elected representatives have helped Americans understand and cherish those ideals.

These ideals—particularly the protection of human life—are also reflected in the Anglo-American legal heritage, starting with the common law that the States adopted in their earliest years. Justice James Wilson, among the first group of Supreme Court justices named by President George Washington, recognized that "human life from its commencement to its close is protected by the common law."

That legal heritage is constantly challenged by culture, technology, and destructive ideas like Marxism.

The late Charles Krauthammer once wrote, "The lesson of our history is that the task of … maintaining strong and sturdy the structures of a constitutional order is unending, the continuing and ceaseless work of every generation."

Our republican—representative—institutions need to be preserved and need to protect human lives. But government can't do it alone. It needs the active assistance of citizens through elections, and through mediating institutions, what some call civil society.

We can see, looking back, that the legal, structural, and cultural support for protecting human life in America didn't exist in the 1960s. More than a dozen states legalized abortion, and then *Roe* happened. The legal, structural, and cultural support for life has improved since *Roe*, but it is entirely possible that the next generation could fail to sustain that support without the assistance of charitable and philanthropic organizations.

As Yuval Levin showed in *A Time to Build*, institutions are needed for reform and renewal. But as he reminded us, "a recommitment to the integrity of our institutions doesn't offer a quick fix to our social problems. It offers hard solutions, but they are the only ones that can be had. Real institutionalism requires the actual practice of some very challenging virtues."

Americans United for Life has been able to flourish for 50 years as an independent, non-profit organization because it combined a number of necessary ingredients. It has been zealously focused on its mission of protecting human life in culture, law, and policy. A series of boards and a series of teams have been stewards of that mission. It has cultivated a team of thoroughbreds, including lawyers who were committed and trained. And it has been sustained by generous, sacrificial supporters from coast to coast. These allies, working together, have been united in the mission and focused on that mission. The momentum of movements depends on strong organizations and institutions, and on recommitment to them.

But, as COVID-19 clearly demonstrated, these bioethical issues affect us every day and are directly related to the flourishing of human beings and families. These issues will affect us for the rest of our lives and those of our children and grandchildren. Commitment to republican institutions, and the charitable organizations that support life, will be necessary if our nation increasingly protects human life generation after generation.

Acknowledgments

We are grateful to Hugh Phillips and Shane Rider for their research assistance and to Regina Maitlen for her research and editorial advice. Thanks also to Tom Shakely, David Mortimer, and Naomi Stringer for improving the manuscript. Thanks, finally, to Steven H. Aden and Carolyn McDonnell for leading the manuscript reviewing team and to each member of the reviewing team: Guzi He, Natalie Hejran, Bradley Kehr, Catherine Kolesar, Caleb Kreft, Danielle Pimentel, Domatius Shafik, Tate Thielfoldt, Hannah Ward, and Danielle Zuccaro.

Acclaim

"So many of us owe so much to those who went before us in the pro-life movement. *Pushing Roe v. Wade Over the Brink* tells the story of the men and women who refused to accept injustice and courageously put their hands to the plow. Clarke Forsythe and Alexandra DeSanctis do us all a service in instructing us on what it took for those who went before us to overturn *Roe*—and highlighting the work left for us to do today to ensure justice for the unborn and their mothers."

Ryan T. Anderson, Ph.D., President of the Ethics and Public Policy Center, and coauthor of Tearing Us Apart: How Abortion Harms Everything and Solves Nothing

"The *Dobbs* case, with the overruling of *Roe*, brought us a gift that some of us thought we would never live to see. Clarke Forsythe and Alexandra DeSanctis provide exactly what we need now: a reminder of that terrain we had to cross. Now, with *Roe* overruled, the sobering and bracing truth comes through: We find that Americans United for Life is needed ever more, because the burdens for the pro-life movement have become even heavier. For the Court in *Roe* had transformed the culture. Abortion was changed from a thing abhorred and forbidden into something to be approved, celebrated, and promoted. States like Illinois, which had been centers for pro-life resistance, have now become absorbed in the block of pro-abortion states, where all the restraints on abortion are in the course of being swept away. The Court in *Dobbs* overruled *Roe*, but it curiously held back from pronouncing and naming the "wrong" that we have worked 49 years to undo. The Court apologized for judicial overreaching, as if judicial activism were its essential error, and then sent the issue of abortion to the political arena. AUL will need to be super-charged just to preserve existing pro-life laws, for energized pro-abortion activists are determined to use the levers of federal power to tear down every restraint on abortion in the law. Our victory in overturning *Roe* was hard-won, but it should not surprise us that we have, even now, steady work to do."

Hadley Arkes, Ph.D., Founder and Director, James Wilson Institute on Natural Rights and the American Founding

"As a progressive anti-abortion activist, I've worked closely with Americans United for Life and have long regarded them as a valuable ally in the struggle to build a culture of life. Clarke Forsythe and Alexandra DeSanctis provide an excellent and highly readable history of the first 50 years of the pro-life movement. There's nothing more encouraging than learning how much those who came before us have sacrificed to get the movement to where it is today."

Terrisa Bukovinac, Founder and Executive Director of Progressive Anti-Abortion Uprising

"In *Pushing Roe v. Wade Over the Brink*, Clarke Forsythe and Alexandra DeSanctis tell the twists and turns of how the pro-life movement persevered against the odds in executing a five decade-long winning strategy that in 2022 finally sent *Roe v. Wade* to the ash heap of history. Now the most important work begins, as pro-life lawmakers in State legislatures and Congress must work to pass laws to protect preborn children and their mothers from the violence of abortion. We must also continue to persuade our fellow citizens that science, justice, and compassion demand protecting the most vulnerable among us. I'm grateful for the leadership of Americans United for Life in helping to bring us to this moment, and in charting the path forward. We cannot rest until the day that every child is protected under our laws and can enjoy our nation's most sacred right — the right to life."

Sen. Steve Daines (R-MT), Founder of the U.S. Senate Pro-Life Caucus

"Americans United for Life remains a beacon of hope for true unity and a truly life-affirming future for American culture and politics alike, despite the intense partisanship and political faction that characterize our politics. *Pushing Roe v. Wade Over the Brink* tells a story that America's young pro-life advocates desperately need to know—the story of the pro-life cause from its very beginnings, from a time when Democrats and Republicans alike were proudly pro-life. Despite the shameful abandonment of the pro-life cause by today's Democrats at the national level, many Democrats serving at the state and local levels across America remain proudly pro-life and millions of Democratic voters remain pro-life, too. With *Roe*'s reversal, I am hopeful that this book will stir Democratic hearts to once more boldly and powerfully advocate for the human right to life."

Kristen Day, Executive Director, Democrats for Life of America

"The victory in *Dobbs* is the culmination of the efforts of millions of Americans joined together in the greatest grass-roots civil rights movement of our time. No aspect of that effort was more important than building the scientific, philosophical, and legal case for protecting the unborn child and reversing *Roe v. Wade*. Clarke Forsythe, a four-decade veteran of this struggle, and Alexandra DeSanctis have written a compelling history of Americans United for Life, the nation's oldest secular pro-life organization, and progenitor of the legal strategy to reverse *Roe*. Readers will learn (some to their surprise) that this strategy is rooted not in any political ideology or theory of constitutional interpretation, but in the core belief that the most fundamental of human rights, that of life itself, must be protected in law lest greater erosions of human rights transpire. For the first time in 50 years, the pro-life movement can engage this struggle on a level playing field. Its success will depend in large part on heeding the wisdom of its founders, in particular those of diverse political and religious commitments who fastened the cause of life to the quest for social justice for all Americans."

Ed Grant, J.D., Adjunct Professor at Georgetown University's Pellegrino Center for Clinical Bioethics and former President and General Counsel of Americans United for Life

"*Pushing Roe v. Wade Over the Brink* conveys the sweeping drama of the nearly 50-year fight to reverse *Roe v. Wade*. Notably, Americans United for Life strategically argued for constitutional personhood in its U.S. Supreme Court *amicus* brief in *Roe* itself. Now that *Roe* has finally been overturned, all Americans who cherish human life can turn their attention to fulfilling America's foremost promise: securing the right to life for all."

Josh Hammer, J.D., Newsweek Senior Editor-at-Large, Host of The Josh Hammer Show, and Research Fellow at the Edmund Burke Foundation

"*Pushing Roe v. Wade Over the Brink* is the superbly told story of the pro-life movement in America, the difficulties of navigating our divided legal, cultural, and moral terrain, and the winning strategies that championed the dignity of human life and pushed *Roe* over the brink. Central to that story is the leading role of Americans United for Life. Clarke Forsythe, one of America's foremost legal experts on the right to life, and his coauthor, Alexandra DeSanctis, do more than chronicle events, however; in describing the people, politics, and principles that built a culture of life, they also illuminate the challenges that remain. One thing is clear: Americans United for Life will neither waver nor rest until all human life is protected in law and cherished in American hearts and minds."

Mary Rice Hasson, J.D., Kate O'Beirne Senior Fellow, Ethics and Public Policy Center

"Through so many of the dark years of the *Roe* regime, Americans United for Life fought the good fight with extraordinary skill and perseverance. Toppling *Roe* happened—something that seemed impossible for decades—because good people at Americans United for Life and in similar organizations never quit. *Pushing Roe v. Wade Over the Brink* is a marvelous read and a reminder that 'the power of the powerless' resides in decent persons refusing to live a lie and insisting instead on living the truth, whatever the cost and however long it takes. The authors have done a great service to the pro-life movement and the women and men who carried it forward."

Francis X. Maier, Senior Fellow, Ethics and Public Policy Center

"Americans United for Life has done a superb job serving as the legal architect of the pro-life movement. Even in the years prior to *Roe v. Wade*, Americans United for Life lawyers were diligently defending laws that protected preborn children. In *Pushing Roe v. Wade Over the Brink*, Clarke Forsythe and Alexandra DeSanctis chronicle the vital role of Americans United for Life in defending both federal and state pro-life laws and crafting legal strategies that ultimately resulted in the reversal of *Roe*."

Michael New, Ph.D., Visiting Assistant Professor at The Catholic University of America and Senior Associate Scholar at the Charlotte Lozier Institute

"In 1990 and 1991, before Americans United for Life reestablished its Washington, DC office, my family lived near Washington and we had an "AUL futon" on which Clarke Forsythe or Guy Condon, AUL's head at that time, slept when one or the other had pro-life business to conduct in the capital. That's one indication of how the David that is AUL went up against Planned Parenthood and other abortion Goliaths: no expensive hotel rooms or fancy dinners, just dogged work year after year when overturning *Roe* seemed hopeless. Now, after the U.S. Supreme Court's excellent *Dobbs* decision, the temptation is to sing, 'Ding dong, the witch is dead,' and to think we're on a yellow brick road that will take us straight to ending abortion. Spoiler alert: *Pushing Roe v. Wade Over the Brink* notes that we should 'erase any notion that abortion will be easily abolished or that the time will soon come when pro-life Americans can pack up and go home.' Sad but true, so it's great that AUL will still be around, making progress inch by inch as it did during the decades this book covers, and challenging notions about prosecuting women or eliminating life-of-the-mother exceptions that a few pro-lifers have put forward, much to the delight of propagandistic abortion activists."

Marvin Olasky, Ph.D., coauthor of The Story of Abortion in America and former Editor-in-Chief of WORLD Magazine

"For over 50 years, Americans United for Life has been a champion for the protection of life in the United States. Its forward-thinking mission enhanced our movement's ability to engage with the hearts and minds of Americans. AUL's focus on conscience protections, clinic safety regulations, and the chronically and terminally ill continue to provide valuable leadership as to where the pro-life movement can focus its time and talents. In light of the Supreme Court's favorable ruling in *Dobbs*, this book is vital for understanding where the movement has been, so that we are better prepared for the promise and challenge of a post-*Roe* world."

Catherine Ruth Pakaluk, Ph.D., Assistant Professor of Economics at The Catholic University of America

"The story of Americans United for Life as recounted in this important book is the story of courageous advocates who worked over may decades to achieve the reversal of *Roe v. Wade*. This fight took them into every state in the Union and into not a few foreign countries and international fora. This noble fight to defend the most vulnerable of human beings achieved a great victory in *Dobbs*, but now must continue in every state and across the world. Clarke Forsythe and Alexandra DeSanctis show that so much of the most crucial human rights advocacy of our lifetimes—advocacy that continues to define Americans United for Life—requires the virtues in abundance, and a willingness to be called every bad name in the book. This book demonstrates that AUL is up to task."

William Saunders, JD, Center for Human Rights, The Catholic University of America

"*Roe v. Wade* is dead. The contentious issue of abortion has been sent to the democratic sphere. In helping to bring the country to this portentous moment, Americans United for Life acted in the grand tradition of social and legal activism that has been a hallmark of the American experience. Clarke Forsythe and Alexandra DeSanctis tell the story of AUL's crucial role and its committed and ongoing engagement in other crucial bioethical issues such as assisted suicide that will determine the morality of American law in the 21st century."

Wesley J. Smith, Chair of Discovery Institute's Center on Human Exceptionalism and Author of Culture of Death: The Age of "Do Harm" Medicine

Made in the USA
Columbia, SC
27 November 2023

52a16bdb-e344-4f68-bc8c-fa1de9d5a016R01